HENCHMEN OF ARES

Warriors and Warfare in Early Greece

By Josho Brouwers

Karwansaray Publishers
2013

Published in 2013 by

Karwansaray BV

Weena 750

3014 DA Rotterdam

The Netherlands

www.karwansaraypublishers.com

The cover design features a side-on view of the famous sculpture from Sparta. It was once believed to represent King Leonidas, but more probably depicts a different warrior. It was found at the temple of Athena Chalkioikos at Sparta and dates to around 480 BC. The forward section of the helmet crest has been restored. The statue is currently on display in the Archaeological Museum of Sparta. The image along the bottom edge of the cover is from a Late Geometric pot and represents a line of warriors equipped with plumed helmets, a set of two spears, and round shields. It is currently on display in Berlin.

ISBN 978-94-90258-07-8

Written by Josho Brouwers

Edited by Jona Lendering

Copy-editing by Duncan B. Campbell

Maps designed by Carlos García

Unless otherwise indicated, all photos © Livius.org, Netjer VOF, or Karwansaray BV

Illustrations by Rocío Espín, Angel García Pinto, Milek Jakubiec, Sebastian Schulz, Johnny Shumate, Graham Sumner

Design and typesetting by MeSa Design, Elst, the Netherlands

Cover design by Andrew J. Brozyna, Longmont, CO, USA

Printed by High Trade BV, Zwolle, the Netherlands

Printed in the EU

Contents

List of maps

Prologue
Homer's shadow

Go tell the Spartans, you who are passing by,
That here, obedient to their laws, we lie.
—Simonides' epitaph at Thermopylae, Hdt. 7.228

King Leonidas was dead, killed in battle. It had been the third – and final – day of fighting in the narrow pass at Thermopylae. Here, the Spartans made a stand against the Persian invader. On this third day, most of the allied Greek troops had withdrawn and Leonidas was left behind with only his chosen body of 300 Spartan warriors, supported by Lacedaemonian auxiliaries, and two contingents of 700 Thespians and 400 Thebans. The Persian host far outnumbered them, but their goal was not to win the battle. Their aim was simply to delay the Persian advance long enough to enable the Greeks further south to prepare for the coming onslaught. Like all Greek commanders, Leonidas had fought in the front rank of battle and – also like so many Greek commanders – he had been slain there.

The final struggle is detailed by Herodotus in his *Histories* (7.24–25). He tells that the fighting on the third day had been particularly grim. The spears of most of the Greek warriors had already been broken in combat and the men had had to continue fighting using their swords. During the struggle, Leonidas was killed. Herodotus does not specify how the Spartan king died exactly, but mentions that a battle broke out between the Greeks and the Persians, in which two of the brothers of the Persian King, Xerxes, died. Finally, the Greeks managed to secure the body and then fended off the Persians four times, before being forced to retreat to a mound away from the area that they were originally defending. Here, they made their last stand, fighting with swords if they still had them, or their bare hands and teeth if they did not. Finally, the Persians succeeded in killing them to a man using missiles.

Thermopylae took place in late summer – August or September – of the year 480 BC. Herodotus wrote his account in the fifth century BC, perhaps as long as fifty years after the fact. Herodotus, often heralded as the 'Father of History', would still have been able to consult eye-witnesses for his scholarly work. But the description of this final struggle at Thermopylae, and the back-and-forth fighting over Leonidas' corpse, echo similar descriptions found in the *Iliad*, the epic poem attributed to Homer that recounts one famous episode in the legendary Trojan War. In the *Iliad*, battles between Trojans and Greeks over the ownership of a fallen

Opposite page: an impression of the fierce struggle that erupted between the Greeks and the Persians over possession of the corpse of King Leonidas in the latter stages of the Battle of Thermopylae. Herodotus' description calls to mind similar battles from Homer's Iliad. *Drawing by Johnny Shumate.*

2

This statue of Leonidas was erected in the modern town of Sparta in 1968. The inscription reads ΜΟΛΩΝ ΛΑΒΕ ("Come and get them"), which Plutarch says was the Spartan King's reply when asked to surrender his weapons. The Battle of Thermopylae is generally regarded as a supremely heroic moment in ancient history, but its historical significance has been greatly exaggerated.

hero's corpse occur relatively frequently; the most noteworthy instance is the battle over the body of Achilles' comrade-in-arms, Patroclus.

The shadow of Homer looms large over the period that this book is about, and would continue to be an influence well beyond the Persian Wars and even into the Roman era. The epic poems attributed to Homer serve as a useful guide to a history of warfare in Early Greece. Not because the mode of fighting or equipment that he describes were characteristic of this period and culture, but because the ethos expressed in the *Iliad* in particular seems to have reflected an ideal that served as an inspiration for at least the upper echelons of Early Greek societies.

• Homer and the Trojan War

Despite the importance of Homer's works, we know almost nothing about the poet himself. 'Homer' might not even have been a proper name, and there is discussion of whether or not the poet who composed the *Iliad* was the same one who later composed the *Odyssey*. For convenience's sake, I will consider Homer as an individual and the poet responsible for both of the works attributed to him. Some minor details about the poet can be added. Homer was active around 700 BC and originated in East Greece. The Greek city of Old Smyrna (near modern Izmir) is a common candidate for his place of birth. Homer composed the poems in so-called dactylic hexameters, using an artificial dialect that combined Ionian Greek with Aeolian elements; this became the standard mode of expression for Greek epic poetry in general.

The Homeric epics, as well as the poet himself, were already fervently studied in ancient times. Their study has again blossomed since the nineteenth century and there are few ancient historians and archaeologists focusing on Early Greece who have not, at one time or another, studied aspects of Homer and his work. Our main point of interest is the content of the poems, especially the *Iliad*, Homer's battle-epic and the earliest known example of Western literature. The story of the *Iliad* is set in the tenth year of the legendary Trojan War, in which an allied force of Greeks besieged the city of Troy and fought against the Trojans and their allies. The theme of the poem is the rage of the main Greek hero, Achilles; the work starts with the word *metis* ('wrath' or 'rage'), and this was probably the title under which the poem was originally known.

The story of the *Iliad* is not set in Homer's own time, but takes place in the distant past. In the epic world, Greece is divided into several small kingdoms governed by lesser and greater kings. All the Greek kingdoms acknowledge Agamemnon, the king of Mycenae, as their overlord, their *anax andron*, during the Trojan War, for reasons not specified by Homer, but known from other Greek myths. These kings are treated as powerful autocratic figures, which must have seemed

A note on periodization

The period between 500 BC and AD 500 is often generally referred to as Classical Antiquity to set it apart from the pre-Classical ancient world. The latter is typically divided into three main eras named after the main material used for the production of tools and weapons, namely the Stone Age, the Bronze Age, and the Iron Age. For our purposes, only the latter two periods need concern us.

The Bronze Age covers the period between roughly 3000 and 1000 BC. It is usually subdivided into three parts: Early, Middle, and Late. This book starts in the Late Bronze Age, which in the case of the Aegean is also referred to as the Mycenaean Age. Absolute dates are problematic. Aegean chronology is, to a large extent, based on the chronology of the ancient Near East and is ultimately connected to Egyptian king lists. Without going into too many details, the absolute dates for the Mycenaean era used in this book range from ca. 1550 to 1100 BC.

The eleventh century BC was a period of cultural impoverishment and depopulation. From about 1000 BC, Greek society slowly began to grow again and this is also the conventional date for the start of the Greek Iron Age. The period between 1000 and 700 BC is referred to as the Early Iron Age. It is uncommon to refer to the Greek Middle or Late Iron Age. Early in the eighth century BC, the Greeks adopted the alphabet from the Phoenicians. With this relatively simple system of writing becoming fairly widespread, Greek history proper begins. Traditionally, it is said to begin with the first Olympic Games of 776 BC.

The historical era is usually divided into three main periods, namely Archaic (ca. 700–480 BC), Classical (480–323 BC) and Hellenistic (after 323 BC). The last period starts with the death of Alexander the Great and usually ends with the Roman conquest of Greek territories. The most common endpoint is the Battle of Actium (31 BC), in which Octavian – the later Emperor Augustus – defeated a Romano-Greek fleet under the leadership of Mark Antony and Cleopatra.

mysterious and foreign to most of those who listened to this poem, as Greek communities in Homer's own time were typically governed by oligarchies – typically aristocracies – rather than monarchies.

The ancient Greeks considered the Trojan War a historic event and even tried to calculate when it had taken place. They tried to estimate the year by counting back in time using genealogies for the most part. Herodotus claimed that the

Trojan War must have taken place 800 years before his own time, or around 1250 BC (Hdt. 2.145). Other ancient Greek scholars came up with different dates that typically fell somewhere in the years around or shortly after 1200 BC. As a result, the conventional date for the Trojan War is usually somewhere around 1200 BC, which means that it took place right before the end of the Mycenaean era proper, around the same time that most of the Mycenaean palaces of the Late Bronze Age were destroyed or abandoned.

It is interesting that Greeks of the Classical era were able to date the Trojan War more or less to the final stages of the Late Bronze Age, during which the country was indeed dominated by small and powerful kingdoms that were ruled over by kings. The political geography of the epic world resembles the situation in the Late Bronze Age. The Greek commander-in-chief, Agamemnon, is also the king of Mycenae, and from the archaeological evidence it does indeed seem that Mycenae was one of the most powerful – if not *the* most powerful –kingdom in Greece. However, by Homer's time, Mycenae had lost its glory and, in later times, was little more than

A map of the ancient Aegean, featuring key sites mentioned in the text.

a small town; it was even destroyed by the city of Argos in the fifth century BC.

Furthermore, the Trojan War is a story that pits the Greek world against Troy, a powerful city in the north-west of Asia Minor. In Homer's own time, Troy was a small Greek town that did not amount to much, but there is compelling evidence that, during the Late Bronze Age, Troy was the capital of a powerful kingdom. During this period, the dominant power in Anatolia was the so-called Hittite Empire, one of four Great Kingdoms that dominate the ancient Near East. The Hittites – who referred to themselves as inhabitants of the Land of Hatti – communicated frequently with their rival Great Kings of Egypt, Babylon, and Assyria. Their records refer to a city known as Wilusa, and it has been convincingly argued that this should be equated with Troy, which the Greeks referred to as Ilion.

A few Hittite letters and a treaty – all written in Hittite cuneiform on clay tablets – have been unearthed that shed interesting light on this period. One of these, the so-called Tawagalawa letter (CTH 181), dates to around 1250 BC and is addressed to the king of Ahhiyawa, named Tawagalawa (probably the Hittite form of a Mycenaean name that would perhaps later be rendered as Eteocles). Specifically, the letter refers to an adventurer named Piyama-Radu, who is claimed to operate under the aegis of the king of Ahhiyawa. The Hittite king – presumably Hattusili III – demanded his extradition. The name Piyama-Radu has been considered a Hittite rendering of a name that in Homer's age would have been written as *Priamos*, that is Priam, coincidentally the name of Troy's king in the *Iliad*.

The name 'Ahhiyawa' has been equated with Achaea. This is the name for at least two regions in Greece in later times; Homer also uses Achaea and Achaeans to refer to Greece and the Greeks. (Our English word for Greece derives from the Latin; the Greeks from Hesiod onwards refer to themselves generally as Hellenes, and their country, Hellas.) However, it is not exactly clear where Ahhiyawa is supposed to be located: it could be in Asia Minor, or it could refer to one or more Aegean islands or a place in mainland Greece. It need not have covered the whole of the Greek culture region and there is no immediately compelling reason to believe that Tawagalawa was an overlord who represented all of the Greeks.

Frustratingly, the Tawagalawa letter is incomplete. At one point, the author refers to a war over Wilusa on which the Hittite king and the king of Ahhiyawa had reached an agreement. If the story of the Trojan War as immortalized by Homer possesses a kernel of historical truth, this almost certainly is it. There are other letters from the Hittite king that reveal further details of the situation in the Late Bronze Age, including the so-called Alaksandu treaty. In this treaty, peace is brokered between the Hittites and the kingdom of Wilusa in around 1280 BC. The king of Wilusa is specifically named as Alaksandu, no doubt a Hittite version of the name that later Greeks would write as *Alexandros* (Alexander), which was also an alternative name for Paris, the hero who took the beautiful Helen from Sparta and thereby caused the Trojan War in the first place.

All of the foregoing is suggestive and supports the idea that the origin of the story of the Trojan War very probably dates back to the Late Bronze Age and quite possibly the thirteenth century BC in particular. The political geography of the epic world also seems to correspond better with the situation in the Late Bronze Age than in Homer's own time. There are other superficial similarities as well. For example, like Homer's kings, the Mycenaean lords resided in palaces and owned vast tracts of land and large herds of livestock.

However, when Homer composed the *Iliad*, the world of the Late Bronze Age was little more than a hazily remembered time of legend. While the framework of his story can be traced back to some five or six centuries earlier, many of the details that he used to flesh out his ancient tale can be positively dated to his own time, sometime around 700 BC or even the first half of the seventh century BC. Homer's kings, like their actual Mycenaean forebears, live in palaces, but their descriptions are completely different from the sprawling citadels of the Late Bronze Age. Homer's kings live in palaces that consist of separate buildings placed within a walled courtyard, where some livestock runs free. The Mycenaean kingdoms were bureaucratic and maintained archives with administrative records. The Homeric kingdoms, however, appear to be positively rural and writing is virtually unknown apart from the story about the hero Bellerophon, told in the sixth book of the *Iliad*.

• The epic world

The world described by Homer can be reconstructed to a reasonably accurate degree, even if some authors disagree about particular details. The epic world is divided into larger and smaller territorial units, each of which contains a number of towns. One town in each territory is the home of a hereditary ruler. Homeric society is divided into four social groups; namely, (a) an 'aristocracy' of so-called *basileis*; (b) a common element, consisting mostly of farmers (smallholders) and a few skilled specialists (craftsmen); (c) a group of landless poor, who work as hired labourers and are referred to as *thetes* (singular *thes*); and finally, (d) slaves (*douloi*). The society of the Homeric world thus seems very similar to common reconstructions of Greek societies of the Early Iron Age and at least the earlier part of the Archaic period.

Nearly all of the main characters in the *Iliad* and *Odyssey* belong to the social group called *basileis* ('chiefs', often translated as 'princes'), who own sizeable tracts of arable land and considerable numbers of livestock. Some of these *basileis* are rated more highly than others, and one of them is the ruler of the whole community. All of the main heroes are either rulers themselves or the sons of rulers. Odysseus, for example, rules (verb, *anasso*) the people of Ithaka. He is assisted in his duties by other *basileis*, specifically the elders (*gerontes*), affluent men who are the heads

The hero Ajax delivers the dead body of Achilles from the battlefield. Both of the heroes are equipped with 'Boeotian' shields, which have scallops cut from the sides and are sometimes considered a 'heroizing' element, rather than a genuine piece of equipment. Attic black figure amphora, dated ca. 520–500 BC. Currently in the National Museum of Antiquities, Leiden.

of their households. The *basileis* who have a say in political matters are sometimes referred to collectively as the *hegetores ede medontes*, 'leaders and councillors' (for example, *Od.* 7.186).

The *basileis*, particularly the leaders, consider themselves to be a superior kind of people; they are the *aristoi*, literally the 'best' that a community has to offer. The leaders distinguish themselves from others by being decisive in battle; they also determine politics and deal with all matters pertaining to law and order within the community (see, for example, *Il.* 1.490–492). Furthermore, they are among the richest of the people in their community, possessing large amounts of treasure (*keimelia*). Naturally, they have illustrious forebears and can recount their ancestries when necessary. They emphasize their wealth by keeping horses. Finally, they engage in a life of leisure and are thus, for example, able to organize and participate in games and feasts.

Social relations in the epic world are horizontal rather than vertical; that is to say, most interaction is between social peers: men associate with other men of equal or similar status (the obvious exception being dependents, especially slaves). The worlds of the *basileis* and of the common people appear to exist more or less side by side; only infrequently do the two social spheres interact directly. Firstly, many of the actions undertaken by the leaders (rulers and elders) are presented as being either in the public interest or otherwise sanctioned by the community as a whole. In the assemblies at home, it appears that a large cross-section of the community was present, even if only leaders were supposed to speak (*Od.* 2.6–259). Secondly, it appears that some sort of tax was levied on the common people that was redistributed in the form of *gerousios oinos*, 'wine of the elders' (*Il.* 4.257–263). Thirdly, a leader might be awarded a *temenos*, a piece of 'public land', for services rendered (*Il.* 12.310–314); no doubt, the other leaders of a community would allocate the land, but it is presented as something approved of by the people as a whole.

Nevertheless, the relationship between the leaders and the rest of the community was normally one of mutual respect, as demonstrated by the description of Nestor and a few thousand of his people sacrificing bulls to Poseidon (*Od.* 3.4–11). The common people simply appear to engage in pursuits different from those of the princes. For example, they do not appear to be present in the Greek camp and might not have any particular role to play in battle. In Homeric descriptions, the leaders among the *basileis* fight and speak, while the *demos* appear to stand by idly. Most modern commentators assume that the *demos* consists of commoners, but this need not at all be the case. Instead, the *demos*, or 'mass' of the people, might equally well have consisted of lower-ranking *basileis*, such as the sons, neighbours, and friends of the leaders; slaves and other dependents might also be included among them. The independent smallholders, presumably the largest segment of society, are perhaps sometimes not present at all.

• Homeric ideals of warfare

The ideals espoused in the Homeric epics would be the same as those pursued by Homer's aristocratic contemporaries and their descendants, and they may have been rooted in an ideology that can be traced back in time and that, to some extent, is found in many comparable cultures, both ancient and otherwise. For Homer's heroes, there are two main ways in which men may distinguish themselves. The first is by being a good speaker in the public arena. Odysseus, in particular, emerges as expertly qualified in this field as a gifted public speaker, storyteller, and liar. The second way is by demonstrating one's prowess (*arete*) on the battlefield. On the Greek side, no hero is as talented when it comes to slaughter as Achilles, son of Peleus, king of Phthia, and commander of the Myrmidons.

An examination of war and violence raises the question of why men in the epic world fight. Insults emerge as the main cause of conflict between communities. Indeed, the main cause of the Trojan War was Menelaus' wounded honour (*time*) as a result of Paris, Menelaus' guest, making off with the king's wife, Helen. In the Homeric world, there are two courses to take when one has been offended. One may exact terrible revenge by retaliating swiftly and dreadfully, or one may seek a diplomatic solution. Both were available to men in the Homeric epics, just as war and diplomacy are options to modern politicians. In the case of the epic world, two instances spring to mind that illustrate the different paths to conflict resolution.

The first is a story told by Nestor in the *Iliad*. His father, Neleus, ruler of Pylos,

A Greek warrior kneels and seems poised to strike down a serpent that has coiled around a column. It may represent the hero Cadmus ready to strike down Ares' dragon near the place where he would found Thebes. Greek artists always depicted ancient heroes in contemporary dress, making artefacts like these valuable sources of information. Laconian plate, dated to around 550–540 BC. Currently in the Louvre, Paris.

once sent a chariot to compete in games held in Elis. The Epeans stole the chariot, thus angering the Pylians. Nestor then led a party of young men on a raid and stole a considerable amount of livestock; they also took a number of prisoners (*Il.* 11.669–704). The second story involves Odysseus in a similar situation, but with a different course of action adopted by Odysseus' father, Laërtes, who was then ruler of Ithaca. Once, the men of Messene had sailed to Ithaca and taken 300 sheep; they also enslaved the herdsmen. Unlike Neleus, who authorized the retaliatory raid led by Nestor, Laërtes and the other elders (*gerontes*) sent the young Odysseus on a diplomatic mission to Messene to ask for suitable compensation (*Od.* 21.15–21). We never learn whether he was successful or not, but it is noteworthy that violence was clearly not the only option available to solve problems.

Despite the Trojan War being presented as a full-scale war between two communities and their allies (Sparta, Mycenae and their allies against the Trojans and their allies), it is clear that, if Menelaus were to die on the battlefield, the war would be essentially over (*Il.* 4.178–181). However, some heroes vow to continue fighting whatever happens (*Il.* 9.40–49). After all, fighting at Troy offers more than just the risk of death, and the other leaders and their men have ulterior motives for fighting. Through fighting and achieving victory (*nike*), men gain *kudos*, the divine glory of success granted by Zeus. *Kudos* leads to the acquisition of both *time* and

A view of Thermopylae as it looks today. Since Antiquity, the sea has retreated, so that the narrow pass of the ancient 'Hot Gates' is now a broad strip of land that would be difficult to defend with a small army. Parts of the Greek coast-line have changed significantly in the course of a few thousand years.

kleos. Time, 'honour', is particularly expressed in material terms: at least some of the booty is regarded as *geras*, a 'prize of honour'. The Greek heroes often ponder the great wealth that is in store for them once Troy is finally captured (for example, *Il.* 2.373–374). Capturing Troy's wealth would immeasurably increase their *time*; the capture of the city itself would add to their *kleos* or 'prestige'. *Kleos* is a man's fame or reputation, and is all that survives after death, so the heroes strive to make

The Aegean in a broader context

To a modern Western mind, Greek civilization looms large. Ancient Greece is commonly regarded as the cradle of Western civilization. That this notion is – for a number of reasons – actually incorrect is of little importance, considering the influence that this line of thinking has had on shaping our society since the Renaissance. But it does ignore one other important fact, namely that the Aegean was – until the time of Alexander the Great –essentially a marginal region on the outskirts of the wider Near-Eastern world.

The main civilizations could be found in Central Anatolia and along the banks of the main rivers in Mesopotamia and Egypt. These core regions gave rise to the civilizations of Sumer and Akkad, Babylon, and Assyria, as well as the Egyptians, Hittites and various important Anatolian cultures, such as the Lydians. Some of them started out as city-states; all eventually came to be territorial states ruled from a central location and often governed by (hereditary) kings. Surrounding the homelands of these civilizations were marginal areas: deserts, various kinds of wild and mountainous countries, and coastal regions. These marginal areas included the Levantine coast, the region around Susa, the island of Cyprus and, of course, the Aegean. These regions were inhabited by nomadic or semi-nomadic tribes or dotted with numerous bigger or smaller city-states.

The main civilizations of the ancient Near East often dominated these marginal areas, engaged in trade with them, or made other uses of their people and resources. For example, wood from Lebanon was exported to Egypt. The kingdoms of the Late Bronze Age and Iron Age also made frequent use of mercenaries recruited from these marginal areas. The so-called 'Apiru' – possibly a general term to denote semi-nomadic roving people who lived outside of civilized society – were used as police forces and soldiers of fortune in the Great Kingdoms of the Late Bronze Age. Similarly, some have suggested that the wealthy Mycenaeans buried in the shaft graves at Mycenae made a living as mercenaries. From the seventh century BC, heavily-armoured warriors from Greece fought in the armies of Egypt and Babylon; they were also known to the Assyrians as brigands and pirates.

A detail of the Amathus Bowl. This silver bowl was found on Cyprus, but is of Phoenician make; it dates to the seventh century BC. The scene shows heavily-armed warriors – perhaps Greeks or even Anatolians – assaulting a Near-Eastern fortified town or fortress. Currently in the British Museum. Drawn after J.L. Myres, 'The Amathus Bowl: a long-lost masterpiece of Oriental engraving', Journal of Hellenic Studies 53 *(1933), plate I.*

a name for themselves and become the object of stories that will be told generations later. By contrast, a man's *time* or honour is lost when he dies: the treasures that symbolize his honour pass on to his heirs (for example, *Od.* 9.263–265).

The Greeks were fascinated by the Trojan War and similarly violent stories, and frequently engaged in war and warlike activities themselves. But like most cultures, they were ambivalent about warfare. This ambivalence is expressed by their possessing not one god, but two dedicated to war. The first of these is Ares, the god of strife and slaughter. The second is Athena, the goddess of wisdom and feminine crafts, and also a goddess of war. Ares revels in slaughter and attack, which makes him careless. Athena, however, is skilled in strategy and defence. When the two divinities meet in battle, Athena handily defeats her reckless and bloodthirsty brother. It is a victory of mind over brute force, of strategy over bloodlust. The endemic nature of warfare in Early Greece is also reflected in the fact that most Greek gods possess martial qualities and were, at one time or another, also engaged in battle, such as the Titanomachy and Gigantomachy, two wars fought against the Titans and the giants, respectively, at the dawn of Olympian hegemony.

• Setting the stage

As is often pointed out, Greece is a poor country. Three-quarters consists of mountains, which limits the amount of arable land. Already in the Bronze Age, Greeks crossed the Aegean to settle in the more fruitful country of western Anatolia, where eventually powerful cities developed in the course of the Archaic period, such as Old Smyrna, Miletus and Ephesus. Between the eighth and sixth centuries BC, Greeks travelled even further afield and founded new towns in the south of France,

Catalonia, Libya, and on the coasts of the Black Sea. Southern Italy and Sicily were so densely settled that these regions together were referred to as *Megale Hellas* by the Greeks and *Magna Graecia* by the later Romans; that is to say, 'Great Greece'. In areas controlled by powerful territorial states or other city-states, the Greeks sometimes founded more humble trading posts, such as at Al-Mina in Lebanon, the location of the old Phoenician city of Tripolis, in the eighth century BC. Greek mercenaries and traders in Egypt were allowed to settle in Naucratis from the seventh century BC onwards.

The different types of evidence used to reconstruct warfare in Early Greece – from archaeological material, such as burials with arms, to iconographic sources like vase-paintings and written texts, such as the Homeric epics – are not spread evenly through the Aegean basin, nor does the evidence of particular regions cover the entire period under examination. A case in point would be the iconographic evidence. For the Mycenaean period, much of it comes from the major centres in southern and central Greece. From the tenth century onwards, the bulk comes from relatively few centres of production (Athens, Corinth, Sparta, and the island of Euboea, as well as some of the other islands in the Aegean and sites in Asia Minor). Syntheses are relatively plentiful, but none focus specifically on depictions of arms and armour or other martial scenes.

Furthermore, the evidence that has come down to us represents only a portion of what must once have existed. For example, we know virtually nothing about early Corinthian poets, such as Eumelus, whose poetry may have added to our insights into warfare in the north-east Peloponnese. In addition, whole classes of material may simply have disappeared. We have no pottery from, for example, Achaea that depicts combat or weapons, but perhaps they instead produced such scenes in other media that have left no trace in the archaeological record (cf. Penelope's elaborate burial shroud for Laërtes in Homer's *Odyssey*, or the chance find of fragments of a wall-painting of the seventh century BC from the remains of the temple unearthed at Kalapodi).

This book is divided into four main chapters that are preceded by a prologue (the introduction you are now reading) and followed by an epilogue that serves as a synthesis of the preceding chapters. The chapters themselves each cover a particular period. The first chapter focuses on the Late Bronze Age and places particular emphasis on the latter centuries of that era, both the heyday of Mycenaean civilization and its collapse. The second chapter examines warfare in the Early Iron Age. The third chapter details warriors and warfare in the Archaic period down to more or less the middle of the sixth century. And the fourth chapter emphasizes developments in Greek warfare set against the backdrop of Greek struggles with the Persian Empire.

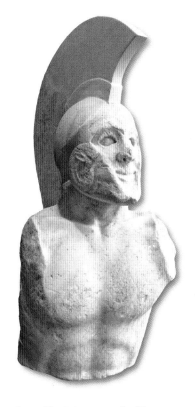

A marble statue unearthed in Sparta and dated to the early fifth century BC; much of the helmet crest has been restored. It has been suggested that this sculpture is a bust of Leonidas, but this seems unlikely. Note the ram's head decoration on the cheek pieces. Currently in the Archaeological Museum of Sparta.

1 Palace warriors

Ascending to Tretus, and again going along the road to Argos,
you see on the left the ruins of Mycenae.
—Pausanias, *Description of Greece* 2.15.4

The Mycenaean Bronze Age is divided into a number of phases, referred to as Late Helladic I–III, each often subdivided into smaller stages using letters, some of which are even further split using Arabic numerals (for example, LH IIIB1). Together, these cover the period between roughly 1550 and 1100 BC, which witnessed the rise, flowering, and eventual demise of the Mycenaean civilization. The latter is dated to the years around 1200 BC; the twelfth century is a period of further slow disintegration. The subsequent eleventh century is a period about which comparatively little is known and it serves as an age of transition to the Early Iron Age, which conventionally starts around 1000 BC and will be the subject of the next chapter.

The period under examination can be divided very roughly into three parts. The first is what we might refer to as a Prepalatial period. It runs down to around 1350 BC and covers the Late Helladic I, II and IIIA1 archaeological phases. The second period witnessed the building of the Mycenaean palaces and encompasses the Late Helladic IIIA2 and IIIB phases, about 1350 to 1200 BC. Mycenaean civilization would reach its zenith in the second half of this age. Around 1200 BC, many of the Mycenaean palaces were destroyed; some were abandoned. After this, the twelfth century or Late Helladic IIIC period is an age in which Mycenaean society managed to cling on before petering out almost completely. Nevertheless, there is continuity from the Bronze Age to the Iron Age, as we shall see.

• The Prepalatial period

Burials with weapons and armour are a feature of Late Helladic I–IIIA1, and again during the Late Helladic IIIC period. The Prepalatial period is characterized firstly by the magnificent finds from the shaft graves unearthed in the grave circles at Mycenae. Grave Circle B, which is located at some distance from the citadel, is slightly older than Grave Circle A, which was in use between ca. 1600 BC and ca. 1500 BC. In the thirteenth century BC, it was enclosed by an extension of the fortification

walls. The shaft graves of Grave Circle A have yielded very rich finds, including sets of swords and the famous gold 'Mask of Agamemnon' (a burial mask).

Another famous find from Grave Circle A is the so-called 'Lion Hunt' dagger. The dagger is made of bronze and features a hunting scene made of inlaid gold and black niello. It shows five male figures hunting lions. Four of them are clearly visible and are naked, apart from a kind of shorts. One of them kneels and fights like an archer. The figure closest to the lions is on the ground and is about to be savaged by a lion. The other three figures are all equipped with very long spears that they hold in an overhand position. Apart from the archer, all figures are equipped with shields. Two of these are so-called 'figure-of-eight shields', whereas the other two are 'tower shields'. Since both types cover the torsos and legs of the owners, they are also referred to as 'body shields'.

Both types of shields were adopted by the Mycenaeans from the Minoan civilization that arose on Crete and came to dominate the Cyclades in the course of the Middle Bronze Age (ca. 2000–1550 BC). For example, tower shields are also depicted on the famous fresco from Akrotiri on the island of Thera. The figure-of-eight shield was also a Cretan motif that was readily adopted on the mainland. Like the tower shield, this type probably consisted of a wooden frame and wicker base, covered with cowhide. It was the height of a man and elliptical in overall shape, with a very slender waist, making it resemble the Arabic numeral 8. Curiously, shields eventually disappear from art in the Palatial period and are not mentioned in Linear B tablets; instead, the figure-of-eight shield is eventually known only as a decorative element used in wall-paintings and jewellery.

The 'Lion Hunt' dagger, discovered in grave-shaft IV in Grave Circle A at Mycenae. It dates to the sixteenth century BC. Men with body shields and long spears, as well as a solitary archer, hunt lion. The body shields come in two types: the figure-of-eight shield and the tower shield. Currently in the National Archaeological Museum in Athens.

A Minoan bronze dagger, dated ca. 1700–1400 BC. The small holes were used for fixing a handle to the blade. The Minoans were accomplished bronze smiths and played a key role in the early cultural development of the Greeks. Currently in the National Museum of Antiquities, Leiden.

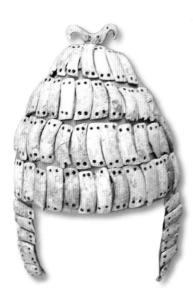

Restored boar's-tusk helmet from Mycenae, dated to the fourteenth century BC. This helmet consisted of slivers of boar tusks that were attached to a leather cap. Helmets like this were in use all through the Mycenaean Bronze Age down to the tenth century BC and perhaps even later. Homer may have seen an heirloom and used it in his description of Odysseus' helmet in the tenth book of the Iliad. *Currently in the National Archaeological Museum, Athens.*

The Dendra panoply

In 1960, Swedish archaeologists unearthed a tomb in the village of Dendra in the Argolid, containing a beaten bronze cuirass made of various parts that is sometimes referred to as a 'lobster cuirass' from its resemblance to the marine crustacean. It has been dated to around 1400 BC. The Dendra panoply is usually interpreted as having belonged to a chariot-borne warrior, who would probably dismount to fight on foot in a manner familiar from the Homeric epics, probably using spears or the rapier-like swords characteristic of the era.

The cuirass itself consists of fifteen plates. One large plate covered the chest and belly; another plate covered the back. The basic structure of these back and front plates is very similar to the later Greek bell-shaped cuirass, discussed in chapter 3. Other bronze elements of this cuirass include a protective plate for the neck, shoulder plates, and a number of interlocking bronze parts that protected the lower body and upper legs. The bronze plates were held together using leather thongs. Other fragments found in the tomb suggest that the panoply further consisted of at least one greave and a gauntlet or lower arm-guard, both also made of bronze, and a boar's-tusk helmet. Associated with the armour were two swords and a long dagger. The grave did not contain either spears or shield; perhaps the warrior needed none.

Bits and pieces of similar pieces of armour have been unearthed in various places on the Greek mainland and in Crete, all in tombs. Metal armour appears only to have been used in the Late Helladic II period and in Late Helladic IIIA, or between roughly 1500 and 1300 BC. In addition to further traces of boar's-tusk helmets, a bronze helmet dated to around 1400 BC has been unearthed at Knossos. These finds are all comparatively rare, but scattered across a relatively large geographical area, so that it is reasonable to assume that metal armour was used fairly consistently in this period. Conversely, there is almost no evidence for armour in the period before 1500 BC, such as the shaft graves in the grave circles at Mycenae, nor in the Late Helladic IIIB period.

Some commentators have suggested that the Dendra cuirass would have been very cumbersome to wear, with some even suggesting that the wearer would have been unable to get up on his own if he were to fall, and that he therefore must have functioned as a chariot-borne archer in the manner of the ancient Egyptians. However, the presence of swords in the tomb strongly argues in favour of the interpretation of the wearer as someone who fought at close range. Furthermore, experiments conducted in the 1980s at the University of Birmingham have demonstrated that the cuirass was, in fact, quite comfortable. One commentator, D.E.H. Wardle, even emphasized how easy it was to walk in the armour and that, if the skirt plates were adjusted, it would even have allowed the wearer to sit.

A stele that marked one of the shaft graves at Mycenae was decorated in low relief with a scene depicting a man in a chariot running down another figure on foot. The charioteer is depicted alone in the chariot. He clasps his rapier-like sword with his left hand, while his right hand appears to hold a long spear or lance that he is aiming at the hapless figure on foot. However, it seems very unlikely that Mycenaeans ran down their enemies in chariots using spears. The Greek landscape is ill-suited to large-scale chariot manoeuvres and it seems unlikely that charioteers would have been able to get close enough for warriors to strike down their opponents with thrusting spears. Instead, it seems far more likely that chariots were used to transport warriors to the battlefield, where they would have dismounted to fight on foot. The scene could therefore be heroizing. Another interpretation is that the man may have served as a mercenary in the east, for example among the Hittites or Egyptians. Certainly, Minoan painters had been employed by the Hyksos kings to decorate the walls of Avaris during Egypt's Second Intermediate Period (1650–1549 BC); it seems likely that Mycenaean warriors could have found employment in the armies of nearby civilizations.

Certainly, the relatively sudden appearance of very wealthy men in Mycenae in the grave circles is something that needs to be explained. The finds make clear that these are high-ranking men: golden funerary masks and the presence of weapons, including the elaborately decorated Lion Hunt dagger, as well as the find of a sceptre prove this fairly conclusively. It has been suggested that these people were part of a royal dynasty that had managed to acquire wealth through long-distance trade. Alternatively, it has been suggested that they may have acquired their riches serving as mercenaries, perhaps on Minoan Crete, and that they thereby gained the necessary experience that would be helpful in conquering the island around 1400 BC.

- **Palatial fortifications**

The most immediately noticeable feature of Mycenaean towns and cities of the Palatial period would have been their fortifications. The Greek archaeologist Spyros Iakovidis, in his *Late Helladic Citadels on Mainland Greece* (1983), has pointed out that fortifications underwent little change down to about 1400 BC. By that time, although some settlements continued to use earlier fortifications, others, such as Kea, had updated theirs with the addition of towers. The walls consisted of stone socles, made of large stones or boulders, topped by mud-brick superstructures. By around 1400 BC, some sites, such as Philakopi on the Cycladic island of Melos, were protected by a double wall built on parallel lines, which were connected by cross walls creating a series of empty spaces between facades.

Many of the Mycenaean palaces after ca. 1400 BC were actually fortified cita-

Ivory plaque of a warrior's head with boar's-tusk helmet. Recovered from a chamber tomb at Mycenae and dated to the thirteenth century BC. Currently in the National Archaeological Museum, Athens.

Reconstruction of the citadel of Mycenae as it would have looked toward the end of the thirteenth century BC. The monumental entrance, the Lion Gate, is clearly visible, as is the palace at the top of the hill. Drawing by Rocío Espín.

dels, though Thebes and Orchomenus in Boeotia, and – if indeed it is a palace – the so-called Menelaion in Laconia, appear to lack fortifications. In the 1990s, geophysical surveys revealed what appear to be fortification walls at Pylos in Messenia, some distance from the palace itself. In the Argolid, a number of fortified citadels are found clustered together, namely at Tiryns, Midea, Mycenae itself and the Aspis hill at Argos. The Boeotian fortress at Gla near Lake Copais is massive, but the L-shaped building inside might not be an actual palace. It is thought that the rulers of nearby Orchomenus had the fortress built. Gla was connected with the system of Mycenaean dams and canals that drained Lake Copais to make it suitable for farming, and it may have served as a refuge site for local farmers.

The fortifications at Mycenaean citadels are built mostly in the then-new, so-called 'Cyclopean' style. This type of masonry consists of large blocks of stone of irregular shape, usually unworked or roughly-worked local limestone, stacked on top of each other without the use of mortar. Cyclopean masonry was not limited to fortifications; it was also used in the construction of other monumental Mycenaean structures, including certain other buildings such as tombs, dams, and bridges.

The middle of the thirteenth century BC saw much activity with regard to the construction of fortifications. At Tiryns, the lower town was originally protected by a stone and mud-brick wall built around 1280 BC; a generation later, this wall

One of the few remaining Mycenaean bridges: a beautiful example of 'Cyclopean' masonry, consisting of loosely fitted large stones and boulders.

A view of the remains of the Mycenaean fortress at Gla in Boeotia.

The Lion Gate of Mycenae, constructed in the second half of the
thirteenth century BC. Note how
the gate is flanked by two walls,
which would have made life very
difficult for any warriors trying to
break down the wooden doors.

was replaced by a more massive Cyclopean construction. Small gates were now also replaced by more monumental constructions; the famous Lion Gate at Mycenae was probably built around 1250 BC. Shortly before the end of the thirteenth century, Mycenae, Tiryns, and Athens undertook efforts to secure a water-supply within the confines of their walls. Such practical considerations suggest that the Mycenaean Greeks were on some kind of war-footing.

Fear of attacks from Central Greece or further north must have been the reason that a huge wall was built across the Isthmus, some time during the Late Helladic IIIB period, at about the same time as the final phases of fortifications at Mycenae and Tiryns. Even after the fall of the Mycenaean palaces, many Bronze Age fortification walls remained visible; some were even extended, repaired, or reinforced, though no new walls of Cyclopean type were ever built. These sites include Salamis, Naxos (Grotta), Siphnos (Aghios Andreas), Kea (Aghia Irini), Melos (Phylakopi and Aghios Spyridon), Paros (Koukounaries), and Tenos (Xombourgo); some, as the Dutch archaeologist Jan Paul Crielaard has pointed out, continued in use until Protogeometric and even Geometric times. Some of these fortifications were still very impressive without being Cyclopean: two fortified *acropoleis* on Salamis, for example, were built wholly of stone.

Mycenaean fortifications were massive, but also relatively straightforward.

This postern gate at Mycenae was constructed at around the same time as the Lion Gate, ca. 1250–1200 BC. It would allow the defenders to send out a small group of men to harass besiegers. The structure of the gate, along with its flanking walls, is similar to the Lion Gate, but more modest in size.

Unlike Hittite fortifications, Mycenaean walls appear not to have been fitted with crenellations. Instead, they appear to have been flat on top. The Lion Gate at Mycenae is a rare example of a more complex form of defensive architecture. Any attackers trying to breach this gate would have been subject to attack from three sides, as the Lion Gate is actually located at the end of a narrow corridor flanked by walls. Furthermore, a small postern gate would have allowed the defenders to sally forth to attack any assailants in the rear who tried to force entry via the Lion Gate.

As regards siege techniques, little can be learnt from the Mycenaean evidence. As a whole, there is little evidence regarding siege warfare in the eastern Mediterranean and the Near East during the Bronze Age. Fortifications predate the Bronze Age, but it seems that siege techniques remained relatively crude overall. The Assyrians were the leaders in the field of siege warfare. Already in the Middle Bronze Age, we find accounts of sieges in which they employed battering rams and towers, but such engines were probably very rare. Typically, fortified settlements were taken through circumvallation and the building of siege mounds; ladders and sappers may also have been used. More detailed depictions of sieges appear on Assyrian reliefs of the ninth century BC and later. But with regards to the Greeks, there is no evidence that they adopted siege ladders, siege towers, or even battering rams before the fifth century BC.

Wall-painting from the palace at Pylos depicting a warrior about to board a chariot (dual type). Note the waisted tunics and the boar's-tusk helmets. Currently in the Chora Museum. Copied from the original by Andrew J. Brozyna.

Tantalizing glimpses of what a siege might have been like in Mycenaean times are afforded by fragments of the so-called 'Siege Fresco' from Mycenae. These fragments of a wall-painting show parts of a town with the characteristic checker-pattern that was used to denote walls, with at least one woman looking out of a window while other figures are shown standing in front of the walls. Other small fragments supposedly reveal the presence of warriors out in the field, possibly archers, and a chariot, but the enemy has not been preserved. A large warrior, clad in tunic and linen gaiters, appears to fall from a roof. The curving line above him is commonly interpreted as part of a horse, and the figure has thus been regarded as forming part of a motif well-known from Near Eastern art and some of the shaft grave stelae, namely that of a warrior being run down by a chariot. According to this view, the warrior does not fall from the roof, but is actually part of a scene perhaps wholly unconnected with the rest of the wall-painting. However, the Dutch scholar Joost Crouwel has cast serious doubt on this interpretation and regards the line and the accompanying change of colour as simply denoting a hill or other change in the landscape, which seems to more accurately reflect what has actually been depicted.

• Soldiers of the Mycenaean kings

During the Palatial period, the heyday of the Mycenaean civilization, burials with arms appear to have been rare. Between Late Helladic IIA and Late Helladic IIIB, or between roughly 1500 and 1200 BC, some members of the elite were buried in so-called beehive or *tholos* tombs. These were large underground burial structures of which the main chamber was shaped more or less like a beehive. Because these *tholos* monuments are rather conspicuous features in the landscape, virtually all of them have been rifled by tomb raiders. As a result, there is little information to be gleaned from graves as far as the appearance of warriors is concerned.

However, the frescoes with which the Mycenaeans decorated the interior walls of their palaces provide a wealth of information regarding the appearance and equipment of their armed forces. Stylistically speaking, Mycenaean art was influenced by the earlier Minoan culture from Crete, but the subject matter is often very different. The Minoans seldom depicted scenes of a martial nature (although they were undoubtedly as warlike as any other ancient civilization), while the Mycenaeans, by contrast, frequently depicted warriors and related themes, like hunting scenes.

Wall-paintings are almost all known from fragments that generally date to just before the palace's destruction. Scenes with martial subjects have been unearthed at the Peloponnesian palaces of Mycenae, Tiryns, and Pylos, as well as in Boeotian Orchomenus. These fragments provide clues concerning the equipment used by warriors. For example, we know that most warriors wore greaves. Fragments

Entrance to the 'Treasury of Atreus', which is actually a tholos *or beehive tomb near Mycenae. It was constructed around 1250 BC; the entrance road or* dromos *would have only been visible when the tomb was opened up to add another burial to the central chamber.*

from the palace at Orchomenus depict walls with figures standing on top of them, whose lower legs are protected by white gaiters. One figure's legs are furthermore equipped with two oval greaves, perhaps made of bronze: such small greaves are typical of the Late Bronze Age. Unlike the bronze greaves in use from about 700 BC onwards, these Bronze Age specimens were clearly strapped or tied on, rather than clipped on.

Shields are never shown in the Palatial iconographic material, apart from the purely decorative figure-of-eight shields. One possible exception is known from Pylos. Fragments of a wall-painting show a figure with a short spear in overhand position; the scene also depicts what could be a shield. Famed illustrator Piet de Jong restored the shield as if it were round and fitted with a double grip. More recently, his British colleague Peter Connolly has interpreted the visible elements of the shield as the upper lobe of a figure-of-eight shield. However, Cheryl Fortenberry, in her important dissertation on Mycenaean warfare, has emphasized the

fragmentary nature of the fresco and believes that the preserved dark band might not be a shield at all; it is perhaps a hill or other element of the landscape. In addition, Fortenberry suggests that the figure is perhaps not even a warrior. Unlike typical soldiers, the figure is not bare-chested, but clad in a tunic. Furthermore, he has no helmet and his spear seems very short. These characteristics strongly suggest that the figure is actually a hunter, rather than a warrior.

Some of the men in the frescoes are equipped with boar's-tusk helmets. Examples of tusk plates have been unearthed at a number of sites, from Middle Helladic II and III down to Late Helladic IIIB, so we know that they may have been relatively common. It has been estimated that some thirty or forty boars would have to be killed to provide the necessary amount of tusks to cut plates from and cover the entire surface of the helmet, from which it has been argued that only the aristocracy could have afforded them. Yet, in Mycenaean art, the boar's-tusk helmet is by far the most popular piece of headgear depicted. It is also represented in Linear B tablets. Perhaps this helmet is closely associated with the palace, which may have handed these out to their soldiers. If true, this means that boar's-tusk helmets are not indicators of social status or wealth, but rather that the person in question – a palace guard or fighting man of the court – worked for the palace and was supplied by it. Of course, they may also have been obtained through trade or could have been handed down as heirlooms.

Horses and chariots are depicted on some wall-paintings, and it is clear that chariots were used by some spearmen to move quickly to the battlefield, where they probably dismounted to fight on foot. Specialization with regards to horses is demonstrated by fragments from Mycenae that show men in tunics grooming horses, while a warrior with boar's-tusk helmet and spear looks on; he is no doubt inspecting the work done by servants. Especially associated with chariots are warriors with linen-wrapped legs. In some cases, these men may be setting out to hunt rather than to fight. Remains of a wall-painting from Tiryns show a (chariot) horse following a tunic-clad figure with linen gaiters holding a dog on a leash. The presence of a dog typically indicates a hunting scene, even though we cannot exclude the possibility that they used war-dogs in battle.

Mycenaeans were familiar with riding on horseback, but depictions are rare. A Mycenaean Late Helladic IIIB pot sherd from a tomb near ancient Ugarit depicts a horseman equipped with a sword. Furthermore, a terracotta figurine of a rider, dated to Late Helladic IIIB1, has been unearthed at Mycenae. However, these examples only prove that people rode on horses; they do not directly support the notion that the Mycenaean Greeks also fought from horseback, although it obviously cannot be excluded. However, similar pictures are known from Egypt, where horsemen clearly served as dispatch riders and scouts. In a Mycenaean army, horsemen perhaps also served in similar capacities. Recreational riding can also not be excluded. Unusual are depictions of female figures, sometimes considered deities, riding side-saddle.

Actual combat between rival armed forces is depicted on a large number of fragments of the wall-paintings that once decorated Hall 64 in the palace at Pylos. This room was probably the first traversed by visitors to the palace, and no doubt served to instil dread in them. The fragments show various scenes of presumably Pylian soldiers fighting so-called 'savages'. The 'Tarzan Fresco' shows similar warriors, clad in short kilts and equipped with linen gaiters and boar's-tusk helmets, attacking men with unkempt hair and clothed in animal skins. Two of the men and one of the savages are equipped with short swords; one Pylian soldier attacks using a long spear. The Pylian warriors also have an oval drawn on their right shins. These undoubtedly represent – bronze? – greaves tied to their legs and covering part of their linen gaiters.

Another set of fragments from the palace at Pylos shows a scene of combat similar to the one just discussed. This time, however, there are no savages. Instead, all men appear to wear some sort of shorts or loincloths; none of them has any leg wrappings. One group is bareheaded while the other group wear helmets of unknown type, perhaps of felt or leather. The helmeted soldiers are probably to be interpreted as Pylian troops, although of a different type from the ones just discussed, and presumably not elite troops or guards, as they lack gaiters or greaves, and have apparently simpler and cheaper helmets. Two warriors fight each other with swords, while one of the bareheaded ones is equipped, if properly restored,

Mycenaean amphoroid krater depicting a chariot following a rider; dated ca. 1300–1250 BC. While horseback riding seems to have been uncommon in the Late Bronze Age, it was not unknown. Currently in the Allard Pierson Museum, Amsterdam.

with a club. Both scenes appear to take place at a river, perhaps representing the boundary of Pylian territory, with brave Pylian soldiers fending off attacks from hostile barbarians and possibly unfriendly neighbours.

The wall-paintings reveal that, while many men wear some kind of – probably linen – gaiters to protect their lower legs, some are also equipped with a single greave. Single greaves are also known from tombs. Again, Cheryl Fortenberry has, in her PhD thesis, suggested that these single greaves, tied to one leg, may indicate status or rank. I would suggest more specifically that single greaves, like boar's-tusk

Artistic rendering of a battle at a river between Mycenaean soldiers and savages, inspired by the 'Tarzan Fresco' from Pylos. Drawing by Angel García Pinto.

helmets, further indicate a connection with the palace, perhaps in combination with the linen gaiters, although there really is no evidence other than that found at the palaces to corroborate this hypothesis.

Hunting scenes are more common than those showing actual combat and no doubt feature high-ranking men. Fragments of a wall-painting from Pylos show a tunic-clad figure aiming a short spear at a deer with antlers. The man is equipped with linen gaiters, like a warrior. Similar-looking figures are also shown on fragments from Tiryns. These, too, wear tunics and are equipped with linen gaiters. They carry a set of two short spears each and must be interpreted as hunters rather than warriors. It seems to me that the short spear is particularly a weapon associated with the hunt. Other fragments, also from Tiryns, again show a very similar figure equipped with two short spears. None of these figures is equipped with a helmet and all of them wear a tunic and linen gaiters.

Furthermore, clothing also indicates relatively high status. Only men associated with chariots and horses – as in the 'Groom Fresco', for example – wear tunics. Hunters and men in procession also tend to be fully clothed and equipped with gaiters and greaves. I would suggest that all of the fully-clothed men include both high-ranking individuals and their personal attendants, including grooms, charioteers, and huntsmen. The men in waisted tunics and associated with chariots may belong to the *heqetai* or 'followers' known from Linear B tablets. By contrast, rank-and-file 'soldiers' are always bare-chested and may have been culled from the lower classes.

• Mycenaean social and military organization

The palaces maintained archives where clay tablets written in so-called Linear B were kept. Linear B was a syllabic script used to write the early Greek language spoken by the Mycenaeans. They had adopted writing from the Minoans of Crete, whose script is referred to as Linear A. Later Greeks claimed that their country was originally inhabited by a people referred to as Pelasgians ('Sea People'), which may have included the Minoans.

The Mycenaeans never intentionally fired their clay tablets: they were accidentally baked in the fires that ravaged or destroyed the palaces in which they had been kept. Many of the tablets thus reflect a situation just prior to the destruction of the Mycenaean centres. The fact that archives have been unearthed in a number of centres (Knossos, Pylos, Chania, Mycenae, Tiryns, and Thebes) suggests that the individual Mycenaean centres were as independent as they were belligerent.

The Linear B tablets provide clues as regards Mycenaean socio-political structure, military equipment, and military organization. Based on the contents of the tablets, it is clear that the palaces produced and maintained at least some of the equipment used in war, including arrows and arrowheads, swords (*pa-ka-na*, probably the same word as the Homeric *phasgana*), spears, javelins, helmets, and chariots, as well as, at Knossos, corslets. As regards the latter, it is often assumed that these were made of metal, but this need not have been the case. However, the palaces did not apparently provide all of the necessary equipment, as there are many tablets in which incomplete chariots are recorded. Some of these list only a single wheel or a single horse. Furthermore, some people may have been awarded land by the palace in exchange for military service, for which they were provided at least part of the equipment, as well.

It thus seems that Mycenaean armies were organized using a mix of private and public – that is to say, palatial – means, with warriors perhaps only needing to provide part of the equipment at their own expense. This fits in well with recent insights regarding the relatively limited extent to which the palaces regulated or controlled economic processes within the territories that they occupied.

The most informative tablets with regard to the socio-political organization in Mycenaean centres come from Pylos and Knossos, which in turn reveal how the military may have been organized. The tablets show that the ruler at both Pylos and Knossos was known as the *wa-na-ka* (*wanax*, 'ruler' or 'king'), who possessed vast tracts of land and employed his own craftsmen, who are called *wanakteros* ('royal') in the tablets. At Pylos, the *wanax* may have had the warlike name *Ekhelawon*, that is 'He Who is Victorious in/over the Host'. Second in command was the *lawagetas* (*ra-wa-ke-ta*), whose name contains the words *laos* and *agein*; the term thus means literally 'leader of the people'. It has been suggested that this was an army-leader – a reasonable interpretation, as *laos* in Homer and later sources is often rendered 'host' or 'army' (the entire body of armed men).

Both *wanax* and *lawagetas* were involved in the organization of feasts; perhaps these places were also the meeting ground of a warrior elite. That such an elite existed is attested by a group of men known as the *heqetai* (singular *heqetas*, from *e-qe-ta*). The later Greek word *hepetas* simply means 'follower'. The British classicist John Chadwick already observed that the *heqetai* were probably elite troops, as well as the commanders of the Mycenaean infantry. On the tablets, they are associated with clothes, slaves, and wheels, and they may have worn a distinctive type of clothing. Other high-ranking figures may have existed, but these did not have as strong a military role to play in palatial organization as the *heqetai*.

Many details are omitted from the Linear B tablets, presumably because these were considered irrelevant. After all, to the scribes and readers of the tablets, there was no need to explain the intricacies of social and military organization, as they would already be intimately familiar with them. Nevertheless, there is a unique set of eight tablets from Pylos that describes the preparations made for an impending attack by apparently seaborne raiders. Two of these tablets – PY An 1 and 610 – give lists of 'rowers', along with their places of origin; five other tablets list the groups (*o-ka*) of people sent out to watch the coast (PY An 519, 653, 656, 657, 661). These groups consist of men from a particular place and led by an individual with a patronymic, an aristocratic feature that undoubtedly identified him as a *heqetas*. The rowers and the men led by the *heqetai* appear to be individuals who had to perform military service for one reason or another, which supports the notion that the palaces were responsible for mobilizing the army as a whole, even though the everyday tasks of command were probably left in the hands of the *heqetai*.

• The fall of Mycenaean civilization

Many of the Mycenaean palaces were destroyed in the early decades of the twelfth century, heralding the start of the Postpalatial period. This period, also referred to as Late Helladic IIIC by archaeologists, essentially covers the twelfth century BC. It is usually divided into three consecutive stages, dubbed Early, Middle, and Late. Much of the evidence for the Postpalatial period dates to Late Helladic IIIC Middle, set some time after the destructions that marked the end of the Palatial period.

The second half of the thirteenth century BC witnessed a marked increase in martial activities, such as the construction of larger fortifications. At least some of these activities were related to an increase in warfare. The clearest example is provided by the continued improvement of swords throughout the Late Bronze Age. The earliest Mycenaean types tend to be long, slender 'rapiers', which must have bent easily, and feature very short tangs that must have made their handles fragile. Many examples of the earliest types (so-called A and B) were clearly repaired multiple times. But in the course of the next few centuries, Mycenaean sword-smiths strove to improve their weapons, making them shorter and stronger, and therefore generally more useful in combat. An example is the so-called type E sword, introduced in Late Helladic IIIA2, which is flat, broad, and relatively short, with small rivet holes and a long tang.

Toward the very end of the thirteenth century, the so-called Naue type II sword was introduced, probably from Central Europe via Italy, which the Mycenaeans may have visited for purposes of trade and exchange. This long sword features a solid tang with pommel extension; the rivet-holes are very small. Aegean sword-smiths added the distinctive 'ears' at either side of the pommel spur. While most swords until now had been intended mostly for stabbing, the Naue-II sword was the first true cut-and-thrust sword. Once adopted, this superior blade spread quickly throughout the Aegean and became the main type of sword in Late Helladic IIIC. During this latter period, the earliest known iron examples of this sword also appeared. This long-lived sword type survived in the Aegean until the end of the sixth century, by which time it was replaced by a shorter Greek sword with cross-guard.

Archaeologist and ancient historian Sigrid Deger-Jalkotzy has published a brief survey of the major Late Helladic IIIC warrior graves, providing summaries of the warrior burials from Perati, and graves from five sites in Achaea, one site in Arcadia (Palaiokastro), one in Thessaly (Trikkala), one on the island of Naxos (Grotta), one on Kos (Langada), and several in eastern Crete, as well as a number of sites without a clearly ascertainable context, including Cephallonia. One of the graves at Grotta contained a man buried with a Naue-II-type sword and accompanied by what the excavators believe to be the remains of a bronze curry-comb for horses, and Deger-Jalkotzy adds that other evidence from Naxos makes clear that horses were part and parcel of the identity of high-ranking Naxian men. This need not surprise us, since horses everywhere in the ancient world are characteristic of elites in general and aristocracies in particular.

Following the collapse of the Mycenaean palaces, there is an apparent increase in the number of burials containing weapons, especially in regions away from the former core Mycenaean centres, such as in Achaea. There is some continuity in funerary practices from the preceding period: most of these burials are inhumations, with many reusing older Mycenaean chamber tombs. As in the preceding periods, the graves contain multiple bodies. The total number of warrior graves in a cemetery is typically very small. Again, Deger-Jalkotzy points out that, of the 219 tombs found at Perati, only two could be defined in any way as 'warrior tombs'. This limited distribution of warrior graves is similar to that of the Early Iron Age, as I shall also note in the next chapter.

The lack of 'warrior tombs' in Late Helladic IIIC Messenia, Boeotia, and the Volos area in Thessaly may be attributed to depopulation following the destruction of the palaces there, but the lack of such burials in the Argolid has no satisfactory explanation to date. However, it should be stressed that most Late Helladic IIIC cemeteries are poorer than in the preceding period, so it should come as no surprise that expensive items such as weapons are perhaps not interred as often. Furthermore, it should be stressed that the total number of Late Helladic IIIC burials with weapons is relatively small. Finally, burials with arms never returned in some of these regions, such as the Volos area, in which case the lack of such graves may simply represent a change in funerary customs.

Recently, construction activities revealed the burial of a warrior near the town of Amphilochia, situated by the Ambracian Gulf. The grave has been dated to the twelfth century BC. The finds included a golden *kylix* (wine cup), a dagger combining bronze and iron, a pair of greaves, an arrowhead, and a spearhead. The grave furthermore contained a pair of bronze swords, one with a bone handle, the other with gold wire wrapped around the hilt. Analysis of the bronze also showed that this second sword was of Italic make. This find emphasizes several characteristically aristocratic aspects, namely warfare (the different weapons, including an arrowhead), consumption of wine (the *kylix*), and overseas activities (the Italic sword).

Some examples of Mycenaean swords. Currently in the Glyptothek, Munich.

• Warriors of the Postpalatial period

With the destruction and abandonment of many of the Mycenaean palaces, wall-paintings also disappeared. Artists of the Late Helladic IIIC period now turned to painting figurative scenes on large vases, especially kraters. Figurative vase-painting flourished in the twelfth century, before petering out toward the end and then disappearing altogether in the eleventh, replaced by a style of vase-painting characterised by abstract, geometric motifs (Submycenaean and earliest Protogeometric-style pottery).

Especially on kraters of the Late Helladic IIIC-Middle style, warlike scenes proved very popular. While there is much variety, warriors on foot were often depicted on these pots equipped with one or two spears, a helmet, dark gaiters, and normally also a shield. The boar's-tusk helmet, so popular in the centuries preceding the fall, all but disappeared. We now encounter a number of different types of helmets that were perhaps cheaper or easier to manufacture. None of these appear to have left any archaeological traces and are known solely from the iconographic evidence.

Perhaps the best-known Late Helladic IIIC artefact is the so-called 'Warrior Vase' from Mycenae. Both sides of the krater show files of warriors. One side shows a line of six men, who are seen off by a woman on the far left; the gesture she makes is either one of farewell or mourning. These men are uniformly equipped. Each carries a crescent-shaped shield, wears dark gaiters and some kind of fringed tunic or perhaps a leather jerkin, and is equipped with a single thrusting spear and a helmet equipped with horns and a plume. If the chariot-borne spearmen are considered leaders, then perhaps these men represent the rank-and-file of a Late Helladic IIIC army. That these are commoners, perhaps even some sort of conscripts, is furthermore suggested by the knapsacks tied to their spears: a high-ranking individual would surely have used servants or slaves to carry his provisions. The other side of the vase shows a group of similarly-equipped warriors, except that they hold their spears overhead, as if ready to attack; their shields are also larger and their helmets are of the so-called 'hedgehog' type. The hedgehog helmet might have consisted of an actual hedgehog-skin stretched over a cap, or it perhaps represents a feathered helmet, raw hide, fur, and so forth.

Depictions of men apparently in some kind of battle stance are also encountered on a Late Helladic IIIC limestone stele, also from Mycenae and generally believed to have been made by the same artist as the 'Warrior Vase'. The object has been damaged and some of the decoration has disappeared over time, but one scene shows a line of five warriors, posed and equipped in a manner very similar to the men shown on the side of the 'Warrior Vase' briefly described above, clad in fringed tunics and equipped with dark gaiters and large shields, and holding their spears overhead, as if ready to strike an (unseen) enemy.

It is unclear what material was used to make the armour shown in the painted scenes. A krater fragment from the island of Euboea shows the body of a warrior, who is equipped with a sword and wears the dark gaiters or leggings so characteristic of Postpalatial vase-painting. The way that the upper body has been rendered is sometimes taken to indicate that the figure is wearing a bell-shaped cuirass, or perhaps some other bronze plate cuirass, fitted with shoulder pieces similar to the chronologically-earlier ones found with the 'lobster' armour discovered at Dendra and dated to around 1400 BC. A second krater fragment, also from Euboea and decorated by a more proficient artist, shows the fringed tunic of a warrior who is equipped with dark gaiters and a sword.

It seems unlikely that the artists meant to represent bronze armour. More likely, all armour at this time consisted of a kind of leather padding, similar to that depicted on other Postpalatial pots. The evidence for the use of metal body-armour other than greaves from Late Helladic IIIA2 or IIIB onwards is, in any case, slight to non-existent. Some bronze scraps have been unearthed at Kallithea in Achaea that date to around 1180 BC and are taken by some to be evidence for metal body-armour with embossed decoration. However, it is far from certain that these are actually armour, and they have since been identified as belonging to a sword scabbard and a type of helmet. Furthermore, the embossed decoration is not typical of the Aegean, but rather seems inspired by bronze armour from Central Europe. A few bronze scales from Greece, Crete and Cyprus suggest that scale armour may have been known in the twelfth century BC, but its use could not have been very widespread. The earliest certain evidence for metal helmets after the fall of the Mycenaean palaces comes in the form of an incomplete bronze helmet with cheekpieces unearthed at Tiryns and dated to the eleventh century BC.

Chariots remained a favourite subject across the Late Helladic IIIB–IIIC divide. It is clear from the iconographic evidence that some spearmen continued to use chariots to transport themselves to the battlefield, as they had apparently done in the Palatial period and possibly continued to do throughout the Early Iron Age, if similar scenes on Geometric pottery are indicative of continuity. Fragments unearthed in Mycenae show at least two chariots, each with a driver and a spearman, both of whom are equipped with round shields that cover most of the body; they may be wearing helmets with spiky crests or feathers. A fragment from Tiryns shows something similar, except that this spearman is equipped with two spears.

This suggests that the origin of the Greek practice of carrying two spears into battle, familiar from some pieces of Geometric and Archaic pottery, as well as – perhaps – the Homeric epics, may have its origin in the Postpalatial period. Further continuity is demonstrated by scenes that depict processions and chariot races. Fragments of an early krater found at Tiryns show a chariot race, probably conducted as a part of funeral games. This krater is among the earliest known depictions of chariot races. Fragments of another krater from Tiryns show a chariot

The 'Warrior Vase' from Mycenae, dated to the twelfth century BC. This side of the vase depicts warriors setting off on campaign, with little knapsacks tied to their spears; a woman at the far left bids them farewell. The other side, not shown, features men holding their spears overhead, as if ready to attack an unknown foe. Currently in the National Archaeological Museum in Athens.

Reconstruction of a warrior of the twelfth century BC,
based on the Mycenaean Warrior Vase. Drawing by Johnny Shumate.

with driver and spearman, the latter equipped with a round shield. This chariot was part of a procession, or perhaps a group of chariots setting off to war. Similar scenes reappear on Attic Late Geometric vases of the eighth century BC.

Comprehensive scenes of battle are rare in Late Helladic IIIC. A number of Late Helladic IIIC-Middle fragments belonging to a krater have been unearthed at Kalapodi, which may depict some kind of siege or an assault on a settlement. The extant fragments show parts of warriors, all equipped with swords; some hedgehog-type helmets are also visible. One warrior carries a large curved stick across his shoulders, from which are suspended two sacks or possibly baskets, perhaps representing a water-carrier. There is also a large, apparently rectangular area filled with a checkerboard pattern, possibly indicating a section of wall or part of a building.

• Summary

The Palatial period saw the flowering of Mycenaean civilization, which had a distinctly martial character, though this should perhaps not be taken to mean that these people were constantly at war. Wall-paintings with martial scenes often adorned specific places within the palace complexes.

The frescoes that decorated Hall 64 at Pylos were probably the first things seen by those who visited the Pylian *wanax*, perhaps to pay homage; the south-west building may even have been the residence of the *lawagetas*. Similarly, the Siege Fresco at Mycenae once decorated the walls of the *megaron*, the central chamber of the palace, where the ruler perhaps entertained his guests. Seen in this light, the wall-paintings conveyed a powerful message: do not meddle with the Mycenaean rulers, lest you suffer forceful retaliation. Similarly, the monumental fortifications that protected most palaces no doubt also served as both a testament to Mycenaean power and a warning to would-be aggressors.

Some of the warriors in Palatial imagery are probably members of the aristocracy, while others may have been culled from a lower stratum of society, perhaps even soldiers in the sense of men who fought for some kind of pay. The aristocratic warriors, especially the *heqetai*, used chariots, probably as a means to get to and from the battlefield. Lower-status soldiers appear to have fought bare-chested and often used relatively short swords; battles look rather like wrestling competitions. The tablets suggest that the palaces perhaps used a kind of conscripts, commanded by *heqetai*, to form the bulk of their army. The palaces provided some of the equipment necessary, though the fighting men appear to have supplied part of it themselves.

Although war in the Palatial period was perhaps not endemic, a military threat does seem to have emerged in the latter half of the thirteenth century, when some palaces turned toward reinforcing or extending their existing fortifications, and

The lure of the sea

Prominent features in Postpalatial vase-painting are ships and scenes of fighting at sea or possibly on the beach; the vessels themselves develop logically from earlier Palatial examples. The pots come from a very distinct geographic area. They are found in Euboea, Kalapodi (Phthiotis), Pyrgos Lagynaton, some of the islands, and even the west coast of Asia Minor (for example, at the Turkish site of Bademgediği Tepesi). Clearly, the fall of the Mycenaean palaces did not bring about a total collapse of the socio-economic system, as these regions at least still built and crewed warships.

A detailed discussion and typology of Aegean ships of the Late Bronze and Early Iron Age has been created by archaeologist Michael Wedde. The Mycenaeans were the first to use the oared galley, at the start of the Late Helladic IIIB period or a little earlier, though not all galleys are, by definition, warships. The first Mycenaean oared galley, type V, developed out of earlier crescent-shaped type IV vessels, which were Minoan. This ship is characterized by a straight keel, vertical stem-post topped by a bird-head device, and a curved or vertical sternpost; some of these vessels were decked. The later type VI is similar, except that the keel extended beyond the stem-post; this feature would later, in the Archaic period, develop into a ram.

The oared galley was long and sleek, with warriors manning the oars. The larger the number of men at the oars, the faster the vessel would move. It is clear, especially in the Late Helladic IIIC period, that these galleys were made for swift assaults on coastal towns. The straight keel, in particular, was presumably designed specifically to make the vessel quick to beach. Furthermore, these vessels may also have been used to attack other vessels, especially heavier and slower merchantmen. During boarding actions at sea, the Mycenaeans would fight with javelins, spears, and swords, in a manner virtually identical to fighting on land. The success of the Mycenaean types is clear when the Iron Age evidence is considered: the galleys depicted on Geometric pottery are clearly developments of the type VI Mycenaean ship.

A copy of the 'Horned God' from Enkomi, Cyprus; the original dates to ca. 1200–1125 BC. The inspiration for such figures comes from the Near East. They remained popular from the end of the Bronze Age down to the Iron Age. Currently in the Allard Pierson Museum, Amsterdam.

some, like Mycenae, sought to safeguard their water-supply. In the years following 1200 BC, many of the palaces were destroyed, and with them disappeared wall-painting, writing, and a relatively complex social organization. But we may also note some examples of continuity after 1200 BC. Rail chariots, for example, continued to be used, and warriors still wore some kind of gaiters to protect their legs. People in Postpalatial times sometimes continued to dwell near the palaces, repairing the older fortification walls when necessary.

A reconstruction of a Mycenaean oared galley. This type of vessel would continue in use and evolve in the course of the Dark Age. Drawing by Sebastian Schulz.

New equipment appeared on the scene. In the iconographic evidence, we now have spearmen equipped with thrusting spears and shields, who also wore some kind of padded tunic or perhaps armour. In iconographic sources, the old boar's-tusk helmets disappear, replaced by a variety of different kinds of helmets, horned or of hedgehog-type, and so on. Prior to the collapse of the palaces, a new type of sword (Naue II) was introduced, which was stronger and better than earlier Mycenaean swords. In the Postpalatial period, this became the dominant type of weapon, and remained in use down to the sixth century. It is frequently found in warrior graves.

The fact that groups of men are often uniformly equipped, as on the 'Warrior Vase', suggests that some kind of central authority survived; indeed, the little knapsacks attached to the spears of these men strongly indicates that they were equipped and provided for by a central body or commanding individual. Only such leaders may perhaps have been awarded the honour of being buried with weapons (see also the next chapter). Warrior graves are very rare in the archaeological record of Late Helladic IIIC, and they are always comparatively rich. However, this is very similar to the situation before the destruction of the palaces, as well as in the Early Iron Age: only a specific group of people – namely, certain high-ranking men – were ever buried with arms in Greece.

2 Raiders of women and cattle

The belly of this amphora is decorated with a procession of chariots. The charioteers wear plumed helmets. The artist has only rendered one horse for each team. The vase's lip and shoulders are decorated with snakes executed in relief. The vase was probably made specifically to serve as a grave offering: the procession would have been in honour of the deceased and the snakes are symbols of immortality. Attic Late Geometric IIB; dated to 720–700 BC. Currently in the Louvre.

I [= Nestor] was driving cattle in reprisal, and he [= Itymoneus], defending his oxen, was struck among the foremost by a spear thrown from my hand and fell, and his people who live in the wild fled in terror about him.
—Homer, *Iliad* 11.673–675

After the fall of the Mycenaean palaces, the societies of the Aegean underwent great changes. As we have seen in the previous chapter, some managed to retain a certain level of sophistication and organization in the twelfth century BC. This is demonstrated by renewed occupation of ancient sites – including Mycenae itself – and by occasional artistic highlights such as large pictorial vases, of which the famous Warrior Vase is a prime example. But overall, we see that the societies of the Aegean Bronze Age disintegrated. Archaeological research, in the form of excavations and field surveys, has revealed that settlements became fewer and smaller, indicating a decline in population. Material culture became more and more impoverished, reaching its lowest point in the eleventh century BC. Figurative art no longer existed, at least not in a form that has left traces in the archaeological record, with pottery styles having transformed into the abstract, geometric patterns characteristic of so-called Submycenaean (ca. 1100–1050 BC).

The period after the fall of the Mycenaean palaces down to the eighth century BC is referred to as a 'Dark Age'. Anthony Snodgrass popularized the use of this term for this period of Aegean history when he wrote *The Dark Age of Greece* (1971). The term became an easy target for critics, who frequently claimed that new discoveries managed 'to shed light' on Snodgrass's Dark Age. In the foreword to the new edition of his book (2001), Snodgrass tackles this criticism directly, maintaining "the view that a prolonged period of cultural, economic and social regression had engulfed Greece after the fall of Mycenaean civilisation" (p. xxiv). The situation in the Aegean was deemed analogous to the fall of Rome in AD 476, which was followed by centuries of cultural impoverishment, movements of people combined with population decline, and general instability, before stabilizing and witnessing the rise of new cultures from the ashes of the old.

There is some evidence that peoples migrated to other places, as a result of whatever caused the collapse of Mycenaean society or in later times, due to population pressures or scarcity of resources. Many Greeks appear to have fled to the island of Cyprus, while others in the once prosperous Peloponnese retreated to the mountains of Arcadia. A later generation crossed the Aegean and settled on the west coast of Asia Minor in the course of the tenth and ninth centuries BC. They sometimes occupied places that had been inhabited by their Mycenaean forebears, such as Miletus (known from Hittite sources as Milawanda) and Ephesus (Apasa). In the seventh and sixth centuries, the Greek settlements in Asia Minor would grow to become wealthy and large, and usually fared far better than the settlements

The 'Cup of Nestor'

When Mycenaean civilization collapsed, the Linear B writing system disappeared along with the associated bureaucracy and scribes. Only on Cyprus, some kind of writing survived. The remainder of the Greek world, however, remained without writing down to the eighth century BC. By then, Greeks had come into contact with Phoenician traders. They had a simple writing system in which each sign represented a particular consonant: as speakers of a Semitic language, they had no need for vowels. The Greeks adopted the Phoenician signs and used some of them for vowels as well as consonants, and thus gave rise to the first true alphabet. Through colonization, it spread to other parts of the Mediterranean. The Etruscans presumably adopted this writing system from the Greeks, and they, in turn, may have passed it on to the Romans.

The earliest extant example of Greek alphabetic writing is provided by the so-called 'Cup of Nestor'. This is a clay cup from Pithecusae (modern Pithecusa) on the island of Ischia, near Naples. This town had been founded by Euboeans, who may have been the first to adopt the alphabet. The cup in question was decorated in Geometric style and dates to the second half of the eighth century BC. It may have originally been produced on the island of Rhodes. At some point, an inscription was scratched into the cup's surface, which reads as follows in the translation found in the Archaeological Museum of Pithecusa:

I am Nestor's cup, good to drink from:
whoever drinks this cup empty, straightaway
will be seized by the desire of beautiful-crowned Aphrodite.

The final two lines are hexameter verses. Hexameter is a metrical line of verse that was the standard for epic poetry, such as Homer's *Iliad*. The lines are intended to be humorous, as they clearly refer to the famous cup of King Nestor, which was decorated with gold and so heavy that only Nestor himself could easily lift if when full (*Il.* 11.632–637). This cup is far more modest in size and value, and the final line clearly emphasizes the humorous intent of the inscription.

on mainland Greece, even if they had to contend with emerging kingdoms and empires further east, such as Phrygia, Lydia and Persia.

There is some continuity from the preceding Bronze Age, including at least the names of many of the principal Olympian deities (first attested on Linear B tablets), as well as ships, chariots, and the megaron, a more or less square room fronted with a columned porch, which formed the heart of the Mycenaean palace and formed the basis for later Greek temples. In other ways, the Dark Age presents a cultural break with the Mycenaean era. For example, kingship appears to have largely disappeared in the course of this period, probably because the small-scale nature of most Dark Age communities made them fairly egalitarian, especially in the eleventh century BC.

Lest we think of this period as one of overall decline, the year 1000 BC traditionally marks the start of the Greek Iron Age. The Early Iron Age covers the years between ca. 1000 and 700 BC, the latter date marking the beginning of the so-called Archaic period, the subject of the next chapter. Iron is more difficult to work than bronze, since it requires higher temperatures to be malleable (the ancient Greeks never succeeding in actually melting iron). However, the advantage of iron is that it is much more common than copper or tin, and Greece itself is relatively rich in iron ore. Since external contacts and trade generally disappeared or were severely curtailed after the fall of the Mycenaean palaces, it stands to reason that the Greeks had to turn to a locally abundant material to continue producing metal tools and weapons.

As far as the material culture is concerned, the main archaeological evidence consists of excavated structures, finds of tools and weapons, and especially pottery. The pottery styles developed out of the abstract Submycenaean pottery. Protogeometric pottery, characterized by large bands and geometric patterns, is typical of the tenth century BC and managed to survive in some regions until later. Athens emerged as an important production centre of the next style of pottery, full Geometric, where the entire surface of the pot tends to be covered in abstract geometric patterns, such as meanders and swastikas.

The communities of the Dark Age were relatively small. Most of these appear to have been relatively egalitarian, to judge from the material culture. From the tenth century BC onwards, some communities appear to become more socially stratified. Ian Morris, in his *Burial and Ancient Society: The Rise of the Greek City-State* (1987), analyzed cemeteries in Attica and proposed an essentially two-part division of society into *agathoi* (elite) and *kakoi* (commoners). It seems likely that communities were typically dominated by a warrior aristocracy comparable to the *basileis* mentioned by both Homer and his near-contemporary, Hesiod. The bulk of these communities would have consisted of farmers, typically small landholders, supported by a small number of craft specialists, such as blacksmiths. They almost certainly used slaves, though not in numbers comparable to Classical Greece or Rome.

The second half of the eighth century BC, toward the end of the Dark Age, in particular presents a watershed, with what appears to be accelerated growth and prosperity. The Greeks also began to look beyond the Aegean basin and started founding new settlements and trading posts elsewhere in the Mediterranean, including southern Italy, Sicily and the south of France. Anthony Snodgrass referred to this period as the 'Greek Renaissance': it is the culmination of his book on the Dark Age and the starting point of its sequel, *Archaic Greece: The Age of Experiment* (1980). Around the middle of the eighth century, figurative art returns in force, with depictions of silhouetted humans and animals on Attic Late Geometric pottery in particular, including fully-fledged battle scenes.

• Burials with arms

Graves with finds of weapons and – more rarely – armour are a comparatively uncommon feature in the ancient Aegean. Geographically, they were limited to certain regions within the area under examination, especially Euboea, Attica (especially Athens), the Argolid (especially Argos itself), Crete and northern Greece (Thessaly and Macedonia). In other regions, only a few such graves – or none at all – have been unearthed. Some examples include a grave at Nichoria in Messenia, dated to around 725 BC and containing an iron sword and spearhead; a grave at Locrian Atalanti that contained an iron sword and a bronze shield boss; and grave XXVIII at Tiryns (dated to the later eleventh century BC), which contained iron daggers, a bronze spearhead, a helmet and a shield boss.

Aside from cemeteries, smaller plots, and isolated burials, the ancient Greeks occasionally used mass graves. When a mass grave contained the remains of dead warriors, it was called a *polyandreion*. *Polyandreia* are mostly a feature of the Classical period. The only Archaic example is from Acragas (Agrigento) in Sicily, dated to the late seventh century BC. It consisted of a pit containing more than 150 Greek vases and the remains of dozens of corpses. Unlike most Classical specimens, this pit was not dug at the battlefield itself, but in a hill at the local cemetery. The contents and location are similar to an earlier, eighth-century *polyandreion* unearthed relatively recently in Paroika, the capital of the Cycladic island of Paros. It featured two large cist graves that together contained around 160 vases filled with the cremated remains of men who were presumably killed in battle. Two of these pots featured warlike scenes, discussed elsewhere in this chapter. This mass burial shows that fighting in this period sometimes led to relatively large numbers of deaths; these may have occurred when the inhabitants fought off a piratical raid, but they might equally well have died in a war against their neighbours.

Turning our attention to other cemeteries, the wealth sometimes encountered in burials demonstrate that certain regions managed to prosper during the Dark Age. The Euboean Gulf region – encompassing the large island of Euboea, as well as Attica and the part of Boeotian opposite the island – appears to have been especially prosperous and outward looking. The best known example is the site of Lefkandi, which is located on the island of Euboea, near the coast, and was abandoned toward the end of the eighth century BC. The settlement was originally located at Xeropolis, a plateau that may have been known in ancient times as Lelanton; or, alternatively, it may once have been the original location of either Chalcis or Eretria. The site is largely known for the many cemeteries on and around Xeropolis, of which the Toumba cemetery has been the most thoroughly investigated.

The heart of the Toumba cemetery was a large *tumulus* or burial mound, which contained the remains of a large apsidal building made from perishable materials on a stone foundation. This large building was constructed around 950 BC and measured some 50m in length and nearly 14m in width. Shortly after its discovery, the original owner of the plot of land bulldozed the site, so that the stratigraphy is somewhat uncertain. It has been speculated that the building was originally the dwelling of the ruler of the settlement. At some point, probably not long after it was constructed, two shafts were cut in the floor of the central room and a monumental krater – a vessel used to mix water and wine – was placed on top of them as a funerary marker.

One shaft contained the ashes of a man, which had been placed in an antique bronze amphora of Cypriot make, with a bronze bowl serving as a lid: it is the earliest of the urn cremations at Lefkandi. The grave goods identify the man as a high-ranking individual, possibly the chief of the community. The finds included an iron sword, a spearhead, a razor, and a whetstone. This shaft also contained the skeleton of a richly-adorned woman, who may have been killed when the man's remains were placed in the tomb. The other shaft contained the unburned remains of no fewer than four horses. The horses must have been yoked to the cart or wagon that originally carried man's corpse to the site where he was cremated. The building may have served as a kind of mausoleum for some time, before it was partially demolished and covered by the burial mound. The size and scope of the burial have been compared with descriptions in Homer, where cremation – a characteristic of the Early Iron Age – is also the norm. After the burial of the building beneath the mound, a cemetery arose at the east end, in front of the building's original entrance, where most of the weapon burials from Lefkandi have been unearthed.

178 tombs and 94 pyres have been excavated or located at Lefkandi; of these, 153 tombs and 73 pyres were fully excavated and published. The burials contained pottery that ranged in style from Submycenaean to Subprotogeometric III, so from ca. 1125–1050 BC to ca. 825 BC in the local chronology. Only 22 graves actually contained any weapons; fourteen of these were unearthed in the Toumba cemetery, in front of the building's entrance. This cemetery was installed shortly after the burial mound had been raised; the graves follow the contour of the mound. The excavators suggest that there were kinship ties between the people buried here and the man interred within the large building; they were therefore probably all members of the ruling elite. It is also possible that some of the men belonged to the leader's followers. The 'epic' characteristics of the tomb have been frequently noted; burials such as this one no doubt inspired descriptions of funeral rites in the Homeric epics.

The interments at the Toumba building seem to have led to a sudden and temporary increase in the number of weapon burials in the period immediately following the construction of the burial mound. More than twenty graves have been unearthed at this cemetery that belong to this period and last perhaps a generation; half a dozen of these graves – over one quarter of the total number, possibly more (depending on exact date) – contained weapons. Excluding graves that straddle the Late Protogeometric and Subprotogeometric I chronological divide, the total number of graves at Toumba from the Subprotogeometric I period onwards is less than forty. In other words, the example set by the burials in the Toumba building appears to have inspired the less grand burials of other dignitaries at Lefkandi. Most of the burials with weapons here are dated to the Late Protogeometric period. When we look at the finds of weapons at Lefkandi, we note that many graves contained knives (nine in all), as well as swords (ten), spearheads (eleven), and, more rarely, daggers (three), axes (five) and arrowheads (two).

Notable are the finds of arrowheads in two of the graves at Toumba. Grave T-26 not only contained arrowheads, but also an iron sword, an iron pin, and a large array of pottery. The more recently discovered grave T-79 contained arrowheads

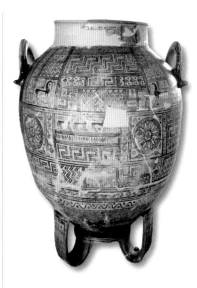

This large Late Geometric vase from Argos must have served as a grave marker. Included amid the pot's decoration are horses, symbols of the wealthy elite. Currently in the Archaeological Museum in Argos.

A beautiful example of a small bronze figurine of a horse. Greek artists of the eighth century managed to capture the essence of this noble animal. Dated to 750–725 BC. Currently in the Allard Pierson Museum, Amsterdam.

as well as a sword, a spearhead, two knives, a large number of pots (both local and Attic), two Phoenician and three Cypriot flasks, a bronze grater (for cheese), two bronze earrings, a set of twelve stone weights, and a seal. This man's cremated remains had also been placed inside a bronze cauldron. In addition, a piece of horn in Toumba pyre 1 may have been part of a composite bow. Clearly, these were affluent and – in the case of T-79 – perhaps well-travelled men, who fought both at close range (with sword and spear) and at a distance (with arrows), like a real-life Odysseus. Of course, the bow may also have been used for hunting, which was presumably even at this early stage already an activity of the upper echelons of society.

The weapons discovered in other cemeteries seem to conform mostly to the pattern encountered at Lefkandi. At nearby Eretria, which may have been founded by settlers from Lefkandi, a small burial plot dated to between 720 and 680 BC has been unearthed near the later West Gate; the gate itself and wall date probably to the sixth century. Six or seven urn cremations were unearthed here, as well as nine or ten child inhumations, which may have belonged to the same family group. A stone triangular feature was constructed on top of the burials. There is further evidence that the area came to be used for feasting and offering, and it clearly had a cultic function, in which Eretrians may have commemorated the memory of the people buried there. The urn cremations show many similarities with the burial beneath the Toumba building and grave T-79 at Lefkandi. The burnt remains were placed inside bronze cauldrons and seem to be centred on what the excavator Bérard has suggested is the earliest grave, number 6. This burial included a large number of weapons: four swords and six spearheads. It also contained a bronze spearhead of the Mycenaean period that may have served as a sceptre.

In Athens, burials with arms have been unearthed at the Kerameikos (the later Potters' Quarter). Some 119 graves have been unearthed here, the earliest of which date back to the Late Helladic IIIC period. As at Lefkandi and Eretria, cremation was the rule. Here, the remains were placed inside a terracotta amphora. The ashes of females were initially placed in belly-handled amphorae (associated with water), and later in shoulder-handled ones. The remains of men were generally associated with neck-handled amphorae. Large pots were used as grave-markers, some of which featured martial scenes. Nineteen graves dated to between Protogeometric III and Middle Geometric II – so between the tenth and eighth centuries BC – have been found to contain weapons. Swords and spears are again the most common types encountered, but one grave also featured arrowheads and three others contained what were probably shield bosses.

Other burials with arms were unearthed in the agora. The Athenian agora is renowned as the civic centre of ancient Athens, but it did not fully acquire this function until the sixth century BC. Earlier, part of the site was used as a cemetery. The earliest burials date back to the Mycenaean era and the Late Helladic IIIC period. Some 80 graves have been unearthed that date to between 1100 and 700 BC. Here, both primary and secondary cremation were practiced, as well as inhumation. Primary cremation refers to when the deceased is cremated at the same spot where he or she is buried; secondary cremation is when the burning takes place elsewhere before the remains and funerary gifts are deposited in the grave. Only five graves contained any weapons, which is nearly a third of the total number of male burials at the agora, but the graves are spread across a period of more than a century. Weapons disappear from the funerary record at the agora after the Middle Geometric I period, around 800, slightly earlier than at the Kerameikos (Middle Geometric II). Swords were recovered from each of these five graves, two of which contained spearheads, while three contained knives. One grave (no. XXVII) contained not only two knives, a sword and two spearheads, but also an axe. Considering the relative scarcity of burials with arms here, one wonders what their significance could be in this specific context. One possibility is that these men somehow represent the cream of the Athenian elite, the heads of important households. However, they might equally well be war-heroes, or men who died in battle.

Over 200 graves, most of which date to the eighth century, have been unearthed in and around the city of Argos; of these, 182 were found in distinct clusters or family plots. Of the 27 burials that are male, no fewer than fifteen contained weapons and also, in three cases, a helmet. The earliest warrior graves date to the Middle Geometric I period (graves T14.2 and GG15). As at the other cemeteries, swords and spears are by far the most common weapons, sometimes found in combination. Some graves even included multiple swords or spears. A similar phenomenon has been observed at Eretria, and here too the larger number of weapons may indicate that these men were high-ranking and warlike individuals, who were probably leaders of men. Two graves contained helmets.

One burial is particularly noteworthy; namely, tomb T45. In this grave were found, among other things, a helmet and a complete bell-shaped cuirass, as well as a pair of double-axes and two strips that may have belonged to greaves. The grave also contained two iron fire-dogs in the shape of ships, which led the original excavator, Pierre Courbin, to suggest that the man may have served as a captain. Anthony Snodgrass questioned this hypothesis, suggesting that he may instead have been a horseman, based on the presence of the cuirass and the double-axes in the grave. I do not believe that these interpretations are mutually exclusive. Instead, the ship-shaped firedogs and the possible connections to horse-ownership ought to be regarded as emphasizing simply that this individual was a powerful and wealthy member of the ruling elite, perhaps even the leader of the local Argive community.

Interestingly, the swords found at Argos tend to be shorter (never longer than 45cm) compared with the ones unearthed in Euboea. For example, most swords at Eretria were over 70cm in length, while those at Lefkandi range between 56cm

This bronze cuirass comes from a deposit of cuirasses unearthed at Marmesse (Haute Marne) in France. It dates from the ninth to the eighth centuries BC. The overall shape is identical to the later Greek bell-shaped cuirass, but the decoration is different and it does not feature the prominent flaring rim at the bottom. The basic structure, with a front and back plate, dates back to at least the lobster cuirass from Dendra, ca. 1400 BC. Bronze cuirasses may have spread from Greece to Central Europe in the course of the Bronze Age and then back again from Central Europe to Greece in the Early Iron Age. Currently on display in the Louvre.

The bell-shaped cuirass

The earliest example of the bell-shaped cuirass comes from the Argive tomb T45. It is named for its distinctive shape, and consists of two plates, front and back, which are connected to each other by hinges on one side and leather straps on the other. The bottom of the cuirass reaches a little below the waist, and would therefore have allowed the wearer to run, squat or even ride a horse. This cuirass is characteristic of the Archaic period. Towards the end of the period, it was replaced by the linen corslet. The metal cuirass survived, however, in a revised form, as the shorter, muscled cuirass. This continued in use during the Classical period, when it became characteristic of cavalrymen and commanders.

The basic form was already used as part of the Dendra cuirass, during the Early Mycenanaean period. This cuirass's front and back plates are shorter and do not feature the distinctive protruding rim, but the principle is the same. It is uncertain if this cuirass is an example of continuity in Greece from the Bronze Age to the Iron Age, with the 'lobster cuirass' slowly losing all extraneous plates until only the core chest and back protection survived. Cuirasses similar to the bell-shaped cuirass – dated to the Bronze Age and often featuring embossed decoration – have been unearthed in Central Europe. Due to the lack of bronze cuirasses in Greece during the Dark Age, it therefore seems more likely that the cuirass was reintroduced to Greece in the late eighth century from regions further to the north-west.

and 74cm. In addition, the swords at Eretria are different from one burial to the next, and may be closely associated with the deceased. The swords from Athens are perhaps more varied than those from Lefkandi, with lengths ranging between 40cm and 90cm. As the Eretrian graves are more or less contemporary with the Late Geometric Argive graves, the discrepancy is even more glaring. Spearheads from both sites are relatively massive, but those from Argos are perhaps slightly larger. They must have been used solely for thrusting.

The combinations of weapons and the general lack of armour offer some tantalizing insights into how these warriors fought, provided that the grave goods are an accurate representation of each warrior's 'typical' equipment. At Lefkandi and Athens, the men fought with spears and swords, and sometimes used shields (of which only the bosses remain). The equipment appears to have been fairly light, allowing for skirmishes and quick raids. The weapons from Eretria are more massive and the swords are very long; these men may have had a proclivity for close-ranged combat. Eretrians are closely associated with horse-riding and a long sword would have offered a mounted warrior the ability to hack away at his enemy below. The

Argives clearly fought on foot: the massive spearheads and especially the very short swords are testament to this, although some may nevertheless have ridden to the battlefield (as has been suggested for the warrior in tomb T45). The bronze armour at Argos furthermore supports the notion that the Argives fought at close range. The finds at Argos and Eretria date to the later eighth century, which can thus be considered a period of change toward a heavier style of fighting. In addition, not all men need have fought with spears and swords, but some were equipped with double-axes (Lefkandi, Athens, Argos), while others may have used the bow as well (Lefkandi and Athens), perhaps even as a secondary weapon.

Why were some men marked as 'warriors', whereas others were not? In the case of the man buried in the building at Toumba, the weapons may have served to underscore his position as a leader. At other sites, too, weapons and armour could have been used to mark someone not merely as 'aristocratic', but as a leader of some sort. This may explain why some of the men in the elite cemetery of Toumba were buried with arms while others were not; these particular individuals may have been leaders of households, or other members of the highest echelons. Similarly, the warriors buried at Eretria's West Gate were no doubt leaders of some accord. Three of them were buried with multiple spears and swords; perhaps these were signs of their power; that is, their ability to command groups of men in battle.

An examination of the Homeric epics, in which burial with arms is also very rare, suggests two other possibilities. The first concerns Andromache's father Eëtion, who was defeated and then cremated in his armour by Achilles, as a sign of the utmost respect (*Il.* 6.416–420). The second concerns Odysseus' unfortunate shipmate Elpenor, who died in an accident; his ghost later asks Odysseus to burn his body in full armour (*Od.* 11.66–78). In both cases, a large mound is raised over the graves. The textual evidence, slim as it is, points in the same direction as the archaeological material: burials with arms are exceptional and serve to mark the deceased as a warrior – Eëtion as an honourable opponent, Elpenor probably to show that, despite the unfortunate circumstances of his death, he was nevertheless a warrior who took part in – and survived – the Trojan War.

• Fortifications

Walls are often the only visible remains of an ancient settlement. Greek fortifications used to receive considerable attention, but interest in walls, towers, and gates has waned in the last few decades, as archaeologists have tried to compensate for their bias towards the most visible remains and tried to focus on other aspects of the material culture of the past. The few standard books on the subject deal with either the Bronze Age or the Classical and Hellenistic periods. Walls of the Early Iron Age and Archaic period have, for a long time, been a neglected subject. Two rela-

tively recent books have tried to fill this particular void. Fortifications of Archaic Greece are discussed by Franziska Lang in her *Archaische Siedlungen: Struktur und Entwicklung* (1996) and, more particularly, by Rune Frederiksen in his *Greek City Walls of the Archaic Period* (2010).

Lang identifies four main types of fortification walls; namely, (1) walls that protected only the highest part of a settlement (the acropolis), as at Emporion on Chios; (2) walls that protected only one side of a settlement, while the other was protected by a precipice, as at Vroulia on Rhodes; (3) walls that enclosed only part of a settlement; and (4) circuit walls that completely enclosed a settlement, as at Old Smyrna. This last type of fortification became increasingly more common from the seventh century BC onwards. To this typology, we may add so-called 'outposts', small fortified sites at some distance from a settlement, such as at Vrachos on the island of Euboea. Unfortunately, the remains of the earliest walls in many places are often too fragmented to say anything conclusive about them. In some instances, the remains may even have wholly disappeared. Nevertheless, some general characteristics can be gleaned from the evidence. It is clear that, in some rare cases, the walls were accompanied by ditches, such as at Vroulia (Rhodes) in the seventh century BC and Samos in the sixth. Furthermore, towers tend to be relatively rare until the later sixth century BC; in many cases, a wall only had a single tower, often close to the gate, so as to form a kind of bastion.

By far the most common type of wall used by Greeks of all periods consisted of

Galleys of the Early Iron Age

Ships are frequently depicted on Late Geometric pots, often within the context of a battle. For the most part, the vessels seem to be descended from galleys used in the final stages of the Late Bronze Age. The earliest representations of ships in Attic art date to the Middle Geometric I period (the late ninth century: a bronze fibula from Kerameikos grave 41) and Middle Geometric II (ca. 800–760 BC: a jug found in Agioi Theodoroi in Kromyon, Corinthia).

We have already encountered Michael Wedde's two main types of warships in the previous chapter. We need only concern ourselves here with the two types that are shown in Geometric art: namely, one with a straight prow and the other with a pronounced forefoot. They clearly developed from the Mycenaean type VI warship. Wedde has convincingly argued that the warships with a straight prow were used for battles at sea (and thus served as fighting platforms), while the vessels with a forefoot allowed them to be beached at speed and were thus made specifically for surprise attacks.

We are fortunate to have a fair number of models of such ships, including a terracotta model from the Amphiareion at Oropos of unknown date. These models are not to scale, but do provide a good idea of what some of these vessels may have looked like. Artists typically exaggerated particular elements of a specific type of ship, especially the forefoot, high forecastle, and curved stern. The forefoot of Wedde's second type of warship ultimately developed into the ram familiar from later types of warships, as described by classical historians. It seems unlikely that ramming was a useful tactic before the invention of at least the two-tiered warship (bireme). The long and sleek vessels of the eighth century BC and earlier would probably not have been sturdy or manoeuvrable enough to make ramming tactics viable.

The vessels depicted on the Geometric vases seem very similar to the galleys described by Homer. Ships in the *Iliad* and *Odyssey* are long, slender, open boats ('long ships'), which are dragged onto a beach and fixed with 'long props' (*ermata makra*) to prevent them from falling to one side. In the part of the *Iliad* known as the Catalogue of Ships, it is clear that most vessels possessed either fifty or twenty oars. The Boeotians are said to have brought fifty ships, each of which carried 120 men, but these may not all have been oarsmen. Ships with twenty and especially fifty oarsmen were regarded as fairly standard types. In the *Odyssey*, a ship with twenty oars is referred to as an *eikosoros*. A fifty-oared vessel is referred to as a *pentekontoros* by Herodotus, but not Homer. This supports the notion that the fifty-oared vessel was the typical warship familiar to Homer, requiring little further description. They were used to transport troops and also to carry out raids on neighbouring towns.

a stone socle with a mud-brick superstructure. We also know from written sources that wooden palisades were used (for example, Herodotus 8.51), but of these virtually no traces survive at all. The use of perishable materials in the construction of fortifications may go a long way to explain the apparent discrepancy in the evidence with regard to the Homeric notion that virtually every independent Greek town was protected by walls of some sort.

Settlements on Crete and the Aegean islands are among the earliest Greek sites to be fortified after the fall of the Mycenaean civilization. Another area with early fortifications is western Asia Minor, where the walls of Old Smyrna must be mentioned, together with Iasus in Caria, Kaletepe in Ionia, and Emporion on the island of Chios, just off the Anatolian shore. Of these, only Smyrna initially possessed a circuit wall that protected a very large part of the settlement, while the earliest fortifications at the other sites are all found only protecting their *acropoleis*. Old Smyrna consisted of dispersed habitation nuclei, around which was flung a large wall, perhaps as early as the late ninth century. Some believe this earliest wall, at least, was actually a retaining wall. If it is a circuit wall, it is the earliest in the Greek world after the Bronze Age. Later building phases have been dated to the middle of the eighth and the late seventh centuries. In each phase, the wall possessed a single tower. The temple to Athena, built in the seventh century, was located on a

A reconstruction of what Old Smyrna may have looked like at her zenith in the seventh century BC. The massive walls are clearly visible; they may have drawn inspiration from fortified Anatolian cities located further inland. These date from the eighth to seventh centuries BC. Inspired by the reconstruction drawing by R.V. Nicholls. Drawing by Rocío Espín.

Typology of Greek masonry styles

Research into Greek fortifications has traditionally concentrated on understanding the chronology and morphology of ancient walls, based on established masonry styles, which are summarized in the table below. Masonry styles can be split into two types, namely coursed and uncoursed. Courses may either be the same height (isodomic) or vary in height (pseudo-isodomic). Aside from using worked stone blocks, which were usually also fairly large, the ancient Greeks also built walls out of readily available, smallish fieldstones. Such simple walls made of unworked stones are still constructed and used by Greek farmers today to build basic enclosures.

Masonry styles may give a rough indication of the age of a particular wall or section of wall. Walls built using curvilinear blocks – also referred to as 'Lesbian' masonry – tend to date to the period before ca. 490 BC, while trapezoidal masonry is characteristic of the fifth century BC and later. The so-called 'Cyclopean' masonry of many Mycenaean structures can be regarded as a rough form of polygonal masonry. Ashlar masonry was used in the construction of Archaic temples, but the notion that it was not used in fortifications from an early date should be dismissed, since ashlar masonry is found not only in the fortifications of Old Smyrna, but also in sections of the Bronze Age walls at Mycenae.

Uncoursed masonry	Coursed masonry
Irregular trapezoidal blocks	Trapezoidal blocks
Irregular ashlar blocks	Ashlar blocks
Polygonal blocks	
Curvilinear blocks ('Lesbian masonry')	

large platform that was part of the circuit wall, close to the north-east gate and the associated tower. The walls themselves consisted of the usual stone socle topped by mud-brick. Despite these impressive fortifications, Smyrna was captured by the Lydians around 600 BC.

The earliest walls on the islands, all dated to Geometric times, are found at Donousa (a small island between Naxos and Amorgos), Minoa on Amorgos, Aghios Andreas on Siphnos, Zagora on Andros, and Xobourgo on Tenos (the latter may be even earlier, possibly Protogeometric). These early fortifications are often quite crude and consist of roughly worked or even unworked local stones. Of particular interest here is Zagora. The town was settled before 800 and abandoned by 700 BC, though the sanctuary near the summit of the town continued in use. The settlement was built on a promontory with a massive 140m-long wall built across the neck to protect it on the landward side. Some of the houses were connected to the wall. The acropolis, located some 150m from the settlement, was unfortified. Traces of three gates have been found. The sections of wall flanking the south gate jut out, giving the impression of a bastion.

More impressive fortifications have been discovered at the site of Xobourgo on the island of Tenos. The site, located in the southern part of the island at some distance from the coast, may have served as a place of refuge in the Early Iron Age. A large 'Cyclopean' wall (Wall A), built using large, undressed granite boulders, either in the Late Bronze Age or Early Iron Age, was discovered with Protogeometric and Geometric cremation graves and pyres in front of it. The finds in the burial area include a ritually 'killed' sword, and there is evidence of post-funerary sacrifices and cult. An extensive settlement existed here in the Archaic and Classical periods, which reused (parts of) the Cyclopean wall. Other parts of the circuit wall were added (or rebuilt) in later periods, including a stretch of coursed and dressed rectangular limestone blocks (so-called Walls AA), dating to the early sixth century BC.

Post-Mycenaean fortifications are rare in mainland Greece before the seventh century BC. However, it is clear that existing Mycenaean fortifications were often reused. One example is Thebes in Boeotia. The acropolis was already fortified in the Bronze Age and continued in use throughout the Early Iron Age and subsequent Archaic period. It has been suggested that the town may also have had a newly-constructed circuit wall as early as 700 BC. Other sites where the Mycenaean fortifications were reused include Athens, Argos, and Tiryns. The modest size of the walls of Mycenae itself made Thucydides remark that they would give one the false impression that it had not been a mighty city (1.10). The town of Eleusis was located on a limestone hill that may already have been fortified in Mycenaean times. Only part of the town was fortified. The Geometric wall, with a socle of crude polygonal stones, was replaced by a more monumental fortification with multiple towers in the sixth century, around the time of the tyrant Pisistratus.

It is often assumed that fear was the main force behind the decision to construct walls. The early circuit wall around Old Smyrna may have been erected because the inhabitants feared attacks from the 'natives' whose country they had just settled. However, Smyrna is exceptional. Most towns in Asia Minor did not construct walls until some time after they had been founded, and a few sites have been continuously inhabited from the Late Bronze Age onward, such as Ephesus and Miletus. There may have been strictly practical reasons, where the walls served to defend the community and to reinforce internal order. Greeks may have built fortifications for reasons other than hostile natives. If we stay within the realm of purely functional explanations, it should be pointed out that Greek towns were perfectly capable of warring with each other, so that the growing power of, and threat posed by, neighbouring Greek cities may have been an important reason for communities to build walls. It is interesting that the wall at Zagora on Andros protects the town from the land-side; the sea-side is protected by steep cliffs. Furthermore, there may have been purely practical reasons for constructing fortifications, especially the walls of newly established settlements. The founders may simply have desired to set the boundaries of the settlement, perhaps to make the allotting of the available farmland just outside the town easier. In this way, walls were used to demarcate the inhabited area and to make it easier to structure the new settlement.

Walls could also be used to divide space and separate the natural from the social orders. In many instances, fortification walls might attain a kind of sacred aspect. The sacred nature of walls is made even clearer in those cases where religious or otherwise cultic buildings are closely connected to a town's defences. At Emporion on Chios, a structure called the 'Megaron' was built up against the eighth-century fortification wall, opposite the main gate, which either housed the local ruler or was used for cultic activities, including ritual feasts. Something similar is also encountered at Kaletepe. At Old Smyrna, a seventh-century temple to Athena – who protected cities – was built atop a large platform that formed part of the circuit wall and was located close to the north-east gate and tower.

The Greek fortifications of the Early Iron Age were relatively simple. They consisted of walls with perhaps one tower near the main gate. We already noted that they usually consisted of a stone socle with a mud-brick superstructure. Not until the later sixth century BC do we see any significant improvements as regards fortifications, when multiple towers were introduced. Clearly, the simple fortifications of the Early Iron Age and most of the Archaic period were sufficient to fend off any but the most determined enemies.

There is some supporting evidence for this in the *Iliad*. All walls in the epic world are taken by storm. The war-god himself, Ares, is frequently referred to as a *teichesipleta*, 'stormer of walls'. In order to capture a fortified settlement (*ptoli-ethron*), one's troops needed to scale the walls and either surprise the enemy or overwhelm them with superior numbers. This suggests that most walls in the epic world were not that high; the same may have applied to the average wall of the Early Iron Age. One portion of the otherwise impressive walls of Troy is specifically singled out in the sixth book of the *Iliad* as being easier to climb, perhaps because it was made largely of mud-brick or rough stones, or featured a more gentle slope, or maybe because it was not as tall as the other sections.

Siege techniques must have been equally rudimentary. The Greeks clearly lagged behind in this field when compared with Assyria. In the Homeric epics, too, no mention is made at all of siege engines; not even (improvised) ladders or simple battering rams. Some heroes use boulders to smash gates and walls, and stakes are employed as levers to topple enemy battlements. Despite the lack of any apparent siege apparatus, siege warfare or, more specifically, the storming and sacking of cities, appears to have been among the most common military activities in the Homeric world. It is certainly no coincidence that war is represented on the new

shield of Achilles by a city under siege. Once again, this suggests that fortifications were rather simple, with most towns having straightforward defences that could be easily climbed, either because of the materials used in their construction (stone foundations with mud-brick superstructures) or because they were not all that high.

Archaeological evidence for sieges – never very abundant in the ancient world, in general – is extremely slight for this early period. In fact, there is only one certain example. We know that Argos conquered and razed the nearby rival town of Asine around 700 BC, probably in a campaign to consolidate control over the coastal areas of the Argive plain. The currently visible remains of fortifications date to the third century BC. However, the so-called 'Crown Prince's Tower', Building B, is thought to date from Geometric times. It was built using large rocks that appear 'Cyclopean' (that is, roughly worked polygonal blocks) but are certainly not Mycenaean in date.

• Depictions of warriors and their equipment

Figurative art reappears in force in the Greek world during the eighth century BC. Athens was a leading centre in the production of Geometric-style pottery and produced a large number of vases with scenes depicting warriors, chariots, ships and battles. Many of these Geometric scenes are found on funerary vases, particularly the large examples from the Dipylon and Kerameikos cemeteries that also functioned as grave markers. These figured scenes generally range in date from the second half of the eighth century BC. The military scenes on Geometric vases have been studied extensively by Gudrun Ahlberg in her *Fighting on Land and Sea in Greek Geometric Art* (1971).

In Geometric scenes, figures are painted as silhouettes. This makes it difficult to say anything about their clothes or lack thereof. Roughly contemporary figurines of warriors found at Olympia and Delphi depict them naked, with sometimes only a belt around their waist for clothing. This need not mean that Greek warriors actually fought in the nude: it might have had a symbolic connotation. Certainly, there are no references in any texts about Greeks fighting naked as a matter of course. The figurines frequently wear helmets, which can be easily recognized by their drooping plumes and are therefore similar to the painted examples. These helmets were probably close-fitting caps made of leather rather than bronze. The plumes are similar to those found on Late Helladic IIIC sherds and are perhaps an example of continuity from the end of the Bronze Age into the Iron Age. A conical helmet with drooping plume adorns the clay head of a warrior found at the Amyklaion sanctuary near Sparta, dated to around 700 BC, and thus offers a three-dimensional view of this type of headgear.

Some warriors in Geometric art are equipped with shields. In Attic Geometric art, we can distinguish between three types of shields, all fitted with a single central grip: namely, a rectangular shield, a round shield, and the 'Dipylon' shield (round or oblong with scallops cut from the side). A fragment of a Late Geometric pot from Athens shows three warriors, each equipped with a helmet, a set of twin spears, and a different type of shield. Toward the very end of the Late Geometric style, round shields were clearly meant to represent Argive shields (round, hollow shields with a double-grip); they sometimes even feature abstract blazons. However, the introduction of Argive shields in the Geometric repertoire did not go hand-in-hand with any other apparent changes, such as the adoption of new types of weapons.

It has been suggested that the Dipylon shield is a wholly fictitious item. However, this viewpoint is unwarranted. In Athens, a small terracotta model of an oblong Dipylon-type shield was discovered that is contemporary with the figured scenes on Attic Geometric pots. The amount of detail present on this model suggests that it was based on an actual shield. The model is convex, with a clearly denoted rim; the outer surface has been decorated with a cross-hatched pattern that suggests the real thing was made of wicker. Furthermore, the inside of the model features cross-staves; no handle is indicated, but perhaps the shield was gripped at the point where the cross-staves overlapped. Shield-types similar to the Dipylon are known from the Persian Empire and were, not very long ago, still used by some African tribes. They are also encountered in Late Helladic IIIC painted scenes and seem similar to shields used by the Hittites; they do not seem to be related to the Minoan figure-of-eight shield, which differed in shape and structure.

In fact, the Dipylon shield has two subtypes: one is circular and relatively flat, while the other – like the aforementioned model – is oblong and convex. They may represent two stages in the development of this shield type, of which the circular, flat one is probably the oldest. Both types are also known from bronze figurines. In addition, the flat and circular subtype disappears at the end of the eighth century, while the oblong and convex type continued in use and was eventually given a double-grip, borrowed from the round Argive shield that will be discussed in more detail in the next chapter. The oblong subtype with double-grip is generally called 'Boeotian', as it later served as the emblem of that region on coins. These developments can be easily traced and argue further in favour of regarding the Dipylon-type shields as having actually existed.

Geometric warriors with shields, particularly those of the Dipylon variety, are frequently associated with chariots, which they apparently used as a mode of conveyance. Usually, four horses form a chariot team, which has led some commentators to regard them as heroizing elements, since four-horse chariots are normally used in races. The war-chariots of the Late Bronze Age are always drawn by two-horse teams, although the Assyrians used massive chariots pulled by four horses in

This Late Geometric stand features a procession of warriors in the top zone. These men are all equipped with plumed or crested helmets or caps, and a set of two relatively short spears. Some of the men carry Dipylon shields, while others carry round shields. The rims on the round shields suggest that these are supposed to be Argive shields. Other scenes are depicted on the legs; the one that is most clearly visible shows a man attacking a wild animal   probably a boar with spear and sword. Dated to the late eighth century BC. Currently in the Kerameikos Museum.

the seventh century BC. In any event, these chariots were at least sometimes used to transport a warrior to, or even on, the battlefield, as demonstrated by the famous image that may depict Actorione-Molione – if the figure is indeed a Siamese twin! – in the heat of battle. Chariots are also sometimes depicted in processions, especially in scenes that feature the *prothesis*, the lying-in-state of a deceased person surrounded by mourners, or the *ekphora*, the funerary procession to the cemetery.

The evidence for horse-riding is slight. One Attic example is a warrior with helmet on a rearing horse; another is a rider with a pair of spears and possibly a helmet with drooping plume. From Skyros, we have a fibula unearthed in a Late Geometric grave at Themis; one side shows a horse, as well as a human figure equipped with Dipylon shield and spear. The position of the figure and the indication of reins leave little doubt that the warrior is actually riding the horse, making this the only depiction – as far as I am aware – of a warrior with a Dipylon shield on horseback. Further elements suggests that he is near the battle, as indicated by the spear set upright in front of the horse and a small arrow inscribed beneath the animal. The reverse shows part of a warship with a Dipylon warrior, who is apparently about to get struck in the back of the head by not one, but two arrows. Late Geometric amphora fragments from the Heraion near Argos depict a diminutive rider on horseback. Particularly common in the Argolid are pots decorated with the motif of the 'horse-leader', a male figure leading two horses (a chariot team?) by the reins. It cannot be said for certain whether they fought from horseback or usually dismounted prior to combat, but the evidence discussed in the next chapter

An example of a horse-leader, a popular motif in Greek Geometric vase-painting of the eighth century BC. Note the exaggerated crest or plume on the warrior's head and the sword at his waist. The two horses were probably intended for a chariot. This cup would have been used to serve alcohol. Currently in the Kerameikos Museum in Athens.

Chariots and horses in the Homeric world

Chariots seem to have been important in Greece during both the Mycenaean era and the Early Iron Age. They also feature prominently in the epic world described by Homer. Chariots and horses, high-status symbols *par excellence*, are repeatedly mentioned in the course of the *Iliad*. However, some confusion arises due to Homeric terminology: the poet refers to both horsemen and charioteers as *hippeis*. At least some of the horses may have been ridden rather than yoked to a vehicle. Horsemen as well as charioteers may have been a regular feature of the epic battlefield.

Within the epic world, horses are particularly common in Anatolia. This reflects reality, since Asia Minor is better suited to the rearing of horses than mountainous Greece. For example, Priam tells Helen of how he once visited Phrygia, where he 'looked on the Phrygian men with their swarming horses, so many of them' (*Il.* 3.185–186). In the tenth book of the *Iliad*, the Phrygians are called *hippodamoi* ('horse tamers'); they may have fought from horseback. On a similar note, it is probably no coincidence that the mythical Amazons, who were presumably envisioned by Homer as horse-riding warrior women, were thought to come from the east, whence they raided the Phrygians and Lycians.

The epic heroes, as the wealthiest combatants in the field, used chariots as their mode of conveyance of choice. Interestingly, Odysseus does not seem to possess a chariot; perhaps chariots and horses are rare on islands. In any event, most chariots in the *Iliad* are drawn by teams of either two or four horses. Each chariot carries two people: a warrior – usually one of the Greek or Trojan heroes – and a charioteer. Chariots are used to transport the heroes to, from, and on the battlefield. Once the hero spots an enemy, he normally dismounts to engage him on foot, his charioteer manoeuvring to a place of safety where he waits for his master to call on him. Rarely do the heroes fight directly from their chariots. Chariot races are mentioned a number of times in the *Iliad*, and a race was part of the funeral games in honour of Patroclus.

The overall picture concerning the use of chariots seems plausible. However, some modern commentators believe that chariots were introduced by the poet in a deliberate attempt to archaize the story. These writers argue that, while the poet describes chariots, he 'actually' had mounted horsemen in mind when describing these scenes. This is unlikely for two main reasons. Firstly, war-chariots remained largely unchanged, structurally speaking, from the Bronze Age down to Classical times, although they may have been used solely in races and processions. Secondly, there is nothing inherently implausible about the Homeric use of chariots as battlefield taxis, especially since we know of recorded uses of chariots later in history – Cyrenaica and Roman Britain, for example – that are comparable.

A Late Geometric pottery fragment depicting a warrior with plumed helmet on a chariot. His oddly shaped body is in fact a so-called Dipylon shield, which he carries on his back, suspended by a shield-strap. Currently in the Allard Pierson Museum, Amsterdam.

would favour the latter interpretation.

There is some diversity with regard to the weapons used by warriors in Late Geometric scenes. Archers are relatively rare. When they appear, they are nearly always shown singly, often kneeling, operating like a modern-day sniper. Interestingly, a Boeotian Late Geometric cup, unearthed at Vougliameni in Attica, depicts a helmeted warrior equipped with a bow. The fact that this warrior is equipped with a Dipylon shield, which is commonly associated with chariots, suggests that he is of relatively high status. Other warriors fight with one or more relatively short spears or use swords; combinations of spear and sword also occur. The position of these short spears (overhead) suggests that they were used especially for throwing. However, we cannot exclude the notion that they were multipurpose, used both for throwing and thrusting, as needed. The importance of the sword in these scenes suggests that a lot of the fighting took place hand-to-hand, at close quarters.

Horses and ships were important constituent elements for ancient aristocrats. They are found united on a locally-made Late Geometric II pottery fragment from Argos. It depicts a ship with rowers and a horse that appears to stand at the bow. Similar depictions of horses on ships will be encountered in the next chapter when iconographic material of the seventh century BC is discussed. It is tempting to regard these scenes as depictions of the legendary Greek journey to Troy, but there is no reason to doubt that early Greeks really transported horses by ship. How else would they have been able to introduce these animals to the islands, for example? A globular wine jug from Argos, dated to either Middle Geometric II or the start of Late Geometric I, depicts a horse-leader positioned between the tail-ends of two confronting galleys.

From at least the late eighth century onwards, Attic Geometric pottery suggests that high-ranking Greeks engaged in 'martial sports'. One amphora depicts a procession of chariots, with warriors alternatively facing forward and backward. Anthony Snodgrass suggested that this represents a martial feat whereby the warrior would make a 180 degree turn. Similarly, some of the scenes of single combat, mentioned above, might represent a dangerous game of some sort (compare Hom. Il. 23.798–825). In addition, wrestling and boxing were important activities; it is interesting that, in some fighting scenes, a man can grab the plume of his opponent's helmet like a boxer grabbing the forelocks of his rival. Such martial sports no doubt served as both entertainment, as a way for men to prove their quality, and as training for battle.

To summarize, the archaeological and iconographic evidence allow us to fairly comprehensively reconstruct what ancient Greek warriors may have looked like during the Early Iron Age. Their nudity may not have been historical; probably they wore simple tunics. Based on bronze figurines, belts may have been ubiquitous. Helmets were simple: presumably leather caps, fitted with drooping plumes, in all likelihood made of horsehair. Warriors were equipped with a sword, presum-

This pyxis *or box was used to store small items, such as items of jewellery. The handle is in the shape of horses. Originally there were four and they must have represented a chariot team. Dated to around 740 BC. Currently in the Allard Pierson Museum, Amsterdam.*

ably suspended by a strap (*telamon*) from the shoulders, and seem to have done the bulk of the fighting using spears. Archers are rarely depicted. Shields could have a variety of shapes, the so-called Dipylon-type being the most common. In addition, the wealthiest of warriors would have travelled to and from the battlefield using chariots.

• Scenes of battle

Attic Geometric vases show both single combat and mass combat. Single combat usually involves men armed with swords, suggesting that warriors in the eighth century engaged in duels, perhaps on the field of battle, or maybe as a dangerous sort of game. However, it is also possible that these scenes of single combat are intended as a kind of shorthand, especially on small pots. In such instances, a scene of combat between two men might actually be a stylized or symbolic representation of battle between opposing armies.

Depictions of mass combat fall into two categories, one type associated with fighting on and around ships, probably on beaches, and the other on land, with no ships present. Of these, the battles associated with ships appear to be more common. Gudrun Ahlberg rightly suggested that the battles depicted in the Geometric vase-paintings were fought between combatants organized into small and mobile

A detail of a large Attic Geometric krater, a mixing vessel for water and wine. Parts of the scene are missing. The main decoration on this vase features two warships, one on either side, flanked by warriors. This detail shows a battle in the rear half of the ship, near the stern. The bird on the ship's tail indicates that we are on or near land; in this case, the ship is probably beached. The figure in the centre seems to be tied down and is perhaps a prisoner. Dated to between 800 and 775 BC. Photo by Marie-Lan Nguyen (via Wikimedia Commons). Currently in the Metropolitan Museum of Art, New York.

groups, rather than in any kind of large formations; in other words, what we might refer to as warbands. The small-scale nature of the fighting, combined with the presence of bands – probably composed of aristocratic leaders and their followers – suggests that most battles consisted of skirmishes fought as part of raids, in which the acquisition of wealth in the form of cattle, women or treasure was a key motive for the men involved.

We may again turn to the Homeric epics for inspiration. Many commentators claim that Homeric warfare consisted essentially of disorganized skirmishing, with individual champions as the poet's focal points. However, such a scheme is applicable only to brawls; it is clear that the fighting described in the *Iliad* is not a free-for-all. Instead, the Homeric *stratos* or army – like any other army at any other point in history, as far as I know – consists of distinct bodies of men (military units), who work together to achieve a common goal. The importance of working together is stressed every so often in the *Iliad*. Homer even suggests that the Greeks are better at co-operating than the Trojans and their allies; perhaps co-operation among the latter is made more difficult by the many different languages that they speak.

In the *Iliad*, military units consist of a leader – often a named hero, such as Achilles or Hector – and his followers, who are collectively referred to as *hetairoi* ('companions'). The leaders use chariots as battlefield taxis, while their followers included spearmen (*aichmetes*), as well as some archers (*toxotes*), and possibly other horsemen (*hippeis*). The men do not manoeuvre in formation; any formations that are adopted arise spontaneously and are always used defensively (that is, statically), rather than offensively, such as when they have to defend the body of a fallen comrade. However, in a few instances, the men do march toward the enemy in 'waves', meaning more or less in ranks.

Homer himself sometimes uses the word *lochos* to refer to a body of men, a 'unit'. This word is also used to denote a small group of men hiding in ambush; the wooden horse is a 'hollow *lochos*' or 'ambush' in the *Odyssey*. These warbands may have numbered around 50 men, or the crew of the average Homeric warship, with their captain serving as leader. A good example is provided by the descriptions of Odysseus' wanderings, where his men look up to him and worry about their leader's safety. When on Circe's island, Odysseus divides the men in two equal parts, appointing Eurylochus as commander of one section and himself of the other. That ships of 50 men were the basis for division of the troops is further demonstrated by the fact that nearly all subdivisions of the army and its contingents are multiples of 50. For example, when Greek sentries are posted to keep watch on the Trojans in the ninth book of the *Iliad*, each of them is given command of 100 troops.

To return to our discussion of battle scenes, we have two amphorae recovered from the *polyandreion* at Paroika, mentioned earlier. One vase is dated stylistically to the end of the eighth century; the other may well be older by a generation or more. On the earlier pot, we have a very dynamic representation of a battle in full swing. Placed centrally is a warrior standing in a chariot. Approaching from the right is a warrior with round shield. He seems to grab one of the chariot's horses by the reins; his other arm is raised, aiming either a spear or slingshot at the warrior in the chariot. Behind the chariot are two corpses, as well as a grazing stag, which perhaps indicates the setting of the scene or suggests that the battle takes place somewhere inland. Further to the left is a warrior with Dipylon shield, who is ready to cut down with his giant sword an unarmed foe to his right. Still more to the left is a second chariot, – to judge from the position of the helmetless charioteer – driving at full speed in the same direction as the first chariot. Two horse riders seem to follow in pursuit; one is beating the hind end of his horse with a baton, while the other is equipped with a round shield and raises his spear. Turned to the other side and facing the first chariot is a group of three helmeted horsemen; all three horses are rearing. Most warriors wear helmets with raised crests. The three warriors that are equipped with a shield carry it on their bodies, leaving their hands free. All in all, this amphora depicts a very vivid and perhaps specific scene of combat. It shows a combination of warriors on foot, chariots, slingers, and horsemen.

On the later pot, we see a violent engagement in which, again, a variety of different types of fighters is involved. The central position in this scene is taken by a fallen naked warrior. To the left appear two archers, six horsemen and three warriors on foot carrying round shields; one of the horsemen is protected by a round shield suspended from a *telamon* (shield strap). The archers fire arrows over the corpse of the fallen warrior toward a group of three men equipped with slings; behind them are two warriors with round shields (a cross-hatched pattern suggests they are made of wicker). The battle scene may depict the violent and noble death of the warrior. The struggle over his corpse is depicted on the belly; the shoulder shows warriors carrying the corpse off the battlefield; the neck depicts his *prothesis* or lying in state. The burnt remains of the warrior were placed in this pot, which thus probably commemorated his moment of glory, and were then buried.

Complex scenes of this type are very rare on Geometric pottery. The manufacture of the two amphorae is separated in time by perhaps one generation, but both seem to depict specific (historical?) events, and maybe even specific people. The later pot clearly renders a single event in three successive scenes. Other indications that we are not dealing with scenes of a generic character are the variety of atypical warriors on both amphorae, as well as unique elements, such as the mourning figure touching the head of the fallen warrior with an arrow in the *prothesis* scene on the later pot. If this conclusion is warranted, these pots present important testimony of fighting in this part of the world during the eighth century. Quite unusual is the appearance of chariots within a battle context, although they are not engaged in actual combat, but are seemingly fleeing from the action. I know of only one other battle scene that involves chariots: namely, a Boeotian Subgeometric vase of the early seventh century BC. This depicts a warrior with round shield engaged in single combat with a warrior carrying an oblong Dipylon shield with pronounced rim, while a third warrior with a square shield and a spear held overhand is carried off on a chariot. On the Parian vase, the horsemen actually fight from horseback, some with spears and at least one with a sword. Although apparently not yet of the Argive type, their shields show that the round form offered the proper protection for warriors fighting on horseback. The scene on the belly of the later amphora also

Opposite page: this scene depicts an assault by seaborne raiders towards the end of the eighth century BC. The attackers have just left their ship, which can be seen in the background. The large, convex Dipylon shields have been drawn after a terracotta model unearthed in the Athenian Agora and dated to the late eighth century BC. Drawing by Johnny Shumate.

Homeric raids for plunder

When Telemachus visits Pylos in search of news about his father, aged Nestor begins his account of the Trojan War as follows (*Od.* 3.103–108):

Dear friend, since you remind me of sorrows which in that country
we endured, we sons of the Greeks valiant forever,
or all we endured in our ships on the misty face of the water
cruising after plunder wherever Achilles led us,
or all we endured about the great city of the lord Priam
fighting; and all who were our best were killed in that place.

The Greeks never established a line of supply back to Greece. Instead, they had to raid the towns and islands close to Troy in order to obtain their 'plunder', *leis*. When Achilles boasts of his military prowess, he recounts how he destroyed (*alapazo*) – that is, captured and sacked – no fewer than 23 towns in the vicinity of Troy, twelve by sea and eleven by land, as part of these raids (*Il.* 9.328–329). With the obvious exception of Troy, walled towns appear relatively easy to take by storm, especially by the presumably large numbers of Greeks led by Achilles. A passing reference in the *Iliad* indicates that most towns were destroyed by burning (*Il.* 21.522–523). Elsewhere, a besieged island-town is described. Smoke rises as the town itself is ablaze. During the night, the townsfolk light signal-fires in the hope that men from neighbouring islands would come to their aid (*Il.* 18.207–213).

The booty obtained in these raids included food, slaves, cattle, and other valuable goods, which were not distributed by Achilles, who apparently led these expeditions, but by Agamemnon, who was the commander-in-chief of the Greek forces and thus nominally in command. Excess goods were exchanged with traders from nearby islands, such as Euneus, son of Jason and a *basileus* of Lemnos (*Il.* 7.467–475). In many cases, raiding and trading probably went hand in hand. However, while *basileis* engage in some trading, they never consider themselves professional traders. All Greek traders in the epic world appear to be *basileis,* who ply the seas as merchants only occasionally. Only Phoenicians are presented as professional traders (for example, *Il.* 23.744; *Od.* 13.272–286, 14.288–298, 15.415–482). Laodamas, a Phaeacian, insults Odysseus by calling him a trader (*Od.* 8.159–164).

Raids are also organized outside the context of open war, typically for the express purpose of acquiring goods or treasure. Such raids allowed a man to increase his honour by capturing *gera* ('prizes of honour') and his *kleos* ('fame') by demonstrating his military prowess or excellence (*arete*) in combat. Raiders are common enough in the epic world to be denoted by a specific word, namely *leisteres*, literally 'booty-takers'. Frequently during his wanderings, Odysseus is asked by his host whether he is on some specific business or 'roving as pirates do'. Crafty Odysseus often responds with a lie.

In one of these lying stories, Odysseus claims he is Castor, son of Hylacus of Crete, who frequently went raiding. Castor mounted nine successful raids, gained much wealth in this manner, and made sure to reward his friends for their aid on these expeditions. This, Odysseus adds, made him 'feared and respected' (*deinos t' aidoios*) among the Cretans (*Od.* 14.234). After the Trojan War, Castor intended to raid Egypt. He arranged nine ships and then organized a six-day feast, apparently to round up some willing crewmen to accompany him on his expedition. When they finally got to Egypt, Castor told his men to wait by the ships as he explored the country; however, they ignored his orders and started raiding anyway, slaying men and carrying off women and children. Soon, defenders came pouring out of the city. Many of the raiders were killed or enslaved, and Castor himself surrendered to the Egyptian pharaoh. On Ithaca, Odysseus largely repeats this story of a failed raid on Egypt to Antinous, with a few minor alterations, in the seventeenth book of the *Odyssey*.

gives us an impression of what war-bands operating on the islands looked like: a mixed lot that might include bowmen or slingers, as well as warriors on foot and on horseback.

• Death and aftermath

We have already touched upon the funerary nature of many of the Geometric vases discussed in this chapter. The funerals generally seem to conform to those described in the Homeric epics. In the *Iliad*, both sides collect their dead at the end of a day of battle, try to identify the remains, and then cremate the bodies. The burnt remains of the Greek dead are buried somewhere close to the battlefield. At one point, Nestor gives the advice to build a funeral pyre close to the ships and have the bones collected to bring back to Greece upon the conclusion of the Trojan War (*Il.* 7.326–335 and 421–432). Funeral games are organized to honour the most esteemed of the fallen warriors, such as Patroclus and Hector; these funeral games

A bronze Assyrian sheet from Olympia with hammered figurative scenes. The zone at the top shows a procession of men. The second zone depicts a woman flanked by bearded men, two of whom wear garments decorated with scales: perhaps they are soldiers. The third zone depicts men fighting griffins. The zone at the bottom shows horsemen. The sheet was originally produced in the eighth century BC and then made its way to Greece, where it was reused for the clothing of a statue and joined to a Greek sheet with depictions of lions and battles. Currently in the Olympia Museum.

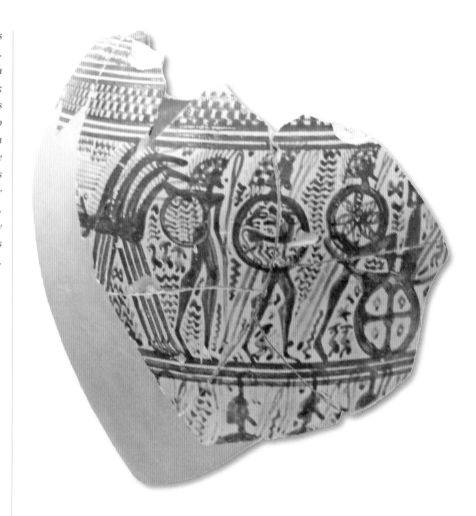

also provide an arena in which those who honour the dead may compete to attain *kleos* of their own.

Despite the fact that great glory could be attained on the battlefield, death is presented in the epics as an unavoidable as well as lamentable part of life. It seems likely that many of the fighters on the battlefield were relatively young men; older men were sometimes exempt from fighting, like Nestor and Priam. Important in this regard is Priam's lament about his advanced age. In this brief passage, he idolizes youth and the brave death of a young warrior, while deploring the death of an older man (*Il.* 22.71–76):

(…) For a young man all is decorous
when he is cut down in battle and torn with the sharp bronze, and lies there
dead, and though dead still all that shows about him is beautiful;
but when an old man is dead and down, and the dogs mutilate
the grey head and the grey beard and the parts that are secret,
this, for all sad mortality, is the sight most pitiful.

When Hector is killed by Achilles, the Greek hero ties the body behind his chariot and drags it back to camp. There, the Greeks gather round to stab and poke the body in order to despoil it, mocking the fallen hero. Afterwards, Achilles in his anger drags the body around Troy behind his chariot (*Il.* 22.395 and further). The gods, however, intervene and preserve Hector's youthful beauty, so that his appearance remains unspoiled. The theme of young men slain in valiant combat is one that will resurface in our examination of the lyric poets in the next chapter.

The so-called Lambros *oinochoe* provides a unique picture of how prisoners of war may have been treated. On this vessel, a number of Dipylon warriors are shown; they lack spears, but each does have a sword and a dagger at his waist. Their arms are not shown and Gudrun Ahlberg has suggested – correctly, no doubt – that their hands were probably bound behind their backs. They are confronted by 'nude' figures, most of whom are also equipped with a sword and a dagger. One of them touches the hilt of a bound warrior's sword; perhaps he is in the process of disarming his opponent. It probably depicts warriors who are being taken prisoner by the other men. One figure appears wholly nude and holds his sword – and possibly the dagger, or else the scabbard of his sword – in one hand, while being confronted by another figure, who brandishes a sword and may be threatening him. The scene also includes two corpses, suggesting that we are dealing with the direct aftermath of a battle.

We may turn to the Homeric poems again to get some insights into what may have happened to prisoners of war. Some of these, particularly women like Briseis and Chryseis, are enslaved. Others are sold off to passing traders in exchange for other goods. A few of the wealthy captives are held for ransom. Ransoming captives appears to be an important means of acquiring wealth in the epic world, although, within the context of the *Iliad*, the Greeks are often ruthless and take no prisoners. For example, when the Trojan warrior Adrestus is at Menelaus' mercy, he begs the Spartan ruler to help him 'and take appropriate ransom', adding that his father is rich and has a considerable amount of treasure in his home (*Il.* 6.46–47). Menelaus prepares to have Adrestus taken back to the Greek camp, when Agamemnon passes by and rebukes his brother for not killing the Trojan outright (*Il.* 6.55–60). When on a night expedition, Diomedes and Odysseus run into a Trojan spy called Dolon, who also asks to be taken captive and held for ransom. However, Diomedes ruthlessly beheads him (*Il.* 10.378–457). Nevertheless, there are other references to men being held for ransom; prisoners of war in general are considered 'prizes of honour' (*Il.* 2.237). Some Trojan prisoners were sacrificed by Achilles at Patroclus' pyre (*Il.* 23.20–23). Even the dead may sometimes be held for ransom; Priam, after all, has to buy back Hector's lifeless body from Achilles in the *Iliad*'s final book.

Some men who surrender are apparently not held at ransom; they might not even end up as prisoners in the usual sense of the word. In the false story told by Odysseus of a failed raid in Egypt, he says that when the battle went awry he dropped his armour and weapons to the ground, went to the Egyptian ruler in his chariot, and clasped and kissed his knees. The king then took pity on him and protected Odysseus, who then spent seven years in Egypt, collecting much wealth in the meantime, until a Phoenician came along and enticed him to travel with him to Libya, intent on selling the Greek there as a slave (*Od.* 14.276–297). Clearly, surrendering was a gamble in the epic world; one might be taken prisoner and held for ransom, killed outright, enslaved, or indeed treated like a guest and apparently subjected to normal laws of hospitality, which included the collecting of gifts.

• Summary

After the fall of the Mycenaean palaces, Greek society seems to have turned more inward during the eleventh century BC in particular. From the tenth century onwards, there are a few bright sparks again in a number of places, demonstrated in particular by rich finds in cemeteries such as at Lefkandi and Athens. Burials

The ancient Greeks did not exist in isolation, but interacted with other peoples in all cardinal directions. For example, we have Assyrian reports of Greeks raiding the Levantine coast in the eighth century BC. The Greeks may have been influenced by the Assyrians when it comes to military matters, such as the use of metal helmets. This relief, which once decorated the walls of the reception hall of a palace, shows Assyrian soldiers forcing an enemy to his knees. Note the spears, raised overhead, the short swords at their hips, and the round shields. From Nimrud, Iraq, and dated to ca. 740 BC. Currently in the National Museum of Antiquities, Leiden.

with arms reappear in the archaeological record, giving an idea of the equipment wielded by warriors of this age, with a heavy emphasis on spears – including combinations of shorter and longer specimens – and swords. Arrowheads are comparatively rare; finds of armour are limited until the end of the period.

Multiple sets of spears and swords found in graves presumably served to underscore the military prowess of the man in question. Vase-paintings and figurines demonstrate how warriors may have been equipped for war. The variety on display echoes the archaeological evidence. Some warriors are equipped with spears, others with swords or bows. Some men fight without any apparent armour with the exception of plumed helmets, while others carry shields of various designs into battle, including round, rectangular and Dipylon shields. The warriors with shields are also frequently associated with chariots that presumably functioned to transport warriors to and from the battlefield, and were normally not used in actual combat itself.

The iconographic material of the eighth century gives us a good idea of what battles may have been like during the Dark Age. Both battles on land and at sea are encountered on painted vases of the eighth century BC in particular. Many battles appear to take place on and around one or more ships that have been dragged onto the beach; seaborne raids were probably common. However, bronze-clad rams and associated naval tactics are unlikely to have been in use at this early stage. To protect themselves from attack, some settlements constructed fortifications that were flung around the settlement or, more commonly, around part of the settlement, such as the town's acropolis. Siege techniques, however, appear to have been fairly unsophisticated.

3   Men of bronze

But when no long time had elapsed, stress of weather compelled some Ionians and Carians, who had sailed out for the purpose of piracy, to bear away to Egypt; and when they had disembarked and were clad in brazen armour, an Egyptian, who had never before seen men clad in brass, went to the marshes to Psamtik, and told him that men of brass, having arrived from the sea, were ravaging the plains.
—Herodotus, *Histories* 2.152

Whatever caused the downfall of the Mycenaean palaces around 1200 BC also managed to bring much of the rest of the eastern Mediterranean to its knees. Egypt had known a period of unprecedented prosperity and stability during the so-called New Kingdom (1549–1069 BC), but suffered various attacks by enigmatic 'Sea Peoples' from the end of the thirteenth to the middle of the twelfth centuries BC. The origins of the Sea Peoples are unclear; they may have included displaced or disgruntled Mycenaeans, among other peoples. After the death of Ramesses IX in 1069 BC, Egypt split up and plunged into the Third Intermediate Period. Parts of the country were held by Nubian kings and rulers of Libyan descent, before the Assyrians established vassals in Egypt.

The Egyptian king mentioned in the quote at the start of this chapter was Psamtik I, founder of the 26th Dynasty (664–525 BC), also referred to as the Saite Dynasty, named after their capital city of Sais in the Western Nile Delta. After his father's death following a failed attempt from a Kushite king to seize control of Lower Egypt, Psamtik mounted a military campaign to unite Egypt again under a single king and free the country from Assyrian influence. By this time, Egypt no longer had a large army of native Egyptians, but instead relied heavily on foreign mercenaries. Among these, the Greeks appear to have occupied a position of considerable importance, as also shown by their commercial activities in Egypt. We already saw in the previous chapter that raids into Egypt were familiar to Homer, as demonstrated by one of the lying stories told by Odysseus.

In Egypt, outside the temple of Abu Simbel, a large and roughly cut inscription can be found on the leg of a giant statue of Ramesses the Great that has been dated to 591 BC. The inscription, mostly Ionic in lettering but Doric in dialect, reads as follows in the (slightly modified) translation by Matthew Dillon:

When King Psamtik came to Elephantine, this was written by those who, with Psammetichus son of Theocles, sailed and came above Circis, as far as the river permitted;

Opposite page: this imaginative illustration shows what the meeting might have looked like between the Egyptian king, Psamtik I, and the Ionian and Carian 'men of bronze'. The latter mercenaries are indistinguishable from each other. Herodotus even suggests that parts of the Greek panoply were actually invented by Carians. Drawing by Johnny Shumate.

While many have tried to read Pelecus (Peleqos) as the name of another human being, Dillon has pointed out that the author was actually using a Homeric pun: Archon wrote the inscription using a weapon, *pelekos* ('axe' or 'blade'), that quite literally was the son of *Oudamos* (Nobody). Most of the other names in the inscription are fairly straightforward. The 'non-native speakers', led as a whole by Potasimto, a known general, were clearly not Egyptians; they probably included the Greek contingent that was led by the son of Theocles. That they came down-river suggests that they travelled by ship along the Nile.

In the inscription, Archon identifies himself as one of the Greeks who followed Psammetichus. This Psammetichus himself was a Greek, the son of Theocles, who was named after the Egyptian pharaoh of the same name; to wit, Psamtik II (r. 595–589 BC). It was common for Greek fathers to name their sons after *xenoi* ('guest-friends'); we know from other documents that some Carian fathers in Egypt also named their sons after the pharaoh. This suggests that the son of Theocles was not simply a mercenary, or even an adventurer; instead, he may well have come along on this expedition up the Nile as a favour to his father's Egyptian friend. While some of these men may have been 'soldiers of fortune' or adventurers, others were some kind of (hereditary) *epikouroi* ('allies', 'mercenaries') – men who came to the aid of either their own guest-friends or those of their fathers.

Greek mercenaries were a common sight in the kingdoms and empires of the ancient Near East from the seventh century BC onwards. For example, we know that East Greek warriors from Ionia and Rhodes, and perhaps also a number of Carians, were stationed at Mesad Haschavjahu, a coastal fortress that lay between Jaffa and Ashdod; it was constructed around 630–620 BC. In these very days, the Deuteronomistic History was written – the historical narrative in *Joshua*, *Judges*, *Samuel*, and *Kings*, which contains a reference to King David's Greek guard, "the Kreti and the Pleti". Greeks had been active in the Near East from an early time onwards. Mycenaean pottery fragments have been found across a wide area, from Italy to Egypt and the Levant. As already said in this book's prologue, Greeks even established a trading post at Al-Mina in Syria in the eighth century BC. From around the same time, namely the reigns of Tiglath-Pileser III (r. 745–727 BC) and Sargon II (r. 722–705 BC), we have Assyrian sources that mention hostile encounters with 'Ionians'. These documents make it clear that some Greeks roamed along the Levantine coast as pirates. The sources also refer to a number of Greek slaves being kept at Nineveh; perhaps these were captured during an Assyrian expedition to rid the sea of Aegean raiders.

The Assyrian Empire fell in 612 BC when an allied force of Babylonians and Medes sacked Nineveh. This heralded the true beginning of the Neo-Babylonian

This sarcophagus belonged to a wealthy man named Wahibree-makhet ('Wahibre is the horizon'); it dates to around 600 BC. His name is actually a reference to the Egyptian king Psamtik I, as his throne name was Wahibre. He was mummified according to Egyptian tradition, but the inscription mentions that his parents were Greeks. By the seventh century BC, Greeks had managed to find employment in Egypt as mercenaries and were also actively engaged in trade. This sarcophagus shows the extent to which Greeks could be assimilated. Currently in the National Museum of Antiquities, Leiden.

Empire, which would take up Mesopotamia and gobble up whatever remained of the Assyrian Empire, all along the Levantine coast. It bordered Lydia in the north-west, Egypt in the south-west, and nomadic Iran in the east. The Greek lyric poet Alcaeus tells us that his brother, Antimenidas, once fought for the Babylonians, possibly in the army of Nebuchadnezzar II (r. 605–562 BC). He may even have taken part in the storming of Ascalon in 604 BC. In one fragment, Alcaeus refers to both Babylon and Ascalon. Alcaeus states that his brother went to Babylon, "serving as an ally", and adds that he was handsomely rewarded for an act of outstanding bravery, as he returned "with the hilt of his sword ivory-bound with gold".

• Who were the men of bronze?

As discussed in the previous chapter, most warriors during the Dark Age seem not to have worn metal body-armour. An obvious exception was the panoply recovered from a tomb in Argos and dated to the late eighth century BC. It seems likely that bronze armour was reintroduced in this general region around that time. Indeed, the north-east Peloponnese appears to have been at the forefront of military developments in the late eighth and early seventh centuries BC. The best proof of this is supplied not by finds of weapons and armour, which will be discussed later,

A bone relief plaque depicting a Gorgon. It may have originally been fixed to a chest or a piece of furniture. The Gorgon, with her fearful appearance and the ability to turn any person to stone at a mere glance, was a popular motif in Archaic Greek art and was also used to decorate shields. Made in Ionia or under Ionian influence in southern Italy; dated to 550–500 BC. Currently in the National Museum of Antiquities, Leiden.

Carian armourers

Carians appear frequently in the Archaic sources. They sometimes collaborated with 'Ionians', a term that in texts from the ancient Near East frequently relates to 'Greeks' and often included other peoples from Anatolia. Herodotus claims that not the Greeks, but the Carians invented three characteristic features of the Greek panoply: a method of fastening crests to helmets, the idea of putting blazons on shields, and attaching handles to their shields (Hdt. 1.171). Until then, shields had been carried from leather straps and suspended from the wearer's neck and shoulder (compare the Homeric *telamon* or shield strap).

Some modern commentators have dismissed the idea that Carian armourers were responsible for the design of what they believe to be typically Archaic Greek war-gear. But there is no compelling reason to dismiss Herodotus. After all, he was born in Halicarnassus, a Greek city in Caria, and may therefore have been familiar with Carian achievements. Carians are also mentioned in other sources and often appear alongside Ionians and other East Greeks, as Archilochus makes clear. Alcaeus, for example, refers in one of his poetic fragments to a "Carian helmet-plume". It therefore seems unlikely that Herodotus' claims are wholly fabricated.

but by the painted pottery produced in Corinth.

Relatively large numbers of figurative painted pottery were made in Corinth from the late eighth century down to around the middle of the sixth, with production petering out altogether in the second half of the sixth century BC. Corinthian pottery tends to be decorated with animals more than humans; but fortunately, whenever humans are depicted, they are often warriors. Like much of the art and architecture of the seventh century, this style of vase-painting seems inspired by art from the ancient Near East; hence, the seventh century BC is also referred to as the 'Orientalizing' period. The earliest style of Corinthian vase-painting is referred to as 'Protocorinthian', essentially an early form of what would later be called 'black figure'. It appeared in the final quarter of the eighth century BC.

An early example of Protocorinthian vase-painting is found on a small perfume bottle from the cemetery at Lechaeum, near Corinth. The diminutive pot features a battle between warriors equipped in a manner familiar from Attic Geometric scenes: they are naked and equipped with oblong Dipylon shields and two spears or a sword; the scene also features a naked, kneeling archer, who is stabbed in the back. Unlike Attic Geometric scenes, the warriors are all equipped with Corinthian helmets. In addition, one warrior differs substantially from the others: he is placed in the centre of the action and is not only equipped with a Corinthian helmet, but is also clothed and equipped with the new Argive shield. His arm has even been unnaturally extended so that we can clearly see the latest innovation on the inside of the shield: the double grip, consisting of a *porpax* (arm-band) and *antilabe* (hand-grip).

The earliest Protocorinthian pottery not only introduces the new Corinthian helmet and Argive shield. Frequently, warriors are depicted on horseback or otherwise associated with horses. Chariots, by contrast, become increasingly rare and are no longer shown in battle scenes until the later sixth century BC, when the context makes it generally clear that we are dealing with depictions of myth. Particularly important for an understanding of the development of Greek warfare is an early Protocorinthian perfume bottle attributed to the 'Evelyn Painter', dated to the late eighth century BC. It depicts a warrior with shield, sword, spear, and helmet, walking behind a youth on horseback. Later scenes usually show the outline of a second horse next to that of the youth; this second horse must belong to the warrior on foot, who has dismounted. Common in the seventh century BC are scenes in which two warriors engage in what appears to be single combat while the mounted youths observe from the sidelines.

The warrior and the youth are usually anachronistically dubbed 'knight' and 'squire'. However, an Early Ripe Corinthian perfume bottle of the last quarter of the seventh century BC provides us with the contemporary Greek – or at least Corinthian – names for these figures. The warrior is called a *hippobatas* (literally, 'horse-fighter'), and the youth, a *hippostrophos*. The name of the youth clearly de-

A small perfume bottle attributed to the Evelyn Painter and dated to the late eighth century BC. It is one of the earliest examples of the motif of the 'knight and squire'. Horse-riding was clearly established in Corinth around this time. Drawn after Peter Greenhalgh, Early Greek Warfare (1973), p. 87 fig. 47.

Typology of Greek helmets

The Greeks may have adopted the use of bronze helmets from the Assyrians at some point in the late eighth century BC. The oldest type of Greek bronze helmet is the *Kegelhelm*. This is the same type as the helmet found in Argos. It is made of five separate pieces of bronze sheet and features a crest raised on a stilt. Early in the seventh century BC, this type developed into the two-piece Illyrian-type helmet, which – despite its name – may actually be a Peloponnesian invention.

The Corinthian helmet is the most typical of the Greek bronze helmets. It is named after the place where it was presumably developed and was made out of a single sheet of bronze. Unlike the *Kegelhelm* and the Illyrian helmet, it covered nearly all of the face, leaving only slits for the eyes and mouth. In the early sixth century BC, an open-faced variant of the Corinthian was created that has been dubbed 'Ionian' and is especially characteristic of Asia Minor. A little later, another variant of the Corinthian was developed; namely, the Chalcidian helmet, which left the ears free and added moveable cheek-pieces; the 'Attic' subtype lacked a nose-guard.

A bronze Corinthian helmet dated to around 600 BC. Corinthian helmets are made out of a single sheet of bronze, making them remarkable examples of the Greek mastery of bronze working. Currently in the Allard Pierson Museum, Amsterdam.

notes what his function was: to take his master's horse when he had dismounted to fight on foot, and 'turn' the animal away from battle to keep it safe. *Hippobatai* and *hippostrophoi* are a fixture in Archaic Corinthian art. Furthermore, both are found in the iconographic material of other regions, including Athens, Sparta, the islands of the Aegean, and East Greece.

The appearance of *hippobatai* and, more specifically, the association of warriors with horses, bronze armour, and the new Argive shield is suggestive. Other authors, such as Anthony Snodgrass, have noted that the bell-shaped cuirass is ideally suited for horsemen. Building on this notion, I would suggest that the Argive shield, too, was made specifically for use by men who spent a good deal of time on horseback. Depictions of men dismounting always show them facing away from the horse, in the direction of the battle itself, as if they simply rode into battle and then launched themselves at the enemy. It would be very difficult to ride around with a single-grip shield strapped to the back or suspended from the neck by a strap, as it would probably bounce off and chafe the hind end of one's horse. With the Argive shield, the double-grip and convex shape would have ensured that it could be comfortably carried on the left side of the body, with the rim resting on one's shoulder and without injuring the horse.

Hippobatai rode to the battlefield and then dismounted to fight on foot. True cavalry – in the sense of mounted men who also fought on horseback and typically did not use shields – do not appear in Greek art before the early sixth century BC.

There is further evidence to suggest that true cavalry was unimportant in much of Greece until long after the Persian Wars. However, some regions – such as Thessaly and Macedon – were known to be good for rearing horses, and true cavalry may have appeared here earlier than elsewhere. This is not to suggest that *hippobatai* would have been unable to fight from horseback if necessary. But, just like those rare instances in the *Iliad* where the men fight from a chariot, these were presumably rare and considered out of the ordinary.

As in other art of the eighth to sixth centuries BC, depictions of archers are rare in Corinthian vase-painting. Whenever they do appear, they are consistently portrayed as kneeling and acting like modern snipers, apparently picking specific targets rather than bunching up with their peers and shooting volleys of arrows high into the sky. Some archers could be at least partially armoured. A 'Middle Ripe Corinthian' fragment of a *pyxis* (box), found at Perachora, shows an archer with helmet, tunic, and greaves, kneeling behind a compatriot and taking aim at an unseen enemy.

Depictions of warriors on Attic pottery also changed and show great similarities with the evidence already discussed. Very late examples of Geometric-style pottery already feature warriors equipped with round shields that almost certainly were intended to be Argive shields, especially those examples featuring abstract blazons. The introduction of this type of shield again does not seem to have introduced any other apparent changes with regard to the nature of the scenes or the style of fighting. Athens abandoned the Geometric style around 700 BC and instead produced pottery in an Orientalizing style termed 'Protoattic', probably influenced by Corinthian vase-painters. Protoattic warriors are nearly always equipped with Argive shields and also wear Corinthian helmets; shield blazons, when visible, still tend to be abstract. There is even a pot from the early seventh century BC that depicts a warrior with Argive shield on horseback, like a Corinthian *hippobatas*. The Attic warriors usually only carry a single, heavy spear, undoubtedly used solely for thrusting, and are sometimes also shown carrying swords. However, bell-shaped cuirasses are, to the best of my knowledge, not attested in Athenian vase-painting of the seventh century BC.

• Lyric poetry

For the Archaic period, we no longer need to rely solely on the poetry of Homer and Hesiod. For the purposes of this book, we now have a large array of additional textual sources available in the form of fragments of lyric poetry. Like the Homeric epics, these poems were meant to be sung, often to the accompaniment of music. The lyric poets were members of the elite; their songs were performed for an immediate audience of friends, but at least some compositions circulated more widely across the Aegean. Lyric poetry is usually categorised according to genre, based on the metres used. Elegiac poetry was similar to epic; suitable for the celebration of war and bloodshed. Many of the elegiac fragments discussed in this chapter come from exhortation poetry; that is, songs in which men are encouraged to stand and fight (Tyrtaeus, Callinus, Mimnermus). Iambic poetry tended to be more varied as far as the subject matter was concerned, ranging from sex to warfare, from (insider) jokes to serious politics (Archilochus, Alcaeus). Much of this poetry was probably intended to be recited during the symposium (literally a 'drinking together') or, in the case of choral songs and iambic poetry, at festivals.

Probably the earliest of the lyric poets is Archilochus. He was a native of the island of Paros and took part in the Parian conquest of the island of Thasos. He was active around the middle of the seventh century BC, a date based on a reference to Gyges, then ruler of Lydia (fr. 19 West), as well as a mention of a solar eclipse (fr. 122 West). He probably also served as a mercenary (fr. 2 West). In one fragment, Archilochus addresses Charilaus as the dearest of his *hetairoi* or 'companions' (fr. 168 West), a term also familiar from Homer. The extant fragments demonstrate that Archilochus was a member of the elite, and therefore concerned himself mainly with "words and deeds" (Hom. *Od.* 2.273); that is, politics and war.

For Archilochus, the main offensive weapon was the spear. As in Homer, the typical warrior is the *aichmetes* or 'spearman'. Archilochus never describes shields

Scene from an Early Ripe Corinthian perfume bottle dated to the late seventh century BC. Like the earlier perfume bottle attributed to the Evelyn Painter, it shows a knight and his mounted squire, but provides them with their Greek names: hippobatas *and* hippostrophos. *Drawn after Peter Greenhalgh,* Early Greek Warfare *(1973), p. 87 fig. 47.*

in much detail, but they were obviously considered bothersome in flight and had to be thrown away if speed was of the essence, as the following fragment demonstrates, in which the poet consciously mocks the heroic code of honour when he had to abandon his shield in a conflict with a Thracian tribe (fr. 5 West):

Some Saian sports my splendid shield:
I had to leave it in a wood,
but saved my skin. Well, I don't care—
I'll get another just as good.

The *telamon*-equipped shields of the *Iliad* were swung around the back when a warrior had to flee. It seems likely that the shield referred to by Archilochus, in contrast, was of Argive type, as it was thrown aside instead.

Archilochus provides us with the first attested use of the Greek word *strategos*. The word is cognate with *stratos* ('army, host') and thus means 'army-leader'; it is typically translated as 'general'. At this early date, the word might simply be an alternative to the Homeric phrase *anax andron*, or the more common *hegemon* or *hegetor*; it seems unlikely that it already referred to a magistrate of some kind, like the Athenian *strategoi* of the later sixth century onwards. Elsewhere, Archilochus refers to a leader as *archos*. Unfortunately, none of the descriptions of battle in the extant fragments attributed to Archilochus are detailed enough to attempt a reconstruction of the style of fighting that he was familiar with.

Archilochus presents a mirror image of the heroic ideology espoused by Homer. In one passage, the poet exhorts fighting men to stand their ground. He warns them not to be "overproud in victory, nor in defeat oppressed". He reminds his audience that, ultimately, the outcome of a battle is "under the gods' control". In a number of fragments, Archilochus mocks the heroic ideals outright. In one fragment, he describes the kind of military commander that he would trust with his life. He claims to prefer "a shortish sort of chap, who's bandy-looking round the shins". That is quite a different kind of leader than tall and handsome Achilles. But it should be pointed out that even in Homer not all heroes conform to stereotype: Tydeus, the father of Diomedes, is specifically said to have been fairly short; Agamemnon, too, was not tall according to Priam, and Odysseus was shorter still. Archilochus' point was no doubt that a smart commander worries about the survival of his men, rather than fretting about his appearance.

A greater sense of realism also pervades Archilochus' treatment of bravery in battle. He sees little point in dying in a blaze of glory if flight meant that you could live to fight another day. Apparently, one of the reasons for fleeing is that "no one here enjoys respect (*aidos*) or reputation (*periphemos*) once he's dead", as the people familiar to the poet only tended to the living. Archilochus openly mocks established ideology, which in turn only demonstrates how entrenched these mar-

Opposite page: a reconstruction of a Corinthian hippobatas or dismounted warrior, and his mounted squire or hippostrophos, ca. 625 BC. Drawing by Graham Sumner.

tial values were at this time. Indeed, battles may have been fairly common: in one fragment, the poet wonders out loud how or to what end another "hapless army" (*anolbos stratos*) is being assembled this time.

Other Archaic poets maintain the Homeric ideals of battle. Callinus, a native of Ephesus and a contemporary of Archilochus, tells the young men (*neoi*) in particular to prepare for war and be ready to "throw your last spear even as you die". After all, Callinus claims, it is no small honour to die while defending one's own community (fr. 1.6–11 West):

For proud it is and precious for a man to fight
defending country, children, wedded wife
against the foe. Death comes no sooner than the Fates
have spun the thread; so charge, turn not aside,
with levelled spear and brave heart behind the shield
from the first moment that the armies meet.

The poet stresses how the brave man, who does more single-handedly than many do together, "ranks with demigods" while alive, and is regarded as a 'tower' or 'bulwark' (*purgos*) by the people; his loss in battle is mourned by people of both high and low standing. Specifically, Callinus appears to appeal to the young men to defend their city, perhaps against attacks by Cimmerians, who we know were roving through Anatolia at this time, or against an invasion by the Magnesians.

Similar exhortation poetry was composed by Tyrtaeus of Sparta, who was active in the second half of the seventh century BC, although his work contains interpolations from the Classical period. Like Callinus, Tyrtaeus extols the virtues of fighting and dying for one's fatherland, encouraging the young men in particular. Men should not fight for personal glory, but for the benefit of the whole community. In a faint echo of Archilochus' more realistic attitude toward warfare, Tyrtaeus

Siana cup showing a symposium scene. A woman is depicted flanked by two men; two other men are shown lying on a couch at the right, with a small table in front of them. The practice of lying on couches was introduced from the East, via Anatolia, and perhaps specifically Lydia. Attributed to the Malibu Painter; dated to ca. 565–560 BC. Currently in the Allard Pierson Museum, Amsterdam.

emphasizes that virtues or good looks are worthless if a man is unwilling to participate in battle. A young man who dies in battle will enjoy everlasting glory, whereas a coward who refuses to fight will be shamed and sent into exile. The man who retreats from battle may die by receiving a spear in the back, between the shoulder blades – a death that is considered especially shameful.

According to Tyrtaeus, a valiant death on the battlefield is the surest path to glory. The community would remember and honour the fallen warrior for many generations, with people being able to point out his grave many years after his death. This suggests that the number of 'honourable dead' was comparatively small, at least in the battles that Tyrtaeus presumably used as inspiration for his songs. No doubt, only members of the aristocracy would have been awarded a burial with full honours and a monument to mark their graves. The survivors would point to such a grave and talk about its occupant, thus keeping the warrior's memory alive and granting him immortality. This is a very Homeric conception of death and glory; compare the description of Achilles' funeral and burial mound (*Od.* 24.80–84):

Around the cremation urns then, we, the chosen host of the Argive
spearmen, piled up a grave mound that was both great and perfect,
on a jutting promontory there by the wide Hellespont,
so that it can be seen from afar out on the water
by men now alive and those to be born in the future.

Dying on the battlefield was, however, not the sole means of acquiring honour and glory. Tyrtaeus tells us that, if a man were to distinguish himself in battle and survive, all the people of the community, "young and old alike", would honour him. He would become something of a local celebrity, respected by high and low, and "all the men at the public seats" would "make room for him". In other words, brave warriors can look forward to enjoying certain privileges. This, Tyrtaeus emphasizes, is the just reward of those who defend their country (fr. 12.35–44 West).

In one fragment, Tyrtaeus distinguishes between two different kinds of warriors on the basis of their armour, making a distinction that is entirely absent in Homer. The relevant passage is the following (fr. 11.35–38 West):

You light-armed men (gymnetes*), wherever you can aim*
from the shield-cover, pelt them with great rocks
and hurl at them your smooth-shaved javelins,
helping the armoured troops (panoploi*) with close support.*

This explicit distinction between *gymnetes* (literally, 'naked men') or light-armed men and *panoploi* (literally, 'all-equipped') or armoured troops is not only new, but also unique among the poets discussed in this chapter. This distinction does

Carpentras

Mantua
Adria

Parma

Felsina

Illirium

Nicaea
Antipolis
Massilia
Olbia

Volaterrae

Arretium
Ancona
Tragyrion
Dimos
Issa

Perusia

Pharos

Corcyra M.

Adriatic Sea

Clusium

Vetulonia
Hatria

Volci
Falerii

Alalia
Tarquini
Caere

Rome

Capua

Lissos

Aegae
Pe

Epidaurus

Epidamnos

Barion

Apollonia

Methone

Po

Tyrrhenian Sea

Cumae
Neapolis
Ischia
Poseidonia
Elea
Pyxos
Laus

Taras
Brentesion
Callipolis
Metapontum
Siris
Sybaris
Thurioi

Corcyra

Ambracia

Anactorium
Leucas
Naupa

Olbia

Tarrae

Sulci
Caralis
Nora

Hipponion
Medma

Crotone

Caulonia
Locri
Rhegium
Naxos
Catana
Megara Hyblaea
Syracuse

Cephalonia

Zakynthos

Elis
Sicyon

Ionian Sea

Panormus
Himera
Zancle

Erice
Segesta
Sicily
Leontini

Hippo Regius
Hippo Diarrhytus
Motya

Utica
Carthage

Selinus
Acragas
Gela
Catania

Cirta

Kosyra

Hadrumentum
Ruspina
Thapsus

Gaulos
Melita

Capsa

Mediterrance

Josho Brouwers
&
José Carlos Garcial

Tacape

Meninx

N

Sabrata
Oea

Leptis Magna

Taucheira

Cyrene
Barke

km 0   400
mi 0   400

not reappear until Herodotus and later writers, when the term *panoploi* has been replaced by the word *hoplites* (literally, 'equipped men'), while *gymnetes* remains in general usage. The passage quoted above suggests that the armoured and unarmoured troops fought closely together, with the light troops apparently seeking protection behind the shields of their better-equipped companions. Some Homeric overtones can be noticed at times; for example, at one point the poet refers to *promachoi*, or 'fighters in the front-rank'.

• Raiders and conquerors

We have seen in the previous chapter how raiding was an important activity during the Dark Age. It continued to be important during the Archaic period, as, for example, the episode with Psamtik makes clear. There are even some rare instances of Geometric motifs executed in an Orientalizing style in the seventh century. An example is an Early Protoattic plaque attributed to the 'Analatos Painter', which was found near the temple of Poseidon at Cape Sounion, the south-eastern tip of Attica. It shows the rear half of a warship (the front part is lost). Five warriors are depicted sitting at the oars, although they are facing the front of the ship rather than the rear, as would be normal for oarsmen, and the oars themselves are not shown. We should perhaps imagine them listening to a rousing speech by their commander or making preparations to jump ashore, while the ship coasts toward the beach. Each of these warriors carries two spears and wears what looks like a Corinthian helmet with stilted crest; their bodies are obscured by large Argive shields. A single figure in the stern is manning the steering oars; he has neither armour nor shield and appears to wear some kind of tunic that may mark him as special, perhaps a specific figure from legend. The plaque must have been intended to curry favour with Poseidon.

A large number of ivory and bone plaques have been unearthed at Sparta, especially at the sanctuary of Artemis Orthia. Among the most impressive is a votive plaque of the late seventh century showing a scene with a warship. Round Argive shields are suspended from the side of the ship; three figures, one wearing a helmet with raised crest, are at the oars. Three other figures are busy with the sail. One man, located in the forecastle, has just hooked a fish, while another squats on the forefoot to defecate. At the stern, a man bids a woman farewell; she clasps his wrist and shoulder. The woman is clothed, while all the men are naked. This is clearly a departure scene and may depict a group of warriors – who would also serve as rowers – about to set out on an expedition for plunder.

There are also rare depictions of battles at sea. One example is an engraved fibula of the early seventh century BC from Sparta. The left-hand ship has a straight keel and a forefoot – clearly a warship. However, the opposing vessel has a rounded

Opposite page: an evocative reconstruction of an early stage in the Siege of Old Smyrna under the Lydian King Alyattes. In order to capture the town, the Lydians built a massive earthen siege mound that eventually towered over the walls of the city and provided a platform for archers. The Lydian warriors in this image are more colourful than their Greek counterparts, despite sharing much of the panoply. The colourful leggings are a very distinct feature of warriors from Western Anatolia. Drawing by Milek Jakubiec.

bottom and must represent a merchantman. Warriors are shown on both ships. A very similar scene is found on the Aristonothos Krater, currently on display at the Musei Capitolini in Rome. This mixing vessel was found in Caere in Etruria and dates to the middle of the seventh century BC. One side depicts the blinding of Polyphemus, while the other again shows a warship attacking a merchantman. Such scenes reveal that raiders not only attacked coastal towns, but also engaged in piracy on the open sea.

Scenes with ships seem to disappear for the most part in the course of the first half of the seventh century BC. Instead, depictions of warriors and combat seem to emphasize, more and more, battles on land, with neither ship nor sea in sight. The reason for this should probably be sought in the developments in the Aegean at this time. From the eighth century BC onwards, Greece became more and more prosperous and outward-looking. There are indications that populations grew at this time, although not as rapidly as was once thought. The city-state probably emerged as the dominant form of political organization in the seventh century BC in central and southern Greece, and may have appeared even earlier in Asia Minor and on the Aegean islands. Territories grew in size and this made conflict between neighbouring polities almost inevitable. The expansion of Argos provides a good example; at the end of the eighth century BC, it destroyed the rival town of Asine, laid claim to the Argive Heraion (an important sanctuary to Hera), and finally extended its influence over the rest of the Argolid when it destroyed Mycenae in the middle of the fifth century BC.

There are some references to early wars, but details are often hazy. One of the first recorded wars after the fall of the Mycenaean palaces is thought to have been the Lelantine War, fought between Chalcis and Eretria over control of the Lelantine Plain in central Euboea. Thucydides claims that this was the only war, between the Greek siege of Troy and the Persian Wars, in which most of the Greek world sided in alliance with either Chalcis or Eretria. Many details have been added by modern scholars, some of whom claim that the Lelantine War should be dated to the eighth century BC and that the abandonment of Lefkandi ought to be attributed to it. Others have dated it to the middle of the seventh century BC and claim that a fragment of Archilochus – in which the poet refers to the fact that the Euboeans were famed for their swords – applies to it (fr. 3 West). Still other commentators believe that the war was wholly a fabrication. The bottom line is that we simply do not know if the Lelantine War ever really happened and, if it did, how it should be dated and what course the war took.

Similarly obscure is the Messenian War. Modern commentators often refer to a First and Second Messenian War; this, however, is a modern convention. Ancient sources only ever speak of 'the' Messenian War, regarding the conquest of Messenia by Sparta as a single, if undoubtedly protracted, event that happened at some time in the distant past. Tyrtaeus mentions that Messenia was conquered in the time

The Lydian Empire

Lydia was an ancient kingdom in western Anatolia. Its fortified capital of Sardis lay east of the Greek coastal city of Old Smyrna. The country was famed for its riches, which it owed to the electrum-carrying River Pactolus (modern Sart Çayı), which flowed from Mount Tmolus alongside the capital city itself. To the Greeks, Lydia was the Near Eastern kingdom that they would have been most familiar with. The city of Sardis was regarded by contemporary Greeks much in the way that we consider a modern city like Paris: metropolitan, glamorous, and cultured, but also prone to decadent excesses.

We know very little about Lydia until the seventh century BC. The account in Herodotus of early Lydian history is a mixture of legend and fact. After the death of King Candaules and the founding of the new Mermnad dynasty by Gyges around 680 BC, we are on firmer ground, at least as far as Lydia's relations with the Greek cities are concerned. Gyges' successors were vigorous rulers who sought to extend the borders of Lydia. Eventually, their empire encompassed the whole of western Anatolia. This naturally brought the Lydians into frequent contact – and conflict – with the Greeks living along the coast, in the Troad, Aeolis, Ionia and Caria, especially since the country lacked good access to the Aegean.

The Mermnad kings therefore frequently waged wars with the Greek cities on the coast, forcing many of them to pay tribute. The cities that could not be easily brought to their knees were pacified through diplomacy; both Herodotus and Thucydides mention alliances made between the Lydians and Milesians, for example (Hdt. 1.22). The Greek cities that actively resisted the Lydians were attacked. The poet Mimnermus of Smyrna, who was active in the mid-seventh century BC, wrote poems to exhort his fellow countrymen to fight. In one fragment, he mentions the valour of a Greek warrior who managed to hold his own against the famed Lydian horsemen (fr. 14 West).

of his fathers' fathers, which is no doubt meant metaphorically, meaning that it was a war that happened long ago. It supposedly lasted for twenty years, or twice as long as the Trojan War; this seems like heroic rhetoric, intended to glorify the Spartan conquest, rather than an accurate assessment of how long it took to pacify the region. Tyrtaeus is clear that the Spartans seized the lands of the Messenians for agricultural gain, as the country was "good to plough and good to plant fruit". The Messenians were not ousted from their lands, but were instead reduced to servile status and required to pay a heavy tax; later sources – starting with Herodotus – refer to these slaves as helots, a word with an obscure etymology. Tyrtaeus mentions how the enslaved Messenians suffered "like donkeys under heavy loads". They were

A warship approaches a merchant-man. This scene is inspired by the Aristonothos Vase of the middle of the seventh century BC. Most of the men are equipped with bronze bell-shaped cuirasses and bronze helmets. Drawing by Angel García Pinto.

thus not sold off or used to work the lands of their masters back in Lacedaemon, but instead were tied to the land. Later Classical sources speak of similarly subjugated populations in the Argolid, Thessaly, and Crete; no doubt these, too, were the result of past territorial expansions.

We are on firmer ground when it comes to the Parian conquest of the island of Thasos, since Archilochus was a part of this expedition. Thasos is located in the northern Aegean, just off the Thracian coast. Interest in this region was due to the

90

presence of gold, both on the island itself, as well as on the mainland across the sea. Archilochus took part in some of the battles against the Thracians for control of the island and its gold mines. Fighting may not always have been necessary, as he also mentions how "Thracian dogs" were bribed (fr. 93 West), probably in exchange for some of the island's gold. The bitter way in which Archilochus couches his remark perhaps suggests that the Thracians had been paid off to stop a siege or other assault on the town of Thasos, for we know from the *Iliad* that defenders could bribe besiegers (*Il.* 22.111–122 and 509–512).

A number of fragments attributed to Alcaeus refer to a clash between Mytilene and Athens. Alcaeus took part in this war, which was apparently fought over control of the city of Sigeum, which lay in the Hellespont near Troy (Hdt. 5.94–96). In one battle, Alcaeus had to abandon – or perhaps even surrender – both his shield and armour, which the enemy then took and hung in the temple of their principal goddess, Athena. One fragment can be taken as a dig aimed at the Athenians, when Alcaeus writes how "she" (probably Athena) tried to inspire a scattered host of men to fight.

The Athenian poet and statesman Solon managed to pass reforms in Athens aimed at preventing the rise of a tyrant there. His military achievements may have been the prime reason why he was entrusted with this responsibility. According to our sources, he inspired the Athenians to continue their long-lasting conflict with Megara over control of the island of Salamis, presumably in the early sixth century BC. Plutarch claims that the Athenians made a law that no one was to mention capturing Salamis, and that, when Solon saw so many "young men" restless, he composed his poem entitled *Salamis*. With this poem, he managed to rouse the Athenians, who went on to wrest control of the strategically placed island from Megara.

Herodotus mentions two battles that can be dated to the period under examination. They are more like anecdotes, but may contain a kernel of truth. His brief description of the Battle of the Fetters, traditionally dated to around 560 BC, in which the Spartans were defeated by the Tegeans and clamped in their own irons, serves mostly to underscore Herodotus' theme of *hubris*, even if he claims to have seen the original fetters in a temple at Tegea (Hdt. 1.66). In the Battle of the Champions, dated to 547 BC and referenced later by Thucydides (5.41), the Spartans had captured a piece of borderland called Thyrea from the Argives. The two sides agreed to settle the dispute in the way of a formal challenge: each side would only leave three hundred of their best warriors to fight, while the remainder of the armies went home to await the outcome. The ensuing battle lasted until nightfall. Only three men survived: two Argives and a Spartan named Othryades. The Argives believed they had won and rushed off to tell their people the news. Othryades, however, remained on the battlefield and stripped the enemy corpses of their armour. Next day, both armies returned to the site and a quarrel naturally arose about who was the rightful victor. Finally, the two sides came to blows in an all-out battle that was ultimately won by Sparta (Hdt. 1.82).

• The nature of battle

Modern researchers have commonly assumed that the introduction of new equipment around 700 BC also led to new innovations in the field of military tactics. Specifically, the appearance of heavily-armed spearmen was considered to go hand-in-hand with the introduction of 'phalanx warfare'. The phalanx, in this case, refers to a formation of heavily-armed spearmen, organized in ranks and files, that was typically broader than it was deep. It applies largely to the Macedonian phalanx introduced by Philip of Macedon in the fourth century BC, which was itself inspired by the slightly earlier Theban phalanx. There is no conclusive proof for the existence of phalanx warfare in the Archaic period, and the word 'phalanx' should therefore also be avoided.

A useful distinction to make is between 'mass combat' and 'massed combat'. The former can be used to describe groups of men working together to defeat the enemy, while the latter refers specifically to men organized in tight formations.

A view across the Argive Plain; the photo was taken from the Argive Heraion. Ancient Greece is a mountainous country with limited areas of flat arable land. The expansion of Argos' influence across the plain can be traced in both the archaeological and textual sources. In the late eighth century BC, Argos destroyed the rival town of Asine. The Heraion itself, located at the edge of the plain, was claimed by Argos and marked one of its boundaries. The expansion of Argos was complete with the destruction of Mycenae in the fifth century BC.

Massed combat requires, almost by necessity, the existence of large armies with a formal command structure. Such a command structure was almost certainly in place during the Mycenaean period, so it stands to reason that the Mycenaeans, like other great civilizations of the Late Bronze Age, made use of massed tactics and formations. But for the Dark Age and the period under examination, down to perhaps shortly before the Persian Wars, there is little evidence for the existence of structures – political and military – that fit with the use of massed formations in battle.

As far as depictions of mass combat in the Archaic period are concerned, perhaps the most famous piece of evidence is the Middle to Late Protocorinthian jug known as the Chigi Vase. It was unearthed in an Etruscan grave; tomb robbers at one point had smashed the vase in their search for more valuable treasure. It is currently on display at the National Etruscan Museum in the Villa Giulia at Rome. Among other things, it prominently features a battle-scene on the upper portion of the belly, showing two groups of warriors (warbands?) right before the moment of impact. Each army consists of spearmen. Perhaps for the first time in Corinthian art, all of the men in the battle-scene wear armour, including bronze greaves and bell-shaped cuirasses. Furthermore, all of the men carry a set of two spears, one of which is shorter and has a throwing-loop; there is no doubt that this shorter spear is intended to be a javelin. It seems likely that the javelin was thrown during the advance, in the manner of the later Roman *pilum*.

This scene is regarded by some modern commentators as the earliest more or less accurate rendering of the Greek phalanx in action. However, this is clearly not the case. The men in the battle scene do not appear to fight collectively in a single block, but are instead split into distinct groups or lines of men. Some of the men are still arming themselves at the far left, while others hurry to catch up with their comrades. These are not supposed to represent men in any kind of tightly-knit formation. The fact that they also wield spears equipped with throwing-loops is a further indication that this is not phalanx warfare of any kind known from Classical sources. Instead, the most natural interpretation of the battle-scene is that we are looking at two forces, both equipped with thrusting spears as well as throwing spears, marching towards each other in 'waves', with each 'wave' consisting of a number of men formed up more or less line abreast. This is a way of advancing across the battlefield known from at least two passages in the *Iliad*.

A similar battle-scene as that on the Chigi Vase is depicted on a Middle Protocorinthian perfume bottle. Here, groups of men advance and fight, while a few of the warriors have fallen to their knees and are about to be slaughtered by their opposite numbers. This scene incorporates the groups of men familiar from the Chigi Vase and then repeats the motif, creating a somewhat disorganized and perhaps realistic feel to the proceedings. The motif of the fallen warriors being killed by their foes is also shown on the 'Macmillan *aryballos*', a Middle II to Late Protocorinthian perfume bottle, which also includes men engaged in single combat amidst the general mêlée. It is similar to the Chigi Vase and may even have been produced in the same workshop. It gives us an idea of what may have happened after the two forces met in battle.

None of these painted scenes represent phalanx warfare. Nevertheless, the presence of a flute-player in the battle-scene on the Chigi Vase has been considered as strong evidence. In particular, it has elicited comparisons with a passage in Thucydides, namely his description of the Battle of Mantinea in 418 BC (5.70). However, the flute-player's function in the battle-scene on the Chigi Vase need not correspond with those of the pipers in Classical times. The warriors may have advanced into battle singing war-songs, or perhaps they raised a paean; it tells us nothing of whether or not the men actually fought in phalanx formation.

• Tyranny in Early Greece

For much of the Archaic period, political power in Greek communities was in the hands of aristocracies, especially particular clans or groups of aristocratic families, such as the Bacchiads at Corinth, the Basilids of Ephesus, and the Eupatrids of Athens. Power vested in the hands of small, exclusive groups of high-ranking families frequently began to cause factional strife or *stasis* (to use the Greek word) among the upper echelons of Greek communities, with other wealthy families also wanting influence in politics. During times of strife, these different groups of families would jockey for power. In many cities, the result of such political bickering was the emergence of a sole ruler, whom the Greeks referred to as a *tyrannos* or 'tyrant'.

To the ancient Greeks – initially, at least – the term *tyrannos* was used simply to refer to a monarch or dictator who had assumed power through illegitimate means. The earliest attested use of the term is found in a fragment attributed to Archilochus (fr. 19 West), where it is applied to Gyges, the King of Lydia. As we have seen, Gyges had assumed the throne and founded his own Mermnad dynasty after

Restored detail of the battle scene on the Chigi Vase. Note how the men seem to advance in waves. Each warrior wears bronze armour and is equipped with two spears, one of which is a short javelin intended for throwing, while the other is a thrusting spear. Currently in the Villa Giulia Museum, Rome.

murdering the last Lydian king, Candaules. In Greece, tyrants appeared from the seventh century BC. The earliest was perhaps Pheidon of Argos, who may originally have been a legitimate king with only limited powers, who decided to wrest control from the ruling aristocracy (Hdt. 6.127).

It was once thought that tyrants relied on the use of mercenaries to seize control, but this does not appear to have actually been the case in most known instances. Instead, would-be tyrants simply relied on their friends and followers to support them in their bid for power, with spear and shield if need be, often in exchange for various promises, such as political power and wealth. In 632 BC, Cylon, an aristocrat and erstwhile victor at the Olympic Games, and his followers – supported by the rival city of Megara – tried to establish a tyranny in Athens. The coup failed, and Cylon and his associates sought refuge at Athena's temple on the Acropolis (Hdt. 5.71). At Mytilene on Lesbos, no fewer than three tyrants rose to prominence: Melanchrus, Myrsilus, and Pittacus. The poet Alcaeus, as a member of the ruling aristocracy, was naturally opposed to tyranny. Interestingly, Pittacus was later regarded as one of the Seven Sages of Greece, and so cannot have been as bad as Alcaeus would have us believe. Alcaus was banished after Pittacus took power, but was apparently allowed to return at a later date.

Tyrants never managed to establish a lasting dynasty. Instead, they seem to have been instrumental in transforming the political governance of Early Greek cities from a narrow aristocracy to a broader oligarchy. At Corinth, Cypselus managed to break the power of the ruling Bacchiads in 657 BC, sending many of them into exile and confiscating a significant part of their wealth. He was succeeded by his son Periander, who ruled in Corinth until his death in 585 BC, when he was succeeded by his son Psammetichus (named after the Egyptian king); but he was ousted after three years. At Athens, the reforms of Solon in the sixth century BC were intended to avoid *stasis*, but the changes merely postponed it. Pisistratus managed to become tyrant in the mid-sixth century BC. He ruled until his death and was then succeeded by his son, Hippias. When Pisistratus' second son, Hipparchus, was murdered in 514 BC (as a result of a personal dispute), Hippias may have become embittered, and was ousted in 510 BC by the Spartan King Cleomenes at the behest of the Alcmeonid clan. With the tyrant gone, Cleisthenes, a member of the Alcmeonids, set about reforming the Athenian constitution and created a direct form of democracy, open only to free male citizens of Attic stock.

• Gifts to the gods

Burials with arms disappeared in central and southern Greece after 700 BC. The change can perhaps be attributed to the emergence of the city-state around 700 BC. (The practice persisted longer in Thessaly and Macedon, perhaps because communities here were organized differently. Macedon preserved a slightly Homeric tinge to their culture all the way down to Alexander, with kings who acted like the *basileis* of old.) Now, Greeks began dedicating arms and armour at important sanctuaries, rather than continuing to deposit them in graves. In the tenth and ninth centuries BC, places of worship had been located in the open air, at remarkable natural sites such as springs or in caves. The earliest temples were built in the eighth century BC, with the specific purpose of housing statues representing the gods, as well as votive offerings deposited by their worshippers.

Among the most valuable offerings deposited at these temples were weapons and armour. The Panhellenic sanctuary at Olympia has yielded the largest amount of weapons and armour. The finds there include a variety of spearheads, including small ones for javelins and massive iron examples used for lances. Only toward the end of the sixth century do we also find examples of the *sauroter* or 'lizard killer', the weighted butt-spike fixed at the end of a thrusting spear to balance the weapon. Swords were not as commonly dedicated at Olympia. The Naue II-type sword, in use since the late thirteenth century BC, was slowly replaced from about the middle of the sixth century BC by a new, shorter type of sword with a straight cross-guard. Arrowheads are comparatively rare at Olympia; most of them date to after the Persian Wars.

As regards armour, nearly thirty bell-shaped cuirasses have been unearthed at Olympia, even though of some only scraps remain. They are dated on the basis of stylistic comparisons with Archaic sculpture, using the cuirass from the Argive tomb T45 as an anchor point. A few of them feature intricate, engraved decorations around the shoulder-blades and have been dated to the mid-seventh century BC. Other finds include a large number of helmets (especially Corinthian), examples of the so-called *mitre* (a bronze abdominal plate, perhaps of Cretan origin), upper arm-guards of the sixth century BC, lower arm-guards (including at least one dated to the late seventh century), greaves, a single bronze thigh-guard, ankle-guards and foot-guards of the mid- to late seventh century BC, as well as the remains of a

A still life from a Corinthian bottle depicting part of the equipment of a warrior. Note the presence of both a short javelin and a longer thrusting spear. The sword and the helmet are suspended from pegs on the wall. A greave – probably a pair shown in profile – is placed next to the spears on the ground, as is the bell-shaped cuirass. The only piece missing is the shield. Dated to around 625 BC. Drawn after Anthony Snodgrass, Early Greek Armour and Weapons *(1964), plate 33.*

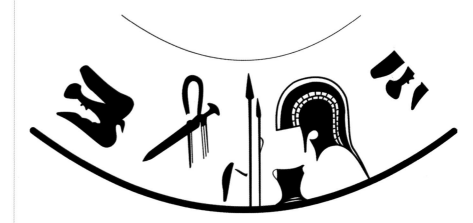

piece of bronze scale armour that may have originally been silver-plated.

Also at Olympia, we have the remains of shields, as well as objects that have been conclusively demonstrated by Anthony Snodgrass, in most cases, to be shield bosses (rather than cymbals). The bosses were used on shields with a single central grip. The shape of the shields is unknown, but they were presumably round or oval, as evidenced from figurines and metal shield coverings of Geometric and Early Orientalizing date. More than seven hundred fragments of Argive-type shields have been discovered at Olympia, including bronze elements from the outside of the shield, rim fragments, handles, and shield band panels. These shields were made of wood, and the rim was generally reinforced with bronze. Furthermore, a number of bronze blazons have been found that were fitted to the wooden shield. Complete bronze facings covering all of the wood on the front are comparatively rare among the finds at Olympia. The shape of the shield and the inner fixtures for the arm did not change dramatically after the basic design was introduced, presumably around the end of the eighth century, with one exception that will be discussed in the next chapter.

Some Argive shields were covered with a thin layer of bronze. This is an example of such a bronze facing unearthed at Olympia. Currently in the Olympia Museum.

Next to Olympia, the Panhellenic sanctuary at Delphi – sacred to Apollo and famed for its Oracle – was the most important cult site in the Aegean. Only small quantities of weapons and armour have been recovered. By far the most interesting finds there are a few early bronze shield facings. These are of the so-called *Herzsprung* or 'Lambda' type and are perfectly circular, with raised concentric circles and a spare triangular area (hence the alternative name based on the Greek letter lambda). *Herzsprung* shields have been unearthed in various regions, including Italy, the Aegean, and Cyprus. The shields at Delphi date to the very end of the eighth century, at the time when single-grip shields were probably phased out in favour of the double-grip Argive shield. It demonstrates contacts between Greeks and cultures further away on the European continent.

Near the modern village of Kalapodi in Phocis, an ancient sanctuary – possibly sacred to Apollo – has been unearthed, with evidence for cultic activity at the site stretching back to shortly before 1200 BC. The metal finds at this sanctuary include copious amounts of weapons and armour. Among the bronze finds there are spearheads, *sauroters*, swords, and arrowheads, as well as various types of helmets (five early *Kegelhelmen*, twenty-nine Illyrian helmets, sixty-two Corinthian helmets, and one late Chalcidian helmet), three greaves, two shields of *Herzsprung* type, and forty-one Argive shields. It should be mentioned that fragments of a seventh-century wall-painting have been discovered that show armoured warriors similar to those depicted on the Chigi Vase.

There have been some attempts to establish what a warrior looked like in the Archaic period, based on the finds of arms and armour at sanctuaries. The evidence in this case suggests, for example, that helmets and shields were more common than cuirasses, and that therefore not all warriors wore bronze armour. This seems logical, but the argument is fallacious. Few greaves, for example, match up with each other, which suggests that they were perhaps not dedicated in pairs and that the distribution of arms and armour is therefore not representative. We simply cannot assume that whole panoplies were dedicated to the gods. Instead, it seems more likely that items were dedicated that had a particular significance; bronze is a high-status metal, after all. Furthermore, shields and helmets could be easily tossed aside in case of a rout and then obtained by the victors, or else were items that were easily removed from the body of a slain foe.

• A Greek way of warfare?

The ancient Greeks themselves had no qualms about admitting that particular items in common use were actually 'Asian' inventions. I have already mentioned how Herodotus attributed certain parts of the Greek panoply to Carian inventors. In fact, it seems safe to say that the Aegean basin and Anatolia were characterized by a certain cultural *koine*; we may also add Italy and other regions to the mix, but the focus for now is on the Aegean. A few examples pertinent to the subject of this book will be discussed in the following paragraphs to further elucidate this point.

It is generally useless to try to distinguish 'Greek' from 'Lydian' warfare. From modern Ikiztepe in Turkey comes a small perfume bottle in the shape of a warrior's head of so-called Rhodian type, complete with Ionian helmet. This may have

Fragmentary metope from the Sicyonian Treasury at Delphi, dated ca. 570–550 BC. It depicts the Dioscuri – Castor and Pollux – and others raiding cattle. Note that both men are carrying two spears in the left hand. Currently in the Delphi Museum.

been an import, but then it must still have had significance to the owner. From the same site also comes a Lydian silver alabastron that features a battle-scene of heavily-armoured men, equipped with Corinthian – rather than the perhaps more expected Ionian – helmets, cuirasses, tunics, greaves, single thrusting spears, and Argive shields. Another interesting element is the fact that something appears to be suspended from the bottom part of some of the shields; perhaps hide with a paw or some kind of tissue with a suspension, perhaps intended for protection of the upper legs. Similar 'curtains' are known from Attic red-figure vases, but these date to the late sixth and fifth centuries BC.

These warriors, both as far as their equipment is concerned and the way they are depicted, elicit comparison with the battle-scene on, for example, the Chigi Vase and Macmillan Aryballos. Note that not all warriors are engaged in a single confrontation; the scene also includes a duel fought between two of the combatants. Clearly, this was a way of fighting that would have been familiar throughout much of the ancient Aegean. Furthermore, we must not assume that warriors

Articulated figurine of a warrior, equipped with what looks like an 'Insular' helmet with a stilted crest. He wears a bell-shaped cuirass; his left arm must once have had a shield. Dated to around 550 BC. Currently in the Antikensammlung in Munich.

Defending the city

Archaeologically speaking, the seventh century BC tends to be less well attested than the sixth. The reason for this is that most sites that existed in the seventh century continued to be occupied in the sixth, and therefore much of the earlier remains were obliterated by new building efforts. Nevertheless, it is clear that new fortifications were constructed in the seventh century BC. Some of these fortifications, such as the mid-seventh century wall at the small town of Vroulia on Rhodes, were reinforced by digging a ditch in front.

The evidence for the sixth century BC is much clearer, with many new fortifications constructed in this period, especially toward the end of the century. Sometimes, we can attribute the construction to specific persons. This is the case, for example, with the fortifications at Pythagorion on Samos, which were instigated by the tyrant Polycrates (r. 538–522 BC). Most walls continue to take the form of a stone socle with a mud-brick superstructure. A new feature toward the end of the sixth century BC was an increase in the number of towers added to the walls.

The poet Alcaeus states that "warlike men are the bulwark (*purgos*) of the city" (fr. 112 Voigt); in other words, without valiant men, a city would be defenceless, regardless of its fortifications. It is also a very succinct way of reminding his audience – fellow aristocrats – that they are the ones who protect their communities. *Purgos* is also found in other poets. Callinus of Ephesus emphasizes how a brave man is regarded as a demigod, and considered a "bulwark" by the people at large (fr. 1.17–20 West).

with Argive shields and bronze body-armour always fought with spears or straight swords; there is some variety in the evidence. A Lydian wall-painting in the Tartarlı tumulus, near Dinar (province of Afyon), depicts a battle-scene between warriors with Argive shields, bronze helmets, and greaves, fighting each other with curved or 'sickle' swords. The date of these wall-paintings has been a matter of some discussion; they are currently dated not to the sixth century, but to around 480 BC. From the Lydian capital of Sardis, we have a number of fragments of a vase depicting riders that are indistinguishable from similar unarmed riders on Greek Geometric and Early Orientalizing pottery.

During the Archaic period, there were frequent contacts between Greeks and Phrygians. Evidence from Gordium suggests that the Phrygians were familiar with 'true cavalry' (men who fought from horseback, rather than *hippobatai*) by the ninth century BC. Within the remains of Megaron 3, possibly the central structure of the citadel, destroyed around 800 BC, excavators found the remains of various items, including some ivory inlays. A square piece of ivory inlay depicts a rider with a round shield (possibly made of wicker), a helmet with cheek-pieces and of a type that appears similar to the so-called 'Phrygian cap', and a long spear or lance. Similar horsemen are shown in a battle-scene on large fragments of a rectangular

Detail of the Siphnian Treasury at Delphi. It depicts part of the Gigantomachy, the battle between the Olympian gods and the giants. Three giants are shown on the right, with the corpse of another on the ground. The giant on the left is trying to run away from the two goddesses behind him; note his bell-shaped cuirass, the sword suspended from a baldric, and the detail on the inside of the shield. Dated to ca. 525 BC. Currently in the Delphi Museum.

piece of ivory inlay; a horse is depicted at the far left (probably a horseman), while an archer at the far right takes aim; there are four horsemen with shields, helmets, and spears, one of whom is holding the spear with both hands in an underarm position. The enemy is unfortunately lost. Interestingly, the richly furnished room in which these inlays were found seems to have been used for drinking and eating, so that among the Phrygian elite we find the same pattern as for the Greeks, namely the association of horses, feasting, and fighting.

Phrygia eventually became part of the Lydian Empire. A clay relief revetment of the sixth century from Pazarli depicts warriors that are very similar in appearance to those found on Greek and Lydian artefacts; namely, men in tunics with some sort of greaves, wearing helmets with stilted crests and equipped with round, possibly Argive shields and single thrusting spears, held in an overhand position. From nearby Lycia, we have Late Archaic wall-paintings in tombs at modern Elmalı-Kızılbel. These include a scene of warriors arming, and another two-horse chariot, as well as a scene depicting a procession of warriors and chariots. Another wall-painting depicts a warrior with Ionian crested helmet, tunic, corslet, greaves, and spear, mounting a chariot drawn by two horses; his charioteer is similarly equipped. Once again, it is clear that equipment and modes of fighting were part of an Aegean-Anatolian *koine*, rather than being distinctly 'Greek' or 'Phrygian' or 'Lydian'.

Outside the military sphere, we have ample proof for cultural exchanges between Greeks and the peoples of Anatolia. One example would be the symposium itself. In the epic world described by Homer, the heroes sit on chairs to feast at tables. But starting in Asia Minor in the early seventh century BC, Greeks began to recline on dining couches. This practice then spread westwards across the rest of the Aegean and was complete by the late seventh century BC. By then, the earliest coins – made of electrum, a naturally occurring alloy of gold and silver – had been minted in Lydia. Coinage would slowly be adopted from the Lydians by the Greeks from about the middle of the sixth century BC onwards.

The front plate of a bronze bell-shaped cuirass dated to the seventh century BC. A warrior wearing a neatly polished bronze cuirass, lit by the Mediterranean sun, must have made a striking impression on the battlefield. Currently in the Antikensammlung in Munich.

• Summary

New types of armour – the metal helmet and the Argive shield with double-grip – were introduced in the late eighth century BC. The metal helmets, at least, may be inspired by Assyrian examples, and there is some evidence for Carian influences on other elements of the Greek panoply. There are many eastern influences on Greece at this time. A leading source of information is the pottery produced in Corinth around this time and throughout the seventh and first half of the sixth centuries BC. This evidence also frequently includes horses, and the motif of the 'knight' and 'squire' – *hippobatas* and *hippostrophos* – soon becomes very widespread. These

Greek men of bronze also found employment as mercenaries by empires of the ancient Near East, and may have been instrumental in the Egyptian efforts to assert their sovereignty.

The century between ca. 650 and 550 BC forms a consistent period, with an abundant amount of evidence – relatively speaking – from a fairly large number of different regions, including archaeological evidence (dedications at sanctuaries, fortifications), figurative art from Corinth, Laconia, the Aegean islands, East Greece, and some other places, as well as ancient texts, especially fragments from poems attributed to Archilochus, Tyrtaeus, Alcaeus, and others. In this period, the equipment of warriors appears to become somewhat more standardized, although small-scale army organization (warbands) and flexible tactics appear to continue; there is no proof to support the existence of 'phalanx warfare' at this time. Bronze armour seems to become more common, but we cannot be sure whether all spearmen were encased in metal armour, or only some of them. The texts and artistic evidence suggests that metal armour was widespread, but they may, of course, not reflect actual conditions in the field. Armies in this period were probably smaller

Bronze elements from an Argive shield unearthed at Olympia. The original shield was made of wood. Along the rim, bronze strips were added for decoration. The shield blazon consists of a composite creature with the legs of a lion and the tail of a fish or aquatic reptilian monster; the main part consists of a winged Gorgon holding serpents. This monstrous blazon was intended to instil fear in the enemy. Currently in the Olympia Museum.

than during the Persian Wars, no doubt due to their being composed of a number of smallish warbands, each consisting of a leader and his followers, with perhaps some lower-ranking people compelled to swell the numbers.

There is a shift away from seaborne raids to battles on land. Depictions of ships become rare after ca. 650 BC, and both the iconographic evidence and ancient texts reveal an interest in conflict between communities. There are accounts of early wars, such as the Lelantine and Messenian Wars, about which there are many uncertainties. Other battles, such as the Battle of the Champions between Argos and Sparta, are largely anecdotal. We are on firmer ground with wars between Athens and Megara, the conquest of Salamis by Athens and of Thasos by Paros, and some battles fought between Greek cities and the Lydian Empire. Conflicts between rival polities were not the only source of discord, however; in many cities, ambitious aristocrats managed to become dictators, *tyrannoi*, but none of them managed to establish any lasting dynasties.

A bronze votive 'Herzsprung' shield with embossed decoration. Such shields were not made in Greece itself, but imported from elsewhere on the European continent. Specimens of such shields have been found in Italy, for example, and they are named after the place in Germany where other shields of this type have been found. Currently in the Delphi Museum.

4 Rebels and empire

Croesus invaded Cappadocia not just out of a desire to add it to his own dominions on account of his confidence in the oracle, but also to punish Cyrus on account of Astyages. Cyrus, son of Cambyses, had subjugated Astyages, son of Cyaxares, who was Croesus' brother-in-law and king of the Medes.
—Herodotus, *Histories 1.73*

Croesus, ruler of Lydia, must not have regarded Cyrus as much of a threat, or else he would never have invaded Cappadocia. But Cyrus was not just another upstart monarch. Persia had been a subject of the Median Empire when he first assumed the throne in 559 BC. He quickly set out to found his own empire – the Persian or Achaemenid Empire – by overthrowing his Median overlords and adding their territory to his own in 550 BC. When Croesus invaded Cappadocia, it brought him into direct conflict with Cyrus. When he failed to convince the Greek cities that were subject to Lydia to revolt, Cyrus marched on to Anatolia and conquered the Lydians by force. He then returned east and added Babylonia to his realm in 539 BC.

The Persian Empire founded by Cyrus the Great was the largest the world had yet seen, spanning a vast territory and incorporating within it various subject nations, including Assyrians, Babylonians, Bactrians, Scythians, Lydians, and many other peoples. The Greeks of Asia Minor were also integrated into the Persian Empire in the second half of the sixth century BC. There is evidence for their intermarriage with Persians, while Greek pottery was traded and Greek coins have been unearthed at numerous places within the Persian empire. Greeks may even have helped build the Persian palaces. But the Greeks never featured heavily in the Persian view of their empire. Persian kings, starting especially with Darius I, emphasized the extent of their empire in royal inscriptions, describing it usually from the core outward. The western fringe included Thracians, Libyans, Carians, and Scythians, as well as Ionians. In the mind of the Persians, the Greeks occupied a position at the extreme fringe of their empire, where they were lumped together with tribal societies like the Thracians and Scythians.

Conflict between the Greeks and the Persians was perhaps inevitable. Following the Ionian Revolt in the first decade of the fifth century BC, the Persians mounted three punitive expeditions into Greece. The first army, in 492, reached Macedon, but was recalled because the Persian navy was unable to round the Athos; the sec-

A scene of men arming for battle; note the man clipping on one of his greaves. Attic black figure wine jug dated to ca. 520 BC. Currently in the Allard Pierson Museum, Amsterdam.

ond one, in 490, was a purely naval expedition against the Greek isles, Eretria, and Athens; and the last one took place a decade later and was commanded by Darius' son and successor, Xerxes, personally. These Greco-Persian wars would loom large in the collective memory of the Greeks, even if they were probably considered less important by the Persians. For the period discussed in this chapter, we are fortunate to have at our disposal the *Histories* written by Herodotus of Halicarnassus (ca. 545–425 BC). The text, which later Classical or Hellenistic scholars divided into nine books, was probably written no later than about 425. The purpose of the *Histories* was to provide both an overview of, and a context for, the Greco-Persian Wars.

From reading Herodotus' prologue, it seems as if the Greco-Persian conflict was a struggle between different ideologies. The historian explains that the Trojan War came about due to differences in culture between the Greeks and the peoples of Asia as regards the abduction of women. It all started, according to Herodotus, when Greeks and Asians engaged in a tit-for-tat raiding of each other's women, including Zeus' abduction of the Phoenician girl Europa (Hdt. 1.1–5). Examples abound in the *Histories* of battles and wars instigated by a desire for revenge. In an important paper, J.E. Lendon has pointed out how fundamental the concept of vengeance was to the ancient Greeks, connected as it was to ideas of friendship and gift-exchange, and the violation of those reciprocal relationships.

A photograph of the place where Xerxes had a canal dug across the Athos peninsula in preparation for his campaign in Greece.

The Persian Wars

The Greek cities in Asia Minor revolted against the Persians in 499 BC, referred to as the Ionian Revolt. In 498 BC, an alliance of Ionian cities – supported by Eretria and Athens – marched to and captured the city of Sardis, the old capital of the Lydian Empire and then the seat of the Persian satrap (governor) of the region. Caria joined the rebels in 496. The Persians struggled to put down the revolt, but they managed to secure a decisive victory at the Battle of Lade in 494 BC. The region was once again pacified in 493 BC.

The support that Athens and Eretria had given to the Ionian Revolt could not go unanswered and the Persians therefore mounted an expedition to teach these cities a lesson. At least, this is what Herodotus says. In 490 BC, Darius' generals led an army into Greece and laid waste to Eretria. Sailing down to Athens, the Persian army landed near the town of Marathon, where it was soundly defeated in battle by the army of the Athenians and a small allied force of Plataeans. With their objectives only half fulfilled, the Persians retreated. When Darius died in 485 BC, he was succeeded by his son Xerxes, who soon swore to take revenge on the Greeks.

The Persian army set off across land in 480 BC, rejoining the Persian fleet every once in a while. At Thermopylae, the advance of the Persian army was temporarily brought to a halt when King Leonidas and his troops blocked off the narrow pass. There was vigorous fighting here, but eventually the Persians succeeded in defeating the defenders and broke through. On the same day, a Greek fleet managed to inflict heavy losses on the Persian fleet off Artemisium. The Persian army arrived in Attica. Athens itself had been largely evacuated and was razed; the insult of Marathon was repaid. However, the Persian fleet was lured into the narrow straits at the island of Salamis and suffered heavily in a naval engagement.

Xerxes returned to his homeland, leaving command of the Persian army in the hands of his general Mardonius, who decided to winter in Thessaly, a region that had sworn fealty to Persia. In 479 BC, he again led an army southwards into Boeotia, where it was defeated by a large army of allied troops under Spartan command at the Battle of Plataea. Mardonius was killed and the Persian army routed. Meanwhile, a Greek fleet was asked by the islands of Samos and Chios to liberate Ionia. Having learnt that a Persian fleet was beached at Mycale, the Greeks broke through the defences and burnt the ships.

LEGEND

Persian:
Garrison ◈
Royal Road ⬧
Satrapy capital ◉
Took part in Ionian Revolt ⬥

Campaigns:

Ionians 498 BC	①
Datis and Artaphernes 494/490BC	②
Mardonius 492 BC	③
Xerxes 480 BC	④
Hellenic League 480/478 BC	⑤
To Andros 480 BC	
To Samos and Mycale 479 BC	
To Cyprus 478 BC	
Sestus 479 BC	⑥

Battles
480 ⊗ Naval
490 ⊗ Land
City ✷ 490 Under siege
492 NAVAL DISASTER

N

Scale:

km 0 25 50 75 100

mi 0 25 50 75 100

A map showing the key sites and movements of troops during the Persian campaign in Greece in the years 480–479 BC.

• Changes in equipment

Attic pottery is an invaluable source of information for tracing changes in this period. In the final decades of the seventh century BC, Attic workshops developed a new technique of vase decoration, the black-figure style. This was essentially a variant on existing vase-painting techniques, in which figures were painted with solid, dark colours, and details later inscribed with a knife or other sharp object. Attic black-figure pots tended to be larger than Corinthian vases. The latter were finally overtaken by Attic pots in trade networks around 550 BC, and most of the extant black-figure vases – of which thousands upon thousands have been discovered – date to this late period, when also a new technique (red-figure) was developed, which will be discussed in more detail in the next chapter.

Initially, the *hippobatai* and *hippostrophoi* of the previous chapter remain a part of Attic pottery. Chariots in a martial context reappear on Attic pottery of the sixth century, but these tend to be associated specifically with myth, such as the Trojan War. However, horses seem to become rarer the closer we get to the Persian Wars. At the same time, especially in red-figure vase-paintings, the bronze cuirass is slowly displaced by the linen corslet, which is sometimes reinforced with scales. When warriors are depicted with bronze bell-shaped cuirasses, they now tend to wear other pieces of bronze armour as well. Particularly prominent are thigh-guards, especially on black-figure vases.

Terracotta votive shield from Corinth with relief decoration showing a hippobatas *jumping off his horse. Dated to the early fifth century BC, it indicates that* hippobatai *were a feature of the entire Archaic period. Currently in the Archaeological Museum of Corinth.*

Thigh-guards make it impossible to ride on horseback. It is certainly no coincidence that some men – if the pictures are correct – apparently began to wear more armour at the same time that horses began to slowly disappear and some warriors turned to wearing lighter pieces of armour (the linen corslet). This suggests that men may now have been required to march to the battlefield, and it is possible that armies were enlarged to include a larger part of society. Lacking horses, rich men may have sought to express their wealth instead by wearing more pieces of armour, to distinguish themselves from warriors whom they perceived as being of lower standing, though obviously not poor. In other words, it seems as if, in the later sixth century, most Athenian warriors were expected to march and fight on foot, instead of riding into battle.

In my opinion, this development can be related to four other new elements that appear at roughly the same time, in the last quarter of the sixth century BC. The first of these new elements is the introduction of the trumpet. An Attic black-figure plate attributed to Psiax shows a male figure with helmet, cuirass, and greaves, blowing a trumpet. Another trumpeter, this time clothed like a Scythian archer, is shown on a bilingual cup signed by the potter Andocides. Trumpets are not necessary when fighting as part of a warband, as one's leader is probably never far away; there are no trumpets in the *Iliad*, for example. The use of trumpets therefore suggests fighting in relatively large armies, commanded by a leader whose voice may not have carried far enough for everyone to hear.

This detail of an Attic black figure plate attributed to Psiax depicts a warrior blowing a trumpet. Such trumpets appear in Greece in the later sixth century BC. Dated to around 520 BC. Currently in the British Museum.

The second element is twofold: the modification of existing types of helmets and the appearance of new ones. Trumpets are good for conveying orders above the din of battle, provided that you can actually hear them. The typical helmet of the period between ca. 725 and 525 BC is the Corinthian, which covers most of the head, including the ears, and only leaves slits for the eyes and mouth. Such headgear is perfectly suitable in situations where one can focus on a few enemies at a time, and one's compatriots, especially the leader, are never far away. But helmets of this type are difficult to use when fighting in close order. In the second half of the sixth century BC, modifications were made to existing types of helmets, and new types were introduced that left more of the eyes (face) and ears free.

The third element is an unusual feature on the inside of Argive shields, which further suggests that some form of more closely-knit fighting in formation was introduced in the late sixth century BC. A good example is provided by the full-length 'portrait' of Achilles found on a red-figure belly-amphora dated to 525–500 BC. Achilles' shield features two hand-grips, one on each side, connected to a rope that lines the inner shield. Allen Pittman has come up with an ingenious explanation for the presence of a second hand-grip (and the rope); namely, that the 'extra' handle was gripped by the man immediately to one's left. This made it much easier to form and maintain a shield wall.

The fourth and last element is a new type of sword. It appears that this may also have been invented for use in a more closely-packed environment. Vase-paintings before the last quarter of the sixth century nearly always feature just one type of sword, the so-called Naue II. However, toward the end of the sixth century, this type of sword seems to disappear quite abruptly, replaced by a sword with a leaf-shaped blade and straight cross-guard. It was also much shorter than the Naue II sword. Shorter blades are more useful in tight formations than in open ones. Examples of this new Greek sword abound in Attic red-figure. Attic black-figure appears to be somewhat more conservative, though examples of these new types of swords are found on a number of vases, some as early as circa 540 BC.

To sum up, I believe that the changes noted here can be related to the introduction of a more close-knit way of fighting in formation; the term 'phalanx warfare' can perhaps be properly applied to it, even if it is somewhat anachronistic for reasons explained in the previous chapter. More specifically, it relates to the emergence of centrally-organized armies of men who fought solely on foot and who replaced the earlier aristocratic warbands. The evidence that supports this notion are the introduction of trumpets, the use of helmets that left more of the ears and

A Scythian archer on an Attic bilingual cup. Dated to around 530–520 BC. Currently in the Louvre.

sometimes also eyes exposed, the introduction of secondary handles on the insides of Argive shields, and the use of a shorter type of sword.

• Greek warriors of the Persian Wars

The *Histories* of Herodotus does not abound with detailed descriptions of arms and armour. However, one notable feature is that Herodotus – like Tyrtaeus, discussed in the previous chapter – makes a fundamental distinction between lightly- and heavily-armoured troops. Whereas Tyrtaeus speaks of *panoploi*, Herodotus uses the word *hoplites*, from which our familiar form 'hoplite' is derived. Hoplites in the *Histories* are equipped with body armour (for example, Hdt. 8.27) and large shields with figurative blazons (Hdt. 9.74; also 8.27). One type of helmet is specifically called Corinthian (Hdt. 4.180). As far as their weapons are concerned, the set of two spears, which we encountered on Geometric pottery and items like the Chigi Vase, seems to have gone out of use by the time of the Persian Wars. Instead, Herodotus' hoplites fight with a single thrusting spear. As always, the sword was used

A butt-spike or **sauroter** *('lizard-killer'), used to balance the spear and to allow it to be driven into the ground when not in use. Currently in the Antikensammlung in Munich.*

Scythian archers

Supposed 'Scythian' archers appear on Attic pottery in the sixth century BC. They typically wear long-sleeved tunics and trousers, often enlivened by decorative patterns. Maria Voss noted that Scythians first appear, although infrequently, on Attic vases of the first half of the sixth century and become more common in the period between 540 and 490 BC; inconsistencies and inaccuracies in the depiction of Scythian archers after 490 suggest, according to Voss, that the archers themselves were no longer available for the vase-painters to imitate.

Scythian archers appear frequently in departure scenes. A black-figure scene of the late sixth century, in which Scythian archers shoot from behind the shields of hoplites, suggests how they were used on the battlefield. It is possible that Athenians hired Scythians as a kind of mercenary troops in combat, as the tyrant Pisistratus supposedly had, or that they were simply part of the following of an aristocratic patron. We know that the Athenians had an active interest in the Black Sea region, where the Scythians lived.

However, Askold Ivantchick has recently argued that the Scythian archers depicted on vases dated 530–490 BC are not really Scythians at all. Instead, he suggests that the clothes worn by the archers were a convention that identified them as secondary characters accompanying a hero, who was always depicted as a hoplite. As such, Scythian dress was indicative of the character's iconographic function, rather than his ethnic origin. I do not believe that Scythian dress was used to denote 'secondary characters'. However, Ivantchick does make a good point in remarking that the Scythian costume may simply represent 'foreigners' of undisclosed origin; furthermore, he makes a valid point by warning us not to overestimate the number of 'barbarian' troops in Athens.

as a secondary weapon, particularly at close quarters when the spear had broken. If a warrior had broken both spear and sword, he would continue the fight with a dagger, or whatever rocks or other makeshift weapons might be at hand.

Herodotus calls lightly-armed men *gymnetes* or, more commonly, *psiloi*. These operated independently from the heavily-armed troops, and were not mixed with them, as in the time of Tyrtaeus. The light troops include javelineers (Hdt. 8.90), as well as archers. The bow and arrow now exclusively appear in the hands of specialist archers, particularly *epikouroi* (for example, Hdt. 3.39). When Pausanias sends a messenger to the Athenians to ask for help, he hopes that they will at least send him some archers (Hdt. 9.60), which suggests that, during this period, archers were relatively plentiful. However, masses of archers are considered a mainstay of the Persian army, rather than the Greek. For example, at the Battle of Thermopylae, when a man from Trachis reported that the Persians could fire enough arrows to block out the sun, one of Leonidas' men is famously said to have regarded this as excellent news, for that meant the battle would be fought in the shade (Hdt. 7.226).

The Athenians at Marathon in 490 BC were noteworthy for possessing neither archers nor horsemen (Hdt. 6.112). Sizeable numbers of Greek cavalry are associated in the *Histories* with specific regions within the Aegean area. Attica is specifically said to be ill-suited to horses (Hdt. 9.13), with the exception of the area around Marathon (Hdt. 6.102). In contrast, the Boeotians possessed bodies of horsemen, commanded by a *hipparchos* or cavalry commander (Hdt. 9.68–69). The Thessalians were also renowned for their horsemen (Hdt. 7.173, 7.196, 8.28); when the sons of Pisistratus enlisted the aid of the Thessalians, they levelled the ground near Phaleron to make it more suitable for horses (Hdt. 5.63).

Greeks from other parts of the Mediterranean also used horsemen, such as the Syracusans (Hdt. 7.154 and 158). Riders were employed to despatch messages by both the Greeks (Hdt. 6.58, 9.54, 9.60) and the Persians (Hdt. 5.14, 9.17); they were also used as scouts (Hdt. 4.121, 7.208). Furthermore, horsemen could seek out and destroy specific enemies (Hdt. 8.138). Certain elite bodies of fighting men had names that imply they once rode to the battlefield, such as the Spartan *Hippeis*, literally "Horsemen" (Hdt. 1.67, 8.124). However, the Persians employed greater numbers of horse troops, often to the detriment of Greek armies. The Lydians were also famous for their horsemen, who used long spears in combat (Hdt. 1.79–80). Persian horsemen apparently fought from horseback using javelins (Hdt. 9.17). It is unclear what weapons Greek horsemen used, and they may perhaps still have dismounted in the fashion of earlier *hippobatai*.

Some of the subject peoples recruited into the Persian army fielded large numbers of horse troops, such as the Scythians and the Lydians. Chariots were a relatively common feature on the Homeric battlefield, but their use was apparently discontinued shortly before the outbreak of the Persian Wars, although the Greeks still used them in races (for example, Hdt. 5.77, 6.35–36), as well as in processions (Hdt. 1.60, 4.180), and also awarded them as prizes of honour (Hdt. 8.124). A chariot was still used by the Persians to transport their king (Hdt. 7.40–41, 7.55, 7.100, 8.115). Finally, chariots were used in war, sometimes alongside horsemen, by a number of foreign peoples, especially Libyans (for example, Hdt. 1.179, 4.170, 7.184), as well as the Cypriots (Hdt. 5.113).

• Mobilization of troops

From the latter half of the sixth century, the earlier warbands seem to have all but disappeared. Larger armies appeared in their stead. The exact mechanism by which armies were mobilized around the time of the Persian Wars is never described by

Attic black figure amphora from Vulci. It depicts two horsemen engaging each other; a warrior on foot is shown falling to the ground, perhaps wounded or dying. The cavalrymen are not equipped with shields and fight using lances. Dated to 510–500 BC. Currently in the National Museum of Antiquities, Leiden.

Sparta

As is well known, Sparta differed to some extent, as far as social and military organization are concerned, from most other Greek cities. For one thing, Sparta was ruled by not one, but two kings, who had the right to declare war against anyone they wished (Hdt. 6.56). Furthermore, at some unknown point in the past, the Spartans had subjugated the other people of Laconia (the so-called *perioikoi*, 'dwellers about') and enslaved the Messenians (called 'helots'). Spartan citizens ('Spartiates'), *perioikoi*, and helots together were referred to as Lacedaemonians and operated as a single armed force, if not on an equal footing (Hdt. 7.235).

By the fifth century BC, the Spartans were renowned for their austere militarism, which was a result of their peculiar socio-political system. The legendary lawgiver Lycurgus was said to have created 'good laws' (*eunomia*) and established three important institutions that – as Herodotus puts it – all concerned warfare; namely, the *enomotias kai triekadas kai sussitia*. Nothing is known for certain as regards the *triekas*. The *enomotia* ('sworn band') was probably derived from a warband or other all-male warrior group, and was no doubt closely related to the *sussitia*, the 'common meals' or 'messes' that Spartan men enjoyed together. Furthermore, Lycurgus is credited by Herodotus with having set up the ephors (Spartan magistrates) and the *gerontes*, the 'council of elders' (Hdt. 1.65), a more formal body than the Homeric *gerontes*, of which the city's two kings were also members. Sparta's rise to military prominence from the latter half of the sixth century onwards is probably also due to reforms that enabled the centralized mobilization of armed forces on a grander scale than had hitherto been possible.

The Spartans' reputation as a military force to be reckoned with pops up regularly in Herodotus. Whenever a polity requires military aid, the Spartans are usually the ones they turn to first; it was even possible for individuals to call in aid. When tyranny had been overthrown in Athens, a number of rival aristocratic factions vied for control. The two most important ones were led by Cleisthenes and Isagoras, both of them members of the Alcmeonidae. Isagoras had a powerful guest-friend, namely Cleomenes, one of the kings of Sparta. Cleomenes sent a herald to Athens, which intimidated Cleisthenes enough to cause him to leave the city. A little later, the Spartan leader arrived in Athens with a small army, where he drove out another seven hundred families. When he tried to dissolve the Council, the latter resisted, forcing Cleomenes and Isagoras to withdraw to the Acropolis, where they were besieged for two days. Cleomenes and his army were allowed to leave on the third day. Isagoras' supporters were executed; Cleisthenes and the other exiles were allowed to return.

Heracles as an archer, from the east pediment of the temple of Aphaea on Aegina. He wears a linen corslet. The kneeling pose is characteristic of early Greek archers, who seem to operate in a manner similar to modern snipers, picking and choosing their targets on the battlefield. Dated to around 500 BC. Currently on display in the Munich Glyptothek.

Herodotus, but personal ties of friendship and blood no longer appear to be a dominant factor. In the later sixth century BC, when the people of the island of Aegina were fighting the Athenians, they asked the Argives for help. The Argive *demos* – in other words, the 'state' – refused to answer their call. However, a thousand Argive volunteers led by Eurybates decided to join the battle, regardless of what their political leaders had decided (Hdt. 6.92). In Athens, a centralized mechanism for mobilizing the army may not have been available until the reforms of Cleisthenes at the end of the sixth century (Hdt. 5.66; cf. 5.78).

The earliest known Athenian decree, dating to between 510 and 480 BC (and broken into seven fragments), happens to inform us a little about the situation at Salamis and what the rights and obligations of the (Athenian) inhabitants were. The text makes clear that the Athenians sent *klerouchoi* to Salamis. This is the first known use of the word *klerouchoi*, indicating Athenians who were given allotments abroad that they could settle without losing their Athenian citizenship. Among other things, the decree states that each *klerouchos* must pay taxes and provide military service to Athens, while providing his own arms to the value of 30 drachmae. Furthermore, the Athenian governor (*archon*) either had to approve the men's equipment or was responsible for mobilizing the colonists in an emergency (the text is poorly preserved and unclear at this point). The text ends in the usual way; namely, that it was approved by the *boule*, the Athenian council.

This is the earliest known reference to men each having to supply their own equipment. These men could then be inspected, and were presumably mobilized, by a representative of the central authority, in this case the *archon* or 'governor'. This is incompatible with earlier forms of army organization, with warbands consisting of leaders and their (personal) followers. The cost of the panoply is interesting as well. Coinage was at some scale introduced in Greece only from 550 BC onwards, even though coins had already been minted in Lydia at the end of the seventh century. It is often difficult to estimate exactly how much an ancient drachma was worth, but 30 drachmae around 500 BC must have been the equivalent of somewhat more than thirty days' worth of wages for a simple labourer. The situation on Salamis was presumably similar to that in Athens at around the same time, with each relatively affluent Athenian subject to some kind of authority figure appointed by the council and having to provide his own military equipment at a (minimum) fixed value.

While the smaller warbands known from Homer and at least some of the Archaic poets are no longer a feature during the Persian Wars, the centrally-organized and larger armies of this period were not inflexible. A leader could detach a small group of warriors from the main force and lead them on specific missions. For example, Herodotus tells the story of the Athenian Aristides, son of Lysimachus. During the Battle of Salamis, he assembled a number of fellow Athenian hoplites from those who were ranged along the shores of Salamis. With this task force, he sailed to Psyttalea, a small island between Salamis and the mainland, where they killed all of the Persians who were stationed there (Hdt. 8.76 and 95). Some believe that this episode was concocted to put down the Themistoclean achievements during the sea-battle. Even if this is true, it had to sound plausible and must somehow have corresponded to a real type of warfare.

Alliances were more formal from probably the later sixth century onwards than they had been before. Alliances – *symmachoi*, literally 'fighting together' – feature in Herodotus, and often are made to defend against a common enemy. They can be large or small. The most famous alliance was that of a large number of Greek states, led by Sparta, against the Persian invaders in 480–479. However, it is characteristic of the argumentative Greeks that this alliance crumbled almost as soon as the invader had been repulsed.

One of the earliest known treaties of alliance was inscribed on a bronze plaque found at Olympia and dated to the later sixth century BC. The text reads as follows in the translation by Russell Meiggs and David Lewis:

This is the covenant between the Eleans and the Heraeans. There shall be an alliance (synmachia) for a hundred years, and this (year) shall be the first; and if anything is needed, either word or deed, they shall stand by each other in all matters and especially in war; and if they stand not by each other, those who do the wrong shall pay a talent of silver to Olympian Zeus to be used in his service. And if anyone injures this writing, whether private man or magistrate or community, he shall be liable to the sacred fine herein written.

The text is essentially a contract, in which both parties (the people of Elis and Heraia) agree to come to each other's aid whenever necessary, especially in times of war; if one side fails to comply with the terms of the agreement, it must pay the appropriate fine. The plaque was set up at the Panhellenic sanctuary at Olympia; the fine had to be paid to Zeus, the protector of oaths, a function he had since at least Homer's time (for example, *Il.* 10.329–330).

• **Army organization**

In the *Iliad*, different types of troops are not separated into distinct homogeneous units; instead, the basic tactical unit is the heterogeneous warband. This also appears to have been the basic unit that lyric poets had in mind. However, it is clear from Herodotus' descriptions of important battles during the Persian Wars that the Greeks by that time, like the Medes and their Persian successors, had divided their troops into largely homogeneous units according to type: that is, tactical units of archers, spearmen, and horsemen. Precisely when this change occurred among the Greeks is never stated explicitly in any of the literary sources, but it obviously must

Attic red figure amphora depicting a Greek warrior attacking a Persian archer. Dated to ca. 480–470 BC. Currently in the Metropolitan Museum of Art, New York.

have happened, if we believe Herodotus, some time in the sixth century, prior to the outbreak of the Persian Wars.

By the time of the Persian Wars, different types of troops no longer intermixed on the battlefield, as they did in Homer and possibly the lyric poets (for instance, Tyrtaeus' *gymnetes* and *panoploi*), but are now each organized into distinct units. The army as a whole is, of course, still called *stratos*, the common Greek word for 'army' or 'host'. Individual units are called *lochoi*, while larger divisions are dubbed *telea* (singular, *tele*). *Lochos* was already used by Homer to refer to a body of men; Herodotus uses it in much the same way (for example, Hdt. 9.53). It is often translated as 'company', numbering up to a few hundred men and commanded by a *lochagos* or 'captain'. The battle-array or order of battle itself may be referred to as *taxis*. This could also mean 'division', in which case it was divided into *lochoi*, as is made clear in Aeschylus' play *The Persians* (298). A *taxis* was commanded by a *taxiarchos*; the army as a whole was commanded by one or more *strategoi* or 'generals' (Hdt. 7.83). The *polemarchos* or simply 'polemarch', a commander-in-chief of the army, was an archon position at Athens (Hdt. 6.109); it was also the title of a high-ranking military commander at Sparta (Hdt. 7.173), though one of the kings always served as commander of the army there.

While we have already seen that Greek warriors tended to band together and

Continued use of mercenaries

In this period, Greeks continued to be used as troops in the armies of foreign empires, although not always as either volunteers or mercenaries: when a Greek city was conquered by the Persians, it often had to provide levies for the army of the King of Kings. If we may believe Herodotus, Greek troops were considered to be among the cream of the military crop; the author frequently points out their superior weapons, armour, and skill, and contrasts them with Persian troops, who are generally – and no doubt rather unfairly – characterized as lightly-armed, unskilled, and disorganized.

Some tyrants used mercenaries to secure their power. Polycrates, tyrant of Samos between 538 and 522 BC, possessed a sizeable fleet of one hundred fifty-oared galleys and an army of mercenaries, including a thousand archers, which he used to conquer a number of cities and islands (Hdt. 3.39 and 3.45). Likewise, the Athenian tyrant Pisistratus, after being ousted for a third time, collected gifts and money from communities that owed him a favour. He then enlisted the aid of Argive mercenaries; furthermore, a man from Naxos, Lygdamis, provided him with both money and men. Pisistratus and his mercenaries then waged a full-scale battle against the – apparently rather small – army of the Athenians and managed to secure a victory (Hdt. 1.61–64).

Detail from the archers' frieze at Darius' palace in Susa, made of glazed siliceous bricks and dated to ca. 510 BC. The men are equipped with long thrusting spears, as well as bows. Currently on display in the Louvre.

fight in groups, sometimes in 'waves', the use of a more rigid formation appears to have been an invention of around the time of the Persian Wars. In Herodotus, the hoplites are arranged in roughly rectangular formations (wider than they are deep), with men arrayed in ranks and files (for example, Hdt. 5.76, 9.18, 9.25). Unlike later Greek historians, Herodotus gives no absolute depths of formations used, so fighting in formation may still have been somewhat looser than would be the case, for example, during the later Peloponnesian War. At Marathon, Herodotus points out that the Athenian line was thinner in the centre than at the wings (Hdt. 6.111), while at Plataea the Spartan formation was much deeper than those of the other Greeks (Hdt. 9.31). However, once battle began, there was still ample room for individuals to prove their worth and subsequently be singled out by Herodotus for special mention.

The ebb and flow of war, familiar from Homer and perhaps some of the lyric poets, during which men might run back and forth between the battle itself and their camp, is absent from Herodotus' descriptions. Instead, the men seem to have stayed put for as long as the battle lasted, and the use of formations ensured that each man had a proper place on the battlefield; the Spartans were reportedly somewhat peeved when Thermopylae-survivor Aristodemus abandoned his position in the ranks to fight the Persians (Hdt. 9.71). In short, I imagine that the bulk of the fighting would have been conducted by those in the front ranks, with the one directly behind his file-leader taking his place when he fell or otherwise had to step back from combat. This mode of fighting probably resembled something of a 'meatgrinder', though it was still relatively fluid when compared to the phalanxes of later Greek history.

In large engagements between groups of allies, the troops were arranged on the battlefield in a specific order of battle, stationed according to regional contingent, in a manner familiar from the *Iliad*. In Herodotus, however, there is a clear hierarchy as regards the exact placement of troops on the line. A battle-line could be divided into three parts: the centre, and the left and right wings (the Greek word for 'wing' – *keras* – originally meant 'horn'). The far-right was considered the place of honour (Hdt. 6.111); this is an element that we have not encountered before. Commanders do not appear to have had a specific place assigned to them, although they did take an active part in the fighting, sometimes leading to their demise (for example, Hdt. 6.114, 7.224); they probably took position in the front rank, to fight as *promachos*, though there is no proof that they took their place at the extreme right, as they did in later times.

Like Homeric armies, Greek armies during the Persian Wars included a number of agents and attendants, as well as a large number of slaves, some of whom may have taken part in the fighting, such as the Messenian helots (Hdt. 9.28). Other agents include the now familiar seers, heralds (for example, Hdt. 9.12), and scouts. Furthermore, it seems that commanders had servants and shield-bearers

Marble sculpture of a warrior from the Heraion at Samos. Note the Ionian helmet with the hinged cheek pieces, and the bell-shaped cuirass. Dated to around 530 BC. Currently in the Archaeological Museum of Samos.

Artist's rendering of the Battle of Plataea. Drawing by Milek Jakubiec.

(Hdt. 5.111, 9.82), and attendants were an apparently common feature in Greek armies (Hdt. 7.229, 9.50).

The *manteis*, seers, often feature more prominently in Herodotus' descriptions than in Homer's (they are absent from the lyric fragments), and few commanders undertook anything without consulting a seer (for example, Hdt. 7.113). A new element is the pre-battle sacrifice, *sphagia* (a word that emphasises the flowing of blood), to determine whether or not one should attack. However, it must be noted that, in Herodotus, this sacrifice is always conducted within the confines of the camp rather than on the battlefield; the latter would become the norm shortly after the Persian Wars. In some instances, a seer was able to give direct tactical advice (Hdt. 8.27).

Spies are fairly rare in Herodotus' account of the Persian Wars, although both the Greeks and the Persians relied on the intelligence provided by traitors and deserters (for example, Hdt. 7.219; also Hdt. 6.101, cf. 6.21). Both sides typically picked their battlegrounds after some consideration; the Greeks specifically decided to make their stand at Thermopylae because the Persians' superior numbers and horses would be of no avail to them there (Hdt. 7.177). Lookouts were sometimes posted to keep an eye on the enemy; they would send out runners to report back any news (Hdt. 7.192). When the Persian fleet was on the move, a squadron of ten fast ships formed an advance guard (Hdt. 7.179). Relatively small ships, such as fifty-oared galleys, were normally used for spying and reconnaissance at sea (for example, Hdt. 1.152).

• The nature of battle

War in Herodotus differs from what we have observed in the Homeric and Archaic texts. On the whole, the scale of the fighting is much larger, involving higher numbers of combatants (although the exact figures are no doubt inflated), and the armies appear to be mobilized by a more or less central authority, with generals often being official magistrates or other appointed individuals rather than charismatic war-lords. Descriptions of battle in Herodotus tend to be rather stylized, but overall there appears to be a shift from the individual to the collective.

It is usually assumed that, once an army was mobilized and on its way to engage its target, a battle would be inevitable. Certainly, this is an impression fostered by both Homer and the lyric poets. However, Herodotus' account contains a large number of expeditions in which opponents never came to blows. Some communities, rather than risking battle with the mighty Persian army, surrendered rather than trying to put up any resistance. For example, when the Persians took Egypt, the neighbouring Libyans, Cyrenaeans, and Barcaeans immediately surrendered (Hdt. 3.13).

Pottery perfume bottle from Rhodes in the shape of a warrior's head. This is a good representation of the Ionian helmet. Dated to ca. 600 BC. Currently in the Allard Pierson Museum, Amsterdam.

In Greece, some people simply abandoned their cities to the encroaching Persian fleet. For example, the Byzantines and Chalcedonians left their cities and fled inland, where they founded a new city. When the Persians invaded Naxos, many of the people there had fled to the mountains. The few that remained were enslaved, after which the city and its sacred places were burnt. Likewise, the Phocians tried to evade the Persians by fleeing to the slopes of Parnassus, to the city of Neon, and to Amphissa in the Crisaean plain; others fled to the islands, or escaped the Aegean altogether. Famously, most Athenians abandoned their city and fled to the island of Salamis in 480, while a few holed up on the Acropolis.

Sometimes, an attack – often a siege – was simply unsuccessful and had to be abandoned. At one point, the Syracusans besieged Callipolis, Leontini, Naxos, and Zancle, but failed to capture any of these cities. The Athenian commander Miltiades suffered from particularly bad luck. In 489 BC, he besieged the city of Paros, telling the islanders that he would not leave until they were dead or had paid him a hundred talents. A short while later, he hurt his leg while leaping over a fence. He abandoned the siege and ultimately died of the wound to his leg (Hdt. 6.133–135). A helmet unearthed at the temple of Zeus at Olympia bears the name Miltiades and may have been dedicated by this famous man.

The land battles described by Herodotus are characterized by large-scale ma-

While most of the Athenians abandoned the city when the army of Xerxes drew near, some instead withdrew to the Acropolis. The Persians besieged the Acropolis, with archers using fire arrows to burn the makeshift wooden stockade. The Athenians rolled boulders and other stone objects down the hill to kill the attackers. Drawing by Angel García Pinto.

Warrior with Boeotian shield, adopting the sideways stance typically used by hoplites in battle. Dated to ca. 510 BC. Currently in the Staatliche Antikensammlung in Berlin.

noeuvres. No longer do the battles consist of fluid, back-and-forth movement of parts of the army. Rather, the core of the army consists of hoplites who move and fight in unison under their general's command. At Marathon (490 BC), the Athenians charged the Persians at a run – perhaps the first *massed* charge, rather than a *mass* charge, in Greek history. The Athenian line crashed into the Persians. In the course of the battle, the Persians managed to break through the thin Athenian centre. However, the wings of the Athenian army were strong and managed to envelop the Persians in a manoeuvre known as 'double envelopment' or the 'pincer movement'. When the Persians routed, the Athenians and their Plataean allies wheeled round and went after the Persians who had broken through the centre, slaughtering many as they fled. The Greeks followed the Persians back to their ships, called for fire, and then proceeded to attack the fleet, capturing a total of seven ships. According to Herodotus, about 6,400 Persians died, while on the Athenian side only 192 men were killed, among them two commanders (Hdt. 6.112–117).

Similar large-scale tactical manoeuvring on the battlefield is clear from other descriptions. At Thermopylae, the Spartans and their allies took up position in the narrow pass and lured the Persians into the funnel by rushing out towards them and then running back when their numerically superior enemy came near (Hdt. 7.202–210). According to Herodotus, the Greeks managed to kill large numbers of Persian attackers. Herodotus further claims that the Persians were at a disadvantage as far as their equipment and skill was concerned. In the end, the Greeks were overrun when Persian troops, using a hidden track through the mountains, attacked their opponents in the rear (Hdt. 7.215–223). The Greeks were also able to fall back in a more or less organized way, as demonstrated by their large-scale tactical retreat just prior to the Battle of Plataea (Hdt. 9.50–52).

Aside from fighting pitched battles, Herodotus' Greeks had no problem making use of ambushes and surprise attacks, in the same way that Homer's heroes had used whatever means were necessary to gain a strategic or tactical advantage. One amusing anecdote concerns a war between the Thessalians and the Phocians. The Thessalians had invaded the lands of the Phocians and the latter had fled up the slopes of Mount Parnassus. There, the prophet Tellias gave them the advice to smear their bodies and armour with white chalk and attack the Thessalians at night, killing any man who was not covered by chalk. When the Thessalian sentries saw the ghostly white Phocians, they were terrified, and the Phocians then managed to slaughter four thousand of the enemy.

There are also a few scattered references to single combat or *monomachia*. One example is offered by Eurybates, an apparently overeager commander of an Argive army of volunteers, who was killed in single combat by the fourth man he had challenged to fight him (Hdt. 6.92). Another example of *monomachia* took the form of a military contest in three distinct stages, where man squared off against man, horse against horse, and dog against dog (Hdt. 5.1); a further example is drawn from myth (Hdt. 9.26). *Monomachia* is also the term used by the Athenians to describe their battle against the Persians at Marathon (Hdt. 9.27); in this case, the term denotes a test of strength between two specific groups.

• War at sea

A modification of the fifty-oared galley, the bireme, was invented by the Phoenicians in the eighth century BC, but appears not have been common in Greece until the sixth century. The bireme featured rowers organized in two tiers, allowing the ship to be shorter and more manoeuvrable. The bireme was probably the first true warship, with the forefoot clad in bronze to make a ram that could be used in attacking enemy warships and crippling their oars. A further refinement of this type of ship was the trireme, with its 170 rowers – who tended to be *thetes* or possibly slaves – organized in three tiers, rather than two. The trireme is first mentioned by the poet Hipponax, in a passage in which he admonishes Mimnes for painting "on a trireme's many-benched side a serpent that runs from the ram to the helmsman; for it is a dangerous omen for the helmsman" (fr. 28.2–5 West). It would become the most common type of warship in the Classical world.

Depictions of ships are somewhat rare in Attic black- and red-figure scenes. One of the earliest is a fifty-oared galley shown on the famous François Krater, dated to around 570–560 BC. From at least the second half of the sixth century onwards, we encounter combinations of armed warriors and unarmed rowers forming crews aboard warships. A platter from the Acropolis, dated to around 530 BC, depicts a galley with a single tier of rowers; we see the oars, but not the men themselves. This ship also features two tall warriors, who may be plausibly identified as *epibatai* or 'marines'. A late variation on the theme of the Aristonothos Krater, discussed in the previous chapter, is found on a black-figure vase dated to the last quarter of the sixth century BC, where a round-bottomed merchantman with no oars is apparently attacked by a straight-keeled warship.

In the Homeric epics, it is clear that ships were owned and operated by private individuals. Apparently not all wealthy members of society owned their own vessels; when Telemachus set off to search for his father, he had to borrow a vessel. By the sixth century BC, we know that the Athenian navy was maintained by some form of official institution. According to Herodotus, the Cylonian conspiracy, mentioned in the previous chapter, was put down by the *prytaneis* ('leaders') of the *naukrariai* (Hdt. 5.71). These naucraries were an organizational unit presumably responsible for the upkeep of ships. The historian claims that, back then, these men effectively ruled Athens (Hdt. 5.71). The word *naukrarias* derives from the Greek word *naus*, meaning 'ship', although Herodotus tells us next to nothing about this institution and later Greek authors regard them as the predecessors of the Cleis-

A Corinthian helmet with decorations along the brow and edges, with a floral motif on the forehead. Greek warriors would have worn a leather or felt cap underneath the helmet. Some helmets also feature holes along the rim so that a leather or felt liner could be attached on the inside; such linings may also have been glued to the inside. Dated to ca. 550 BC. Currently in the Allard Pierson Museum, Amsterdam.

The Phoenicians developed the bireme probably in the eighth century BC. The bireme had rowers staggered in two tiers. There are some Greek Geometric vase-paintings that depict what look like biremes, but these vessels do not appear to have been common in Greece until the sixth century BC. Drawing by Sebastian Schulz.

thenic demes (*demoi*), and therefore subdivisions of the four Ionian *phylai* ('tribes'). By the time of the Persian Wars, the *prytaneis* of the *naukrariai* were probably the ones who were responsible for getting their ships and crews ready for war.

Herodotus is the first to describe naval warfare, in the sense of battles fought

out between rival fleets. Two sea-battles are described in some detail: namely, those of Artemisium and Salamis, both fought in 480 BC. Under pressure from the Persians, the Athenians under Themistocles initiated a large-scale ship-building programme, funded by the revenue from the silver mines at Laurion. Herodotus only mentions two types of vessels: namely, the *pentekontoros* (presumably the fifty-oared galley familiar from Homer, if not a bireme with 25 men staggered on each side across two tiers), and the trireme.

Like the land battles, the sea battles are characterized by large-scale co-ordinated movement, with fleets even deployed in simple formations. Most ancient sea-battles from this time onwards appear to have been fought with vessels formed up line abreast, rather than line ahead. At the Battle of Artemisium, the Greeks used the *diekplous*, a tactic in which ships sought an opening in order to ram an enemy vessel and break the line of Persian ships (Hdt. 8.9). At Salamis, the naval equivalent of Leonidas' tactic at Thermopylae was used by luring the Persian ships into a narrow strait where they could be easily attacked by the numerically inferior Greek ships. Herodotus claims that the Persians were relatively quickly disordered by the tactics used by the Greeks (Hdt. 8.86), which might suggest that the Greeks were better organized.

The trireme was the typical warship of the Persian wars and after. It was probably invented in the late sixth century BC and had about 170 rowers. Drawing by Sebastian Schulz.

A reconstruction of what a Greek hoplite may have looked like during the Persian Wars. Drawing by Graham Sumner.

• The aftermath of battle

Epic tinges in Herodotus have been noted earlier; the battle around Leonidas' corpse is a fine example of a Homeric-style struggle over a fallen comrade (Hdt. 7.225). Herodotus rarely mentions the stripping of the enemy dead of their weapons (and, in the case of the Persians, jewellery) following a battle (Hdt. 9.80), but these were undoubtedly a major part of the spoils of war and probably taken for granted. The stripping of the enemy fallen of their armour also plays a crucial role in his account of the older Battle of the Champions (Hdt. 1.83), discussed briefly in the previous chapter.

Distribution of booty may have taken place shortly after victory, prior to the burial of the dead (for example, Hdt. 9.85). A portion of the spoils, usually a tithe, was to be dedicated to the gods (for instance, Hdt. 9.81), and the generals were expected to be given their own portions (for example, Hdt. 9.81), probably before the rest was distributed among the remaining warriors in the army. The spoils naturally consisted of arms and armour, and whatever else might be found on the bodies of the dead or in their camp. For example, after the Battle of Plataea, the Greeks discovered considerable treasures in the Persian camp that were originally intended to bribe the Greeks into submission (Hdt. 9.41). Prisoners of war were enslaved (Hdt. 1.151, 6.45, 6.106), held for ransom, usually at a fixed price (Hdt. 5.77, 6.79, 9.99), or executed (Hdt. 1.167, 4.202, 8.127, 9.120); only rarely were prisoners ritually sacrificed (Hdt. 7.180).

Whereas in Homer and the Archaic poets each death is lamented and honoured individually, in Herodotus the war-dead feature as a collective. Enemy Persians, at least, were left unburied, scattered across the battlefield. (This is perhaps a more complex issue than at first appears, for Persian religion forbade burial and cremation. Bodies were exposed to the birds until the early 1970s in "towers of silence".) When the Spartans learnt of the Athenian victory at Marathon, they set off for the place and looked at the corpses littering the field, then commended the Athenians on a job well done (Hdt. 6.120). The natural impulse for some men was to mutilate enemy corpses; Lampon suggested to Pausanias that he defile the body of Mardonius in order to avenge the death of Leonidas, who was also mutilated by the Persians after he and his men had been defeated at Thermopylae (Hdt. 9.78–79).

Herodotus does not say what happened to the 192 Athenian dead at Marathon, but Thucydides mentions, in the famous funeral oration attributed to Pericles, that they were buried where they fell (Thuc. 2.34). Excavations carried out from the end of the nineteenth century onwards have revealed several mass graves in the area, one of which is ascribed to the Athenians, and another possibly to their Plataean allies and slaves (free Greeks were cremated, slaves inhumed). The men who died at Thermopylae were also buried on the battlefield, covered by a burial mound. Three inscriptions, one for all the dead collectively, one specifically for the Spar-

Warrior ready to strike an unseen enemy or engaged in some kind of dance. He is equipped with an Attic helmet, which is essentially a Chalcidian helmet, but without a nose guard. Attic red figure cup; dated to ca. 510 BC. Currently in the Allard Pierson Museum, Amsterdam.

Painted copy of the stele of Aristion, a young Athenian who was killed in battle. Made of pentelic marble; decoration in low relief. The ancient Greeks originally painted their sculptures in bright colours. Dated to around 510 BC. The original is currently in the National Archaeological Museum in Athens.

Displays of martial prowess in peace-time

In the epic world, funeral games were organized for noteworthy heroes who had been killed in battle, such as Patroclus. These games typically had a martial component, including friendly duels, javelin-throwing contests, and chariot races. Such games continued to be held in the Archaic period and down to the Persian Wars, even though funeral games as such seem to have disappeared shortly after 700 BC.

A footrace-in-arms – the *hoplitodromos* – was introduced in Olympia probably around 520 BC. Shortly thereafter, naked runners equipped with shields and helmets are depicted on Attic wares, especially in red-figure style. In addition, we find depictions of the so-called 'Pyrrhic' or 'Pyrrhic Dance'. Perhaps the earliest example is a picture of a warrior on an Attic black-figure Siana cup from about 570 BC. The figure wears a tunic and animal skin, and is equipped with a Boeotian shield, spear (with thong), greaves, and helmet with stilted crest. The position of his legs and his stooped appearance suggest that he is dancing. Of course, there can be no doubt that the Pyrrhic is intended in scenes which include not only the armed dancer, but also a flute-player. Examples include an Attic red-figure cup attributed to the Poseidon Painter and dated to the end of the sixth century, as well as a cup attributed to the Eucharides Painter and dated to around 490 BC.

Some high-ranking men were identified as warriors on their grave monuments. Many of the earlier Geometric vases were originally intended for funerary use, with some of the larger examples used as grave markers in high-ranking burial plots in Athens. From the sixth century onwards, graves also began to be marked by stone stelai. One of the earliest of these has been unearthed in the Kerameikos cemetery in Athens. It has been dated to around 560 BC and depicts a standing naked young man, equipped with a sword and holding a spear in front of him. Similar in pose is the well-known stele of Aristion, dated to around 510. Unlike the earlier figure, Aristion is fully clothed, wearing a tunic with linen corslet, as well as greaves; his head presumably once sported a helmet, pushed up. He lacks a sword, but like the earlier figure holds a spear in front of him. These stelai served to immortalize the dead men, whom they commemorated as warriors, as men who fought and possibly died on the field of battle; they were both the leaders and the protectors of their communities.

tans, and one for the Spartan soothsayer Megistias (an act of friendship on the part of his *xenos* Simonides, son of Leoprepes), were placed at the site (Hdt. 7.228). After the Battle of Plataea, each of the Greek communities buried their dead in separate mass graves. Herodotus adds that other Greek communities erected burial mounds at Plataea in order to pretend to have fought there as well (Hdt. 9.85).

• Summary

Like Homer, Herodotus distinguishes between troops on foot (*pezoi*) and troops on horseback (*hippeis*). Similar to Tyrtaeus, he makes a fundamental distinction between heavily-armoured warriors on foot – *hoplitai* – and lightly-armoured troops – *gymnetes* or *psiloi*. Most of his descriptions of battle focus mostly on the hoplites; in some cases, such as at the battles of Marathon and Thermopylae, it seems as if these are the only Greek troops engaged in the fighting. In contrast, the Persians are called *gymnetes* and said to employ large numbers of archers. Horsemen, in the sense of men who fought from horseback, were limited to specific regions in Greece, especially Thessaly and Boeotia, and some Eastern peoples, such as the Lydians, are singled out as horse-masters.

By the time of the Persian Wars, small warbands no longer dominate the battlefield. Instead, large armies, mobilized through a central authority, were used by major Greek communities. Descriptions of combat tend to be stylized. These battles are different with regards to scale and organization from those familiar from Homer and the Archaic poets. Hoplites, *psiloi*, and horsemen no longer mingled freely on the battlefield, but operated instead in separate units, referred to as *telea* or *lochoi*. The fluid back-and-forth characteristic of Homeric battle – and perhaps also of the lyric poets – has gone. Instead, hoplites now operated in roughly rectangular formations – that is, the so-called 'phalanxes' – that were generally wider than they were deep, even though Herodotus never specifies the exact depth.

The information gleaned from Herodotus seems to be supported by inscriptions as well as the iconographic evidence. An inscription from Salamis makes clear that some people, at least, were required by law to purchase a set of armour and report to a government official. Another inscription proves the existence of formal alliances between Greek states, rather than a reliance on guest-friendship alone to smooth diplomatic relations. The iconographic evidence also points toward an increase in scale, especially with regard to the increased use of linen corslets, which may have been easier to procure than bronze cuirasses, as well as trumpets and the use of helmets that left the ears and eyes unobstructed and thus made it easier to observe commands on the battlefield.

Achilles hiding behind a bush, preparing to ambush the Trojan hero Troilus. To the ancient Greeks, there was nothing dishonourable about killing from ambush or mounting a surprise attack. Attic black figure oil bottle; dated to ca. 490 BC. Currently in the Allard Pierson Museum, Amsterdam.

Epilogue
Henchmen of Ares

I am a henchman of the lord god of war
and skilled in the lovely gift of the Muses.
—Archilochus, fr. 1 West

Warriors in Early Greece were not simply men who waged battle; they were regarded as being in league with Ares himself. In the *Iliad*, Homer sometimes refers to the Greeks as a whole – as well as some individual heroes – as "henchmen of Ares". The set of attributes ascribed to Ares, the god of war or – more appropriately – the god of slaughter and warriors, tells us a great deal about how ancient Greek warriors regarded themselves, or wished to be regarded. Ares is the swiftest runner of all the gods and a fine dancer – in other words, a fit individual. Perhaps these aspects are what make him irresistible in the eyes of the opposite sex. After all, Ares' lover, from at least the *Odyssey* onwards, is none other than the goddess of love and beauty herself, Aphrodite.

Ares is strong and tends to come across as courageous, sometimes even foolhardy. He revels in causing strife and spilling blood; in his battle-frenzy, he might strike down both friend and foe. He is accompanied by the Keres, female death-spirits that suck the blood of those who have fallen in battle, both the dead and the dying. But Ares is not invincible. Of all the Olympian gods, he is the one who has, on more than one occasion, not only been wounded, but even mortally so. Only the eating of nectar and ambrosia preserved his existence when mortal men would long ago have perished. In the *Iliad*, he is struck down by Diomedes with the aid of Athena (as briefly mentioned in this book's prologue); there are a number of stories in which the god is captured by his enemies and has to be freed by another deity or demigod. This vulnerability is a characteristic trait of Ares. Similarly, Greek warriors would have been aware of the risks they took in battle.

But before turning to a discussion of the cultural significance of warfare and warriors in Early Greece, a summary of the developments in Greek warfare from the Mycenaean Bronze Age down to the Persian Wars is necessary. Looking back, it is clear that there are at least three points in time when major changes can be noted. The first is around 1200 BC, when most Mycenaean palaces were destroyed and abandoned. The large armies that were probably fielded by the Mycenaean kings disappeared, to be replaced instead by smaller warbands. The mode of fighting presumably changed little from the twelfth century down to the end of the eighth century BC. The Naue II sword, introduced late in the thirteenth century, remained in use and was even translated from bronze to iron quite early. Rail chariots and characteristically sleek warships continued in use throughout the Greek Dark Age, the latter developing a more pronounced forefoot in the course of time, the ancestor of the later bronze-clad ram. Large armies had been replaced by smallish warbands that consisted of a high-ranking leader and his followers.

The second period of change can be dated to around 700 BC and was more or less complete by around 650 BC. During this time, the emphasis in art shifts from ships and battles on beaches to encounters on land. The warriors were now equipped with bronze helmets and greaves; some of them also wore the bronze bell-shaped cuirass. Their most distinguishing feature is the Argive shield, a heavy, convex shield about a metre in diameter, which featured a double grip, spreading the weight of the shield across the bearer's arm and shoulder. At the same time, chariots disappear from the battlefield and horses are now ridden instead. A common motif is that of the 'knight' and 'squire' or, as per the inscription on a Corinthian perfume bottle of the late seventh century BC, a *hippobatas* and *hippostrophos*. Battles may now have been fought between neighbouring polities for ownership of borderland, and we also know that some wars were fought for conquest. Yet it seems likely that the armies of this age were still organized based on personal ties, and that warbands were still a feature until well into the sixth century BC.

The third and last significant moment during the period under examination can be placed in the second half of the sixth century BC. In this period, we see the emergence of a stronger central authority in places such as Athens. Inscriptions testify to the creation of formal alliances between polities, as well as to rules that set down the requirements for military equipment and made the central authority responsible for ensuring that those rules were followed. Various small changes, such as the introduction of trumpets and helmets that left the ears and face exposed, suggest changes in military tactics. Together with the evidence gleaned from Herodotus, this seems to be the period in which an early form of phalanx warfare was introduced. Perhaps these changes went hand-in-hand with the looming threat posed by the Persian Empire.

• Early Greek warrior societies

For much of the period under examination, military matters were within the purview of what we might term the aristocracy. Warfare, in the broadest sense of the word, emerges as a constituent lifestyle among Early Greek elites and can be seen as a defining characteristic of aristocracy. This is expressed quite succinctly in the *Iliad*. When Sarpedon storms the walls of the Greek camp, he calls out to Glaucus, pointing out that they always enjoy good food, wine, and land in their native Lycia, and that this obliges them to fight (*Il*. 12.315–321):

Therefore it is our duty in the forefront of the Lycians
to take our stand, and bear our part of the blazing battle,
so that a man of those close-armoured Lycians may say of us:
"Indeed, these are no ignoble men who are lords of Lycia,
these kings of ours, who feed upon the fat sheep appointed
and drink the exquisite sweet wine, since indeed there is strength
of valour in them, since they fight in the forefront of the Lycians."

This is not to say that the lower classes were excluded from taking part in war, but they were not considered decisive in battle. Economic factors no doubt played a role here, in that only the wealthy were able to equip themselves with good armour and weapons.

That warfare was an important part of the elite lifestyle seems clear from even a cursory examination of the evidence. Weapons are only found in the graves of some high-ranking individuals, and these must have been leaders within their community or particularly important warriors. These men took part in martial games and may have been the principal competitors at Panhellenic Games, and were presumably among the people who dedicated arms and armour to the gods. The iconographic evidence depicts men fighting using expensive kit, often engaging in small-scale raids. Descriptions in Homer emphasize the warriors supplied by aristocratic families. The lyric poets likewise leave an impression of war as the province of the elite. Characteristically, war is beyond the purview of the farmer-poet Hesiod.

Aristocratic men fighting in small groups or warbands are characteristic of the Early Iron Age and Archaic period. In many engagements, they may have physically excluded commoners from taking part, as much as possible. This may have been a function of scale; during the heyday of Mycenaean civilization, there is evidence for larger armies in which commoners could probably be conscripted. Likewise, at the other end of the period under examination, we have Herodotus. His descriptions of massive armies and the appointment of officers who had no close personal ties to their men, suggests that the Postmycenaean aristocratic warbands disappeared completely in the latter half of the sixth century BC.

Nevertheless, the one constant is the importance of warfare in the aristocratic lifestyles of elites in Early Greek communities, from the people buried in the Mycenaean grave circles down to Herodotus' own time. Again, this is not peculiar to the Greek situation. Paul Treherne has pointed out that this lifestyle seems to focus on aspects of the body in particular. He argues that the appearance of 'warrior graves' can be related to the development of a specific form of life, a lifestyle, among an emergent warrior elite, which marked the growth of a new understanding of personhood – specifically male self-identity – rooted in both social practices and cultural representations. Treherne adds that this lifestyle, and the male body's place in

A beautiful example of a late Corinthian helmet. The helmet almost completely encased the warrior's head, rendering him anonymous. Combined with other shining pieces of bronze armour, a warrior wearing this helmet must have made an impressive sight; even more so if a tall horsehair crest had been fixed to the helmet. Dated to ca. 500 BC. Currently in the Antikensammlung in Munich.

it, is only to be understood in conjunction with an equally important 'death-style', a socio-culturally prescribed way of expiring. Central to both life and death was a specific form of masculine beauty unique to the warrior.

Treherne's observations are based on Bronze Age Europe, but they can be usefully applied to the Greek situation. The collapse of the Mycenaean palaces may have disrupted the existing balance of power and led to the emergence of either a new elite or a weakened, older ruling social group that tried to reclaim some of their bygone glory. These elites emphasized a military – or at least violent – ethos by burying some of their men with weapons and, in a few rare instances, armour. This group of people shared a similar lifestyle and attempted to reinforce their lifestyle in death.

Four main themes are at the core of this lifestyle. These include warfare, as demonstrated by the presence of weapons; consumption of alcohol, as shown by drinking vessels; riding horses and/or driving chariots; and also ornamentation of the body. To Treherne's four themes we can add a fifth: namely, seafaring and overseas activities, as demonstrated by the importance of ship iconography and the presence of imported artefacts in burials and other archaeological contexts. The wide geographic distribution of this lifestyle and its associated 'death-style' can be attributed to interactions between elites from various regions and cultures. Public displays of wealth, of power and prowess, tie all of these aspects together.

• Symbols of power

Weapons are characteristic symbols of power. They represent a man's ability to protect himself, his family, and his property. As a general rule, the stronger the central authority, the more weapons will be limited to a certain subset of people. This seems likely to have been the case in the Mycenaean Bronze Age, when armies seem to have been under the command of the palatial authorities. Our examination of the Mycenaean evidence revealed the existence of more or less uniformly equipped Mycenaean soldiers during at least the thirteenth century BC, wearing boar's tusk helmets and equipped with spears and short swords.

With the disintegration of the palaces, it is possible that weapons became more widespread. Certainly, if we can use the Homeric epics as a historical source for the situation in the eighth century BC or even a little later, it seems that high-ranking men did not go anywhere without either their sword or a spear. Similarly, Late Geometric scenes depicting processions and mourning scenes commonly depict men equipped with at least a sword. The close association of an aristocratic man and his weapons no doubt explains why some high-ranking men, presumably leaders of the community, were also buried with arms. Funerals would have allowed the conspicuous display of armed men, including sometimes the deceased himself, and could also be accompanied by funeral games, in the case of a particularly note-worthy person. These funeral games would have featured a wide array of martial sports; descriptions in the *Iliad* include a duel, a chariot-race, and an archery contest.

The public display of mourning and remembrance, including the organization of funeral games, and the connections that this emphasized with the deceased, should not be underestimated. Paying respects to the honoured dead was not only a way of keeping the memory of the deceased alive, for public veneration at tombs also served to underscore any potential achievements of one's ancestors. Greek aristocrats were fiercely competitive, striving to always be the best; the word *agon* – 'strife' or 'contest'; it also means 'battle' – perhaps best summarizes the lifestyle of the elite. Strife requires an arena for public display of merit and wealth, and the funerals and associated rites and customs of other high-ranking men offered opportunities for such displays.

Burials with arms disappeared in the course of the eighth century, at around the same time that deposits at sanctuaries, including metal items such as weapons and armour, increased. Some, like archaeologist Catherine Morgan, have suggested that this indicates a shift from the private sphere to the public, but there was noth-

The best of the Greeks

The ancient Greeks are renowned for their competitive spirit. Certainly, it is no coincidence that they did not engage in team sports during funeral games or at the Panhellenic Games. Each strove always to be the best. We find an excellent expression of this mentality in Homer's *Iliad*, where Nestor recalls the advice that Peleus gave to his son Achilles (*Il.* 11.783–784):

And Peleus the aged was telling his own son, Achilles,
to be always best in battle and pre-eminent beyond all others.

Achilles is the champion of the Greeks and shares may characteristics with Ares. He is repeatedly said to be the swiftest of all the Greek warriors, as well as the most beautiful. But unlike Ares, who appears to be wholly destructive, later traditions record that Achilles was also a great healer. Similar to warrior-poets like Archilochus, he is able to play the lyre and sing of famous deeds (*Il.* 9.185–191). However, he is also prone to bouts of furious anger; the *Iliad* begins with the word *menis* ('rage' or 'wrath'), and deals with the rage of Achilles. As such, the hero served both as a role model and as a warning to temper emotion with reason.

Opposite page: this illustration shows what the inside of Alcaeus' great hall may have looked like. The poet himself is standing and delivering one of his poems, while his drinking companions listen intently. Weapons and pieces of armour line the wall or are suspended from pegs. Drawing by Sebastian Schulz.

A Late Geometric jug that combines the theme of horses with the consumption of alcohol, two key aspects of the aristocratic lifestyle. This object was also deposited in a grave, tying it into the owner's 'death-style' as well, emphasizing his elevated position to those who bore witness to his burial. Dated to ca. 725 BC. Currently in the Allard Pierson Museum, Amsterdam.

ing particularly 'private' about aristocratic funerals. Instead, it seems more likely to me to denote a shift from a local to a regional or, indeed, in the case of Panhellenic sanctuaries such as Olympia, supraregional level. Both funerals and sanctuaries offered public arenas for rival men to compete. The first was public but destructive (weapons were interred, the body cremated, and so on), while the second was public and permanent (weapons and armour on display).

Fortifications may have been among the largest building projects to be undertaken in Early Greece. Some of these walls may have been built in response to attacks; coastal and island towns had every reason to fear seaborne raiders. However, many fortifications were built only around part of a settlement or just the acropolis. The exact reasons for this cannot yet be answered, but it seems clear that military concerns alone did not always prompt the construction of walls. In many cases, walls may have been a powerful statement that served both to deter would-be attackers, as well as to demonstrate the ability of the community's leaders to harness available manpower. In some cases, it may even have been prestigious not to have walls; Sparta was still unwalled by the time of the Peloponnesian War (Thuc. 1.10), and Alcaeus emphasized that men, not walls, were a community's main defence (Alc. fr. 112 Voigt).

• Fighting and feasting

The evidence shows that there was a strong link between fighting and feasting. Some burials with arms also contained spits or other implements associated with roasting meat in particular; virtually all high-ranking burials also contained pottery specifically made for the consumption of alcohol. The literary evidence further attests to the importance of organizing feasts in forging friendships, in male-bonding, and in recruiting troops (for example, Hom. *Od.* 14.248–291); consuming food and drink at another man's expense naturally created an obligation to return a favour. A fragment attributed to the poet Alcaeus gives some idea of what a room might look like that was used for feasts between companions (fr. 140.3–16 Voigt):

The high hall is agleam
with bronze; the roof is all arrayed
with shining helms, and white
horse-plumes to ornament men's heads
nod from their crests. Bright greaves
of bronze to keep strong arrows off
cover the unseen pegs,
and corslets of new linen, and
a pile of convex shields.

Chalcidian swords are there,
and belts in plenty, tunics too.
We can't forget this store
now that we've taken on this task.

It seems likely that Alcaeus and his drinking comrades – no doubt including his brothers – were supposed to use this store of arms and armour in their struggle to oppose a would-be tyrant at Mytilene, perhaps Pittacus himself. Certainly, the amount of arms and armour mentioned seems more than sufficient to equip a small number of men, perhaps those who did not or could not procure any equipment of their own. The fight to defend the position of the ruling elite is presumably the "task" referred to in this fragment (fr. 140.16 Voigt). The description of the store of weapons and armour resembles similar descriptions found in the Homeric epics. A practical interest in the quality of the equipment is revealed when Alcaeus describes the linen corslets as "new", that greaves offer protection against arrows, and that the swords are of Chalcidian make.

Drinking parties between companions need not have taken place at private houses. Sometimes, an ostensibly public building could also be used. An example is the second Hekatompedon – that is, a temple measuring 100 feet in length – on the island of Samos. It dates from the middle of the seventh century BC and was constructed, at least partially, of stone; its roof was covered with tiles, marking it as a particularly expensive and prestigious building at this early date. A stone block has been unearthed that was possibly once part of the frieze that adorned this temple. It features the engraved heads of warriors and the upper parts of their spears. The excavators believed that the temple was also used for banquets, as they reasoned that raised areas along the inside of the walls were used for reclining couches. This building was probably used by a group of high-ranking men who ate together and – based on the warrior frieze – presumably also fought together.

The groups of men who congregated in the second Hekatompedon at Samos, or the men who dined in Alcaeus' *megas domos*, no doubt formed warbands in the manner of the Homeric heroes – a mode of military organization that probably emerged following the fall of the Mycenaean palaces and was eventually replaced, perhaps only as late as the final decades of the sixth century, by larger and centrally-organized armies, commanded by men who did not possess a close personal tie with the men under their command.

Furthermore, I would suggest that war was an affair of high-ranking men and their male next of kin. This further strengthens the notion that, in Early Greek society after the fall of the Mycenaean palaces, war was the concern of a limited group. Young men, presumably sons, younger brothers, and so forth, would serve as attendants to their older brothers and fathers. In the Homeric epics, we have references to *kouroi* ('young men'), who perform services such as filling drinking bowls (Hom. *Il.* 9.173); a statement in the *Odyssey* suggests that young men also undertook small expeditions themselves (Hom. *Od.* 4.642–644). In iconography, mounted warriors are generally accompanied by mounted youths. Furthermore, it is possible that semi-naked warriors, such as those on the Chigi vase, are supposed to be younger men cutting their teeth on the field of battle; a Laconian plate of the sixth century shows young men carrying the bodies of bearded warriors. In sum, war may have been a craft passed on from father to son, like Peleus passing his mighty spear on to Achilles.

• Ownership and use of horses

Horses were demonstrably hallmarks of the aristocracy. Chariots are common in Palatial, Postpalatial (Late Helladic IIIC), and Late Geometric art, where they mostly served as vehicles to transport warriors to and from the battlefield. The main difference lies in the number of horses that formed the chariot teams: in the Bronze Age, a chariot was only ever drawn by two horses, whereas three or four horses are a feature of the Iron Age. The argument that the use of chariots in Homer and their depiction on Geometric vases is incorrect and inspired most probably by chariot races can be dismissed. We know, for example, of chariots being used in war in a similar way – as 'battlefield taxis' – in Cyrene in the historical period. And the Assyrians of the Iron Age also fielded chariots on the battlefield pulled by teams of three or four horses.

Horse-riding was known in Late Helladic IIIC, but rarely portrayed; it becomes common in Corinthian art from the end of the eighth century onwards. The introduction of the Argive shield and metal armour at the end of the eighth century BC went hand-in-hand with horseback riding, according to the iconographic evidence. To judge by the iconographic evidence (and some of the literary material, as well), mounted warriors were so common that the horse appears to have been just as fixed an element in a warrior's accoutrement as was his shield or spear. Indeed, by the middle of the sixth century BC, the poet Theognis was able to write the following in an offhand, matter-of-fact way (frr. 549—554):

The voiceless messenger, shining from the far-gleaming lookout, is raising fearful war. Come, place bits on the swift-heeled horses, for I think they'll meet the enemy. The distance between is not great; they'll get there, unless the gods deceive my judgement.

Theognis sees that a fire has been lit, signalling that they are under attack; he immediately tells Cyrnus – who perhaps acted as his squire or *hippostrophos* – to ready the horses. It seems like the standard response to an invasion or a raid. In other words, this can be taken as proof that at least some men in the period between ca. 725 and 525 BC may have typically ridden to the battlefield, rather than marching on foot.

Furthermore, horse-hair was generally used in the production of helmet plumes and crests. The plumes would call to mind the tails of horses, while the crests would remind one of the manes on the head and neck of a horse. Both would serve to give the warrior a horse-like aspect, even when dismounted or not accompanied by a horse. In some cases, the names used to denote certain groups or even an aristocracy as a whole referred to the ownership of horses; examples include the Spartan elite unit referred to as the *Hippeis* ('Horsemen'), familiar from Herodotus, and who may once have consisted of warriors who rode to the battlefield, as well as the *Hippobotai* ('Horse Breeders'), who were the horse-owning gentry of the Euboean city of Chalcis.

• The masculine body

The importance of the male body is central to the way that (high-ranking) Greek men represented themselves. Though not fighting in the nude, their body armour nonetheless served to emphasize their bodies and even enhance their physique. Bronze plate armour as used by Greeks and other peoples can be aesthetically pleasing; the bell-shaped cuirass has a relatively narrow waist, while at the same time making the chest seem broader and more masculine, with lines indicating pectoral and abdominal muscles. Similarly, greaves and arm-guards, with their moulded musculature, served to emphasize the male body.

Once highly polished, a man's armour would also gleam in the sun. 'Shining' is an adjective often used to denote something that is grand or awe-inspiring, including armour (*Il.* 3.83, 5.680, and 4.422–432; Alc. fr. 140.3 Voigt). The gods themselves are often described as 'shining', or otherwise radiant in some fashion; for

A warrior's beautiful death is embodied in this sculpture showing a dying Trojan warrior, from the east pediment of the temple of Aphaea on Aegina. Dated to around 500 BC. Currently in the Munich Glyptothek.

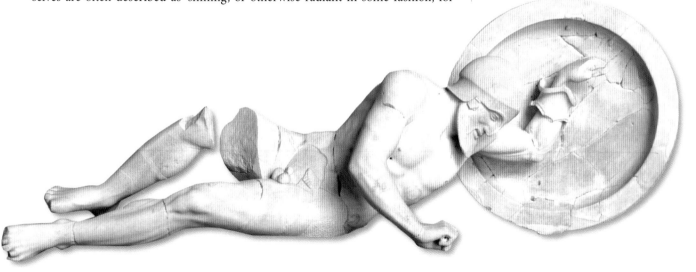

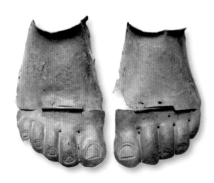

A pair of bronze foot guards from Ruvo, Italy. Pieces of armour not only protected parts of the body, but also drew attention to them or could enhance them. Neatly polished, the bronze body parts must have given the wearer an aspect of the divine. Dated to 520–480 BC. Currently in the British Museum.

example, *Phoibos Apollon* ('Shining Apollo') or *Glaukopis Athena* ('Athena with the flashing eyes' or 'bright-eyed Athena'). Men who walked onto the battlefield in their gleaming bronze armour may have possessed something of the divine. The armour may even have given the men a sense of empowerment. When Hector puts on Achilles' cuirass, the poet comments that "Ares the dangerous war god entered him, so that the inward body was packed full of force and fighting strength" (*Il.* 17.210–212).

Warriors were concerned with looking after their general appearance. Hair was used as a distinguishing feature. In the more detailed art of the seventh and sixth centuries, boys and young men are beardless and often have close-cropped hair, whereas more mature men have beards and long hair. Homer frequently describes his warriors as possessing long hair; Archilochus specifically asks for a commander who is good at his job, rather than one who is more concerned with his wavy hair; a late sixth-century statue from Samos depicts a warrior with Ionian helmet, finely-made bell-shaped cuirass, and long hair. When a Persian spy was sent to the Spartan camp at Thermopylae, he saw that some of the warriors were engaged in athletic competitions, while others calmly combed their long hair (Hdt. 7.208).

The central importance of the body is clear when we look at descriptions of death. The ideal dead warrior is young, cut down in the prime of life, and his body must be secured at all costs. Compare the battle over Patroclus' body in the *Iliad*. The young warrior is beautiful, whereas the old man is hideous, grey, and weak (e.g. *Il.* 22.71–76). Such sentiments are also found in the lyric poets. A good example is provided by Tyrtaeus, where he encourages the young men not to abandon the fight, but to stand and protect the older veterans of war (fr. 10.15–21):

It is disgraceful when an older man
falls in the front line while the young hold back,
with head already white, and grizzled beard,
gasping his valiant breath out in the dust
and clutching his bloodied genitals,
his nakedness exposed: a shameful sight
and scandalous.

A lifestyle that puts so much emphasis on the body may also prefer cremation as a means to dispose of the bodies of dead warriors. By reducing the body to ashes, the flesh cannot be corrupted in the soil; the (memory of the) dead warrior is, in essence, preserved through burning. Importantly, we know from the *Iliad* that particularly outstanding warriors were burnt in full armour, which offers new insights into interpreting burials with arms; these are not merely high-ranking men, but an elite within an elite, famed fighters or especially remarkable leaders of either the community at large or their followers. However, it should be pointed out that some localities nevertheless preferred inhumation and that cremation was also not practised by the Mycenaeans.

The male body and the ideology of male prowess formed a single unit. But aristocratic men did not exist in a vacuum; they were part of a community, a *polis*. Status groups as well as the community as a whole accepted and strove to maintain that unity, to prevent it from dissolution. Aristocratic men were the leaders of their communities, the preservers of the body politic. They were accepted as leaders and in exchange they had to act as the protectors of their communities. In exchange for their exalted status within the communities that they ruled, they were expected to sacrifice themselves when necessary.

• Ships and seafaring

The evidence for seafaring among the Mycenaeans is relatively slight. We know that they must have used ships frequently for trade and conquest. Perhaps their ships looked similar to Minoan vessels, which have been depicted, for example, in a fresco discovered on the volcanic island of Thera (Santorini). Some very early depictions from the late third millennium BC already show long and sleek ships with a straight prow. Certainly, oared galleys with a flat keel-line and vertical stem-post are attested for the thirteenth century BC. By the eighth century BC, this type of vessel has evolved to include a pronounced forefoot, which, along with its straight keel, would have aided in quickly beaching the vessel for an attack. With the invention of multi-tiered vessels, the forefoot was clad in bronze and transformed into a weapon used in ramming operations.

During the Dark Age and probably also in the period down to around 550 BC, ships were probably owned by private individuals. Only after 550 BC – perhaps earlier in Athens – do we see the appearance of navies that are operated in name of the state at large. Certainly, by the time of the Persian Wars, Themistocles was able to convince the Athenians to spend the revenue from the silver mines at Laurion on building a new fleet of warships. Of course, the nature of war at sea also changed. Whereas earlier, we have the painted testimony of scenes such as those on the Aristonothos Krater, in which a single pirate apparently attacks a lone merchantman, for the Persian Wars we know of large-scale encounters at sea, between massive fleets of warships that managed to pull off tactical manoeuvres, such as the *diekplous*.

For the period between at least the fall of the Mycenaean palaces down to 550 BC, there is a great deal of evidence that demonstrates the significance of ships and seafaring to Greek aristocrats. Indeed, it seems likely that only the well-to-do were able to afford the building and maintenance of seaworthy vessels, and galleys in particular. The Argive tomb that included the earliest known Greek bell-shaped

Neoptolemus strikes down the elderly Priam at the altar. Whereas the death of young men in battle was worthy of song, the sight of elderly men dying in combat was considered wretched. Attic black figure amphora from Tarquinia; dated to 520–500 BC. Currently in the National Museum of Antiquities, Leiden.

cuirass, also featured a pair of firedogs in the shape of ships. Many of the burials at Lefkandi included finds that came from a long way away, such as items from Cyprus and Egypt. Such objects underscored the deceased's long-range contacts, which may have included prestigious *xenoi*, or 'guest friends'.

• Closing remarks

Ares, the god of war, received little in the way of sacrificial favours. There were few major temples dedicated to him. In the *Iliad*, Zeus specifically tells Ares that he hates him the most out of all his children, because he delights in endless strife and slaughter. Yet the Greeks believed that war was a necessary part of life. Martial symbolism permeated much of ancient Greek culture and was a constituent element in the identity of high-ranking Greek men. This ambiguous relationship between the Greeks and warfare is expressed in an epitaph from the island of Corfu, dated to ca. 600 BC and presented here in the translation of M.L. Lang:

This warrior is equipped with a Boeotian shield decorated with scales and the head of a fearful Gorgon. He wears greaves and a bronze cuirass. His single thrusting spear is held overhead. Dated to around 500 BC. Currently in the Staatliche Antikensammlung in Berlin.

This is the tomb of Arniadas whom flashing-eyed Ares destroyed as he fought beside the ships in the streams of Arathus. He was the bravest by far in the wretchedness of war.

This epitaph is similar to one from Athens, dated between 540 and 530 BC, in which we are asked to mourn for Croesus, "whom raging Ares once destroyed in the front lines". These epitaphs call to mind the Homeric echoes that we have encountered throughout this book. Both reflect the ambiguous attitude of the Greeks toward war. On one side, battle was glorious and enabled men to demonstrate their physical prowess and skill in serving as protectors, and to attain immortality by having their deeds remembered. On the other side, war is seen as a force of destruction and death, bringing nothing but misery and pain. In the *Iliad*, Achilles summarizes the choice that each man has to make:

For my mother Thetis, the goddess of the silver feet, tells me
I carry two sorts of destiny toward the day of my death. Either,
if I stay here and fight beside the city of the Trojans,
my return home is gone, but my glory shall be everlasting;
but if I return home to the beloved land of my fathers,
the excellence of my glory is gone, but there will be a long life
left for me, and my end in death will not come to me quickly. (Il. 9. 410–416)

Eternal glory would be the reward of the man who was willing not only to excel in combat, but even to sacrifice himself, if necessary. Fame was the only way to achieve immortality; once dead, one's shade would roam grey and lifeless through the Underworld. To those who wished to be remembered for generations to come, nothing could be more glorious or everlasting than a valiant death on the battlefield. The Early Greek warrior ethos, which found its most eloquent expression in the immortal epic poems of Homer, would continue to be of major importance in the Classical world (ca. 500 BC to AD 500). Alexander the Great is said to have slept with a copy of the *Iliad* under his pillow. Later still, the Roman poet Virgil would take the end of the Trojan War as the starting point for the history of the Roman people in his *Aeneid*, chronicling the adventures of the Trojan hero Aeneas. To the ancient Greeks and their successors, great men walked in the looming shadow of the war god; they were – in every sense – henchmen of Ares.

List of dates

This list of dates aims to provide a concise overview of important periods, people, events, wars, and battles in Early Greece. The different periods follow the scheme used in this book, divided into the Bronze Age (chapter 1), Early Iron Age (chapter 2), Early Archaic period down to around 550 BC (chapter 3), and finally the Late Archaic period, from the second half of the sixth century BC to the early decades of the fifth (chapter 4). As a rule, absolute dates before the end of the sixth century BC get progressively less exact the further back in time we go; from a little before the Persian Wars, dates are generally reliable. All dates are BC.

• The Bronze Age (chapter 1)

2000	Emergence of Minoan palace civilization on Crete.
1650–1500	Period of use of the shaft graves at Mycenae.
1500–1200	Construction and use of underground *tholoi* or beehive tombs by the Mycenaean Greeks, of which the so-called Treasury of Atreus near Mycenae is a good example.
1425	Destruction of palaces on Crete, presumably as a result of the Mycenaean conquest of the island. Only Knossos remains in use as an administrative centre.
1400	Date of the Dendra panoply (end of Late Helladic II period). The Mycenaeans adopt the syllabic system of writing, referred to as Linear B. Mycenaean pottery found from Italy to the Levant and Egypt.
1300–1200	Late Helladic IIIB period. Mycenaean civilization reaches its zenith. Great activity with regards to the construction of fortifications at important Mycenaean centres, such as Tiryns, Mycenae and Athens.
1200	Widespread destruction and abandonment of Mycenaean palaces. Many signs of upheaval in the Eastern Mediterranean at large around the same time, including the collapse of the kingdom of the Hittites in Anatolia, the destruction of the Levantine city-state of Ugarit, and the attacks by the 'Sea Peoples' in Egypt.
1200–1050	Late Helladic IIIC period, the final cultural period of the remnants of Mycenaean society. Pictorial decorations on large kraters (vessels for mixing wine and water) reach new heights during the Late Helladic IIIC (Middle) period, roughly 1130–

	1090 BC; an example is the Mycenaean Warrior Vase.
1193	Traditional date of the destruction of Troy.
1050–1000	The second half of the eleventh century BC sees further impoverishment of Greek material culture and the appearance of Submycenaean-style pottery; this brief period links the Bronze Age to the subsequent Iron Age.

• The Early Iron Age (chapter 2)

1050–950	Greeks found new settlements in the Aegean and along the coast of Asia Minor. Mycenaeans had already inhabited some centres in Asia Minor, such as Ephesus and Miletus.
1000	Traditional date of the beginning of the Greek Iron Age.
1000–900	Pottery produced in Protogeometric style, developed out of Submycenaean. Characterized by the use of dark bands and abstract geometric patterns that typically do not cover the entire surface of the pot, unlike the later Geometric-style of decoration.
950	Construction of large apsidal building at Lefkandi with 'heroic' burial. The evidence from Lefkandi presents a picture of an outward-looking people, with contacts extending to Cyprus and Egypt.
900–700	Geometric pottery in Athens. Various local schools surface in other regions in Greece, producing similar-looking pottery.
825	Euboeans establish a trading post at Al-Mina in the Levant.
814	Traditional date of the founding of Carthage by Phoenicians.
776	Traditional date of the founding of the Olympic Games.
775–750	First settlement by Euboeans of Pithecussae on the island of Ischia, near Naples in Italy, signals the start of the Greek colonization of southern Italy. The site – selected for its commercial value as a trading post with the Etruscans – has yielded finds of Mycenaean pottery, so Greek interests in the region may date back to the Bronze Age.
750–650	Approximate dates of the composition of Homer's *Iliad* and *Odyssey*, as well as the suggested floruit of the poet Hesiod, who composed the *Theogony* and the *Works and Days*.
745–705	Assyrian sources dated to the reigns of Tiglath-Pileser III (r. 745–727) and Sargon II (r. 722–705) record hostile engagements with 'Ionians', who probably roamed the Levantine coast as traders and pirates. A number of Greek slaves, perhaps captured during one of the Assyrian expeditions to rid the sea of

	Aegean raiders, are held at Nineveh.
735	Greek colonization of Sicily begins with the founding of Syracuse by the Corinthians.
730–680	Commonly suggested date range for the Lelantine War, the earliest known war after the Trojan War. It was fought between the Euboean cities of Chalcis and Eretria for control of the fertile Lelantine plain.
725	Greeks establish a settlement at Cumae on the Italian coast.
720	First Greek colonization of the Chalcidice peninsula in the Aegean.
706	Traditional date of the founding of Taras by Sparta.
700	Earliest attested forays of Greeks in the Black Sea; Byzantium is founded in 658, with other settlements following soon afterwards.

• The Early Archaic period (chapter 3)

700–650	Approximate dates of the reign of Pheidon, tyrant of Argos.
669/8	Date of the so-called Battle of Hysiae, in which the Spartans are defeated by the Argives. However, this battle is perhaps fictional.
680–644	Approximate reign of Gyges of Lydia, founder of the Mermnad dynasty. Assyrian sources from the archives of Assurbanipal suggest he may have signed a treaty with Psamtik I of Egypt and sent Lydian and presumably also Ionian and Carian mercenaries to the Egyptian king between 662 and 658.
660	Ionian Greeks and Carians enrol as mercenaries in the army of the Egyptian king Psamtik I (r. 664–610), founder of the 26th or Saite Dynasty. These mercenaries were to be instrumental in freeing Egypt from Assyrian dominance. Rise of Greek trade with and in Egypt; founding of Naucratis.
657–627	Reign of the tyrant Cypselus in Corinth. Upon his death, he is succeeded by his son Periander.
650	Floruit of the poet Archilochus of Paros, who also took part in the Parian conquest and settlement of the island of Thasos.
644	Roving Cimmerians under the command of a man called Lygdamis attack and sack Sardis, the capital of the Lydian Empire; Gyges is killed in combat. The kingdom survives and Gyges is succeeded by his son, Ardys.
640	Approximate date of the Chigi Vase.
640–620	Reign of the tyrant Theagenes at Megara.

632	Attempted tyranny by Cylon at Athens.
630	Cyrene in north Africa founded by settlers from Thera.
627–585	Reign of the tyrant Periander at Corinth. Upon his death, he is succeeded by his son Psammetichus. The latter would be ousted after three years in favour of an oligarchy.
626	Founding of the Neo-Babylonian Empire.
625–600	Reign of the tyrant Thrasybulus at Miletus.
620	Approximate date of Draco's laws at Athens.
612	An allied force of Babylonians and Medes manages to capture and destroy Nineveh, causing the fall of the Neo-Assyrian Empire.
604	Ascalon, the last city of the Philistines, captured and sacked by Nebuchadnezzar II (r. ca. 634–562) of Babylon, with its people sent into exile. Alcaeus's brother Antimenidas may have taken part as a mercenary in the storming of Ascalon.
600	Old Smyrna taken and destroyed by Lydian King Alyattes. Alyattes wages war against Colophon and Clazomenae, as well as in Caria. Foundation of Massilia (modern Marseilles) by Phocaeans.
595–570	Reign of the tyrant Cleisthenes at Sicyon.
594/3	Solon's archonship in Athens.
591	Greek inscription by a mercenary named Archon, son of Amoe bichus, on the leg of one of the giant statues of Ramesses the Great at the temple of Abu Simbel, with a reference to King Psamtik, no doubt Psamtik II (r. 595–589).
590–580	Reign of the tyrant Pittacus at Mytilene.
585	Battle of the Eclipse, between the Lydians and the Medes near Pteria, results in the establishment of the Halys River as the eastern boundary of the Lydian Empire.
582–573	Spread of Panhellenic Games at Olympia, Delphi, Isthmia and Nemea. This is probably the earliest date for truly Panhellenic games, regardless of the traditional founding date for the Olympic Games.
580	Foundation of Acragas from Gela on Sicily.
569–526	Reign of Ahmose II in Egypt; he is succeeded by his son, Psamtik III, who would be the last ruler of the Saite Dynasty prior to the Persian conquest of Egypt.
566	Reorganization of Panathenaic Festival in Athens.
560	Approximate date of the Spartan defeat at the hands of the Tegeans at the Battle of the Fetters.
560–547	Reign of Croesus, king of Lydia. Croesus follows his predecessors in putting pressure on the Greek cities of Asia Minor to squeeze

tribute out of them and ensure Lydian control over the western half of Asia Minor.

559–530   Rule of Cyrus the Great, founder of the Persian Empire.

550   Floruit of the poet Theognis of Megara, who lamented the loss of traditional aristocratic values.

• The Late Archaic period (chapter 4)

560–546   Activities of Pisistratus in Athens.

547   Spartan victory over the Argives at the Battle of the Champions.

546–540   Persian conquest of Lydia and the Greek cities in Asia Minor. The city of Sardis becomes the capital of the new Achaemenid satrapy of Sparda, the most important of the satrapies on the western frontier.

546–510   Pisistratid tyranny in Athens firmly established and lasts until the overthrow of the tyrant's son Hippias in 510. This period sees Athens emerge as the main cultural centre of the Greek world.

540–523   Reign of the tyrant Polycrates at Samos.

539   Persian conquest of Babylon.

535   An allied Etruscan-Carthaginian fleet is defeated by a Greek fleet near the Greek colony of Alalia (modern Aléria on Corsica). However, the costly victory leads the Greeks to abandon Corsica and flee to southern Italy. The island is left in the hands of the Etruscans, while the Carthaginians take control of Sardinia.

525   Persians under Cambyses II conquer Egypt (Battle of Pelusium); Psamtik III is executed. Attic red-figure vase-painting appears and slowly begins to displace the older black-figure style, which largely disappears after the first quarter of the fifth century.

525–500   Approximate date of the oldest known Greek treaty of alliance, found engraved on a bronze plaque at Olympia, recording a formal alliance (*symmachia*) between the Eleans and Heraeans.

521   Darius I becomes king of Persia.

520–ca. 490   Reign of Cleomenes at Sparta.

512   Darius of Persia conquers Thrace.

508/7   Reforms of Cleisthenes in Athens form the foundation of Athenian democracy. Cleisthenes is the maternal grandson of the tyrant Cleisthenes of Sicyon. He reforms the constitution and may have introduced the practice of ostracism.

506   Spartans, Chalcidians and Boeotians invade Attica. The Spartans withdraw, but the Chalcidians and Boeotians are defeated by the Athenians.

501	First election of the ten generals (*strategoi*) at Athens.
499–493	Revolt of Ionian Greeks against the Persians in Asia Minor, supported by Eretria and Athens; Sardis is captured and destroyed in 498. Revolt in Caria against the Persians in 496. Decisive Persian victory in the naval Battle of Lade in 494; the Persians continue to subjugate the remaining rebels down to 493.
498	Reign of the tyrant Hippocrates at Gela.
493	Themistocles becomes archon at Athens.
492	Expedition by Mardonius – the son-in-law of the Persian King Darius I – to subjugate Thrace again; Macedon is forced to become a client state (vassal) and Thasos is conquered. Expedition ends when the Persian fleet is wrecked off Mount Athos and Mardonius is injured during a raid by a Thracian tribe.
491	Reign of the tyrant Gelon at Gela.
490	Expedition of the Persians under Darius against Athens and Eretria. The latter city is besieged and captured by the Persians. But the Persians are soundly defeated at the Battle of Marathon by the Athenians, assisted by a small force of Plataeans.
489	Unsuccessful siege of Paros by Miltiades.
488–472	Reign of the tyrant Theron at Acragas.
487	Earliest attested use of ostracism in Athens.
485	Gelon becomes tyrant at Syracuse.
483	Themistocles persuades the Athenians to construct a fleet of warships, funded by the revenue of the silver mines at Laurion.
481–480	Formation of the Hellenic League against the Persians under Spartan leadership, following a conference of Greek cities, first at Sparta and then at the Isthmus of Corinth.
480–479	Expedition of the Persians against the Greeks under Darius' son, Xerxes. Persian victory at Thermopylae and the naval Battle of Artemisium, both in 480. The tables are turned when the Greek fleet defeats the Persians a little later in the same year at Salamis. In 479, the Persians under Mardonius manage to sack Athens. New revolt against the Persians in Asia Minor. The Persians are later defeated at the Battle of Plataea in Boeotia and the sea battle off the coast of Mount Mycale in Ionia, near Samos. Theban leaders executed for having supported the Persians.
478	Greek siege of Persian-held Sestus in the Thracian Chersonese; the Persians flee in the night and the Athenians take control of the city. The Greek allies also send a fleet to Cyprus; they appear to have raided the Persians there. The fleet then sails to Byzantium, which is besieged and captured by the Greeks.
477	Founding of the Delian League.

Bibliographic notes

Much has been written on ancient Greek warfare, but certain topics have traditionally received greater attention than others. Modern scholars – who are frequently Classicists or historians – have generally favoured the study of ancient texts over the archaeological evidence. Iconographic material, such as vase-paintings, is often only used to illustrate a point observed in texts or, in rare cases, to serve as a counterpoint. Noteworthy histories of ancient Greek warfare that are also accessible to the general reader include *Greek Warfare: Myths and Realities* (2004) by Hans van Wees and *The Ancient Greeks at War* (2007) by Louis Rawlings. A general reference work that strives to incorporate as much of the textual evidence as possible – with some archaeological supplementary material – is the collection of volumes on *The Greek State at War* by W.K. Pritchett. Note that the first volume in this series was published under the title *Ancient Greek Military Practices* (1971).

Less frequently has the archaeological material been used as a source worthy of inquiry on its own. Particularly important are Anthony Snodgrass's *Early Greek Armour and Weapons* (1964), which focuses on the period between ca. 1200 and 600 BC. His shorter follow-up, *Arms and Armour of the Greeks* (1967; extended edition 1999), extends his earlier work in both directions and gives a good overview of developments in arms and armour from the Bronze Age down to the age of Alexander the Great. Tim Everson's *Warfare in Ancient Greece: Arms and Armour from the Heroes of Homer to Alexander the Great* (2004) serves as an update to Snodgrass's work. A valuable study of Greek burials with arms is provided by Andrea Bräuning in her *Untersuchungen zur Darstellung und Ausstattung des Kriegers im Grabbrauch Griechenlands zwischen dem 10. und 8. Jahrhundert v. Chr.* (1995). More particularly on body-armour is Eero Jarva's *Archaiologia on Archaic Greek Body-Armour* (1995). Of course, some archaeological sites have yielded finds of weapons and armour in such quantities that they warrant the publication of separate volumes. Such is the case, for example, with Olympia, the grandest of the Greek sanctuaries. *Die Angriffswaffen aus Olympia* (2001) by Holger Baitinger is one of the most recent fruits of the German labours at the site.

We are fortunate that the ancient Greeks produced large amounts of figurative evidence for much of the period under examination. This iconographic material tends to be found collected in museum catalogues or in relevant volumes of the massive *Corpus Vasorum Antiquorum*, as well as in studies of more limited scope, which I will discuss below for each chapter of the book. Vase-painting is an especially important source of information. Some general works that may be of interest include John Boardman's *The History of Greek Vases* (2001), as well as his *Greek Art* (second revised edition, 1985). Another useful introduction is *Looking at Greek*

Vases (1991), edited by Tom Rasmussen and Nigel Spivey. William R. Biers's *The Archaeology of Greece* (second edition, 1996) offers a useful and broad treatment of ancient Greek art and architecture.

As regards ancient texts, I have tried to make use of standard editions and translations whenever possible, particularly the relevant volumes of the Loeb Classical Library. For translations of lyric poets, I have relied on M.L. West's *Greek Lyric Poetry* (1993). I have used Richmond Lattimore's translations of Homer's *Iliad* and *Odyssey*, as well as Hesiod's *Works and Days* and *Theogony*. For Herodotus, I used Henry Cary's venerable translation of the *Historiae*. I have generally avoided using my own translations, but did adapt certain translations whenever I felt the meaning could be rendered more precisely in English. Occasionally, I have changed the English spelling in translations to make it fit the style used in this book.

• Prologue: Homer's shadow

The quote at the start of this chapter is the epitaph written by Simonides to honour the Spartan dead at Thermopylae and recorded by Herodotus. The story of Thermopylae is known especially from the seventh book of Herodotus' *Historiae.* The figures cited by Herodotus for the size of the Persian army in particular are often rightfully treated as suspect and will be discussed in more detail in this book's fourth chapter. The term 'Early Greece' is not an invention of my own, but generally can be used to refer to Greece from the Late Bronze Age down to the Persian Wars, in the manner of, for example, Moses Finley's *Early Greece: The Bronze and Archaic Ages* (1970).

Much has been written about Homer, and new articles and books appear frequently. Opinion is divided as regards the usefulness of the Homeric epics as a source of historical enquiry. This depends on whether or not one believes that the epic world described in the poems is internally consistent. Authors such as Anthony Snodgrass believe that the Homeric world was a mishmash that incorporated elements from both the Late Bronze Age and the Early Iron Age. Snodgrass has explicitly argued – in 'An historical Homeric society?', *Journal of Hellenic Studies* 94 (1974), pp. 114–125 – that the different elements can no longer be untangled and that the epics are thus useless as reliable sources of information for any period of Greek history.

However, other authors are not as pessimistic. Moses Finley argued, in *The World of Odysseus* (second edition, 1978), that we should look at the structure of Homeric society, rather than trying to determine which (material) elements are Mycenaean or Archaic. Ian Morris disagrees, suggesting instead that one ought to examine Homeric 'culture', in the sense of 'taken-for-granted attitudes about how the world works', rather than its social 'institutions and forms of behaviour'; see his 'The use and abuse of Homer', published in *Oxford Readings in Homer's Iliad* (2001), pp. 57–91, edited by Douglas Cairns (the quotes are from p. 57). Both argue that the epics are not only internally consistent, but can also be used as a source of information for a particular period in time. The question then becomes which period?

Following the spectacular discoveries made by Heinrich Schliemann at Hissarlik (Troy) and Mycenae in the later nineteenth century, it was long maintained that the world described by Homer corresponds to that of the Late Bronze Age; that is, the 'Mycenaean' period. Others, including Ian Morris, instead have argued that the Homeric world more closely resembles the Early Iron Age or, more specifically, Homer's own age. Finley suggested, in his *World of Odysseus,* that the Homeric world ought to be dated to the ninth century BC (p. 48), but archaeological evidence collected by Jan Paul Crielaard strongly favours a date in the early seventh century. For details, refer to Crielaard's paper, 'Homer, history and archaeology: some remarks on the date of the Homeric world', in his edited volume, *Homeric Questions: Essays in Philology, Ancient History and Archaeology, including the Papers of a Conference Organized by the Netherlands Institute at Athens, 1993* (1995), pp. 201–288.

The emphasis placed in this book on the importance of Homer can be largely attributed to the influence of two important authors; namely, Hans van Wees and J.E. Lendon. Van Wees has written extensively on Homer. I should like to single out his monograph *Status Warriors: Violence and Society in Homer and History* (1992) as the one publication that I found most useful in examining the *Iliad* and *Odyssey.* But he has also written a number of articles that shed important light on aspects of war and society in the Homeric epics. On military organization, see his article, 'Leaders of men? Military organisation in the *Iliad*', *Classical Quarterly* 36 (1986), pp. 285–303. Van Wees has shown – in his 'Kings in combat: battles and heroes in the *Iliad*', *Classical Quarterly* 38 (1988), pp. 1–24 – that the heroes almost never operated alone on the battlefield, but were always accompanied by their followers and thus formed warbands. Finally, differences and similarities between Homeric modes of fighting and later phalanx tactics are discussed in his two-part article, 'The Homeric way of war: the *Iliad* and the hoplite phalanx', *Greece & Rome* 41 (1994), pp. 1–18 and 131–155.

J.E. Lendon's *Soldiers and Ghosts: A History of Battle in Classical Antiquity* (2005) is very much based on the cultural approaches to the study of Greek warfare espoused by French scholars. The ethos expressed in the poems of Homer looms large in his work. *Soldiers and Ghosts* offers a useful overview of Greek warfare and also contains a very extensive bibliographic essay (pp. 393–440) that interested readers will find useful. The passage in my text on the role of vengeance as a cause of war owes a great debt to Lendon's paper, 'Homeric vengeance and the outbreak of Greek wars', published in the volume *War and Violence in Ancient Greece* (2000), pp. 1–30, edited by Hans van Wees.

The text box on Greek periodization is not meant to be controversial. Absolute dates before 500 BC are by necessity all approximations, and the further one goes in time the less secure the dates tend to be. For the Bronze Age, absolute dates are usually based on synchronisms with the ancient Near East and especially Egypt; virtually all absolute dates for the ancient Mediterranean and Near East can be traced back to lists of Egyptian kings. Absolute dates are invariably disputed; I follow here the so-called 'short' chronology, in which the Mycenaean era starts more or less at the same time as the Egyptian New Kingdom, ca. 1550 BC. Readers should not be surprised to see alternative dates in other scholarly publications. For a brief overview of the problems and complexities concerning absolute chronologies from an Aegean perspective, consult Oliver Dickinson's *The Aegean Bronze Age* (1993), pp. 17–21.

The Hittites wrote in the Hittite language when communicating with their vassal states, rather than using Akkadian, the *lingua franca* of the ancient Near East and the language used in texts sent to other Great Kingdoms such as Egypt. For further details, see Trevor Bryce, 'Anatolian scribes in Mycenaean Greece', *Historia* 48.3 (1999), pp. 257–264. References to the Hittite tablets use CTH numbers, which refer to the *Catalogue des textes Hittites*, which began publication in 1971. For an accessible overview of the letters sent by Hittite kings, refer to *Letters from the Hittite Kingdom* (2009) by Harry A. Hoffner Jr. Those more broadly interested in correspondence in the ancient Near East may also want to consult Trevor Bryce's *Great Kings of the Ancient Near East: The Royal Correspondence of the Late Bronze Age* (2003) or William L. Moran's *The Amarna Letters* (1992).

There have been some heated debates on Ahhiyawa, but the notion that this refers to Greece or some Greek territory in or around the Aegean seems no longer to be too controversial. Hans Güterbock wrote a number of articles on the subject. See his articles: 'The Hittites and the Aegean world: Part 1. The Ahhiyawa problem reconsidered', *American Journal of Archaeology* 87 (1983), pp. 133–138; 'Hittites and Akhaeans: a new look', *Proceedings of the American Philosophical Society* 128 (1984), pp. 114–122; and 'Troy in Hittite texts: Wilusa, Ahhiyawa, and Hittite history', in the volume *Troy and the Trojan War* (1986), pp. 33–44, edited by M.J. Mellink. Trevor Bryce has contributed a great amount to publishing data on the Hittite world in English and also touches on the Ahhiyawa issue and the historicity of the Trojan War in a number of his publications. Those interested are recommended to read his book, *The Kingdom of the Hittites* (new edition, 2005), as well as its companion volume, *Life and Society in the Hittite World* (2002).

Some of the passage on Homeric society is informed by reading Hans van Wees's *Status Warriors*, cited above. For details on the Homeric concepts of *anax* and *basileus*, refer to N. Yamagata's '*Anax* and *basileis* in Homer', *Classical Quarterly* 47 (1997), pp. 1–14. In my original PhD thesis, I emphasized that all the warriors in the Homeric epics appear to have been aristocrats, but I no longer wish to maintain this as fervently. Suffice to say that the aristocratic element dominates, but this does not necessarily preclude the presence of commoners, who may have been mustered through some form of conscription. Omitted here is a discussion on the polite form of address, *daimonie*, which appears in Homer – for example, *Il.* 2.188–206 – and later texts and can be translated as 'dear sir' or 'dear madam'; those interested may refer to E. Brunius-Nillson's *Diamonie: An Inquiry into a Mode of Apostrophe in Old Greek Literature* (1955).

Vengeance was a cause of war, but one should not assume that insults always had to be repaid. A useful article written from an anthropological perspective is D. Dawson's 'The origins of war: biological and anthropological theories', *History and Theory* 35 (1996), pp. 2–28. Specifically, Dawson points out that "Primitive peoples may say they have to avenge injuries for the sake of honor, but the selectiveness and manipulativeness [*sic*] of their memories for these injuries has often been noted: they can 'forget' stains on their honor a long time until they find it convenient to 'remember' them" (p. 27–28). Those interested in learning more on biological and anthropological reasons for war and conflict in the epic world – and through that lens, human society in general – are urged to consult Jonathan Gottschall's *The Rape of Troy: Evolution, Violence and the World of Homer* (2005).

The section on *kudos*, *time* and *kleos* owes a great deal of inspiration to Bart Natoli's unpublished Master's thesis, *A Heroic Trichotomy: kudos, kleos* and *time in Homer's epics* (2006). Of course, Van Wees in his *Status Warriors* (1992) has argued that war in the *Iliad* is status warfare: a kind of warfare in which men raise their social standing by performing noteworthy deeds in battle (esp. pp. 206–207). This does indeed seem to be the ideal, but in actual practice the fighting in the *Iliad* appears only to *reinforce* the status of the heroes. The actual status of a hero remains essentially the same and is measured by the number of 'gifts of honour' (*geras*) or booty that he receives. For this, see also J.L. Ready, 'Toil and trouble: the acquisition of spoils in the *Iliad*', *Transactions of the American Philological Association* 137 (2007), pp. 3–43. Thus, Agamemnon – as the commander-in-chief of the Greek forces and the greatest of the rulers – receives far more of the spoils than men who are arguably better fighters, as Achilles bitterly points out (*Il.* 1.225–244).

The text box on the relative insignificance of the Aegean until the Classical period is of key importance, I believe, in properly evaluating the place of ancient Greece in world history. Too little research has thus far been devoted towards studying Greece from the perspective of the wider ancient Near Eastern world. It is a characteristic of the Classical period of western history – ca. 500 BC to the fall of the Roman Empire, or around AD 500 – that originally marginal areas such as Greece, Persia and Rome come to the foreground and get to dominate the political and cultural realms, reducing the earlier great civilizations to mere shadows of their former glory.

• Chapter 1: Palace warriors

Chopping the Late Bronze Age into a Prepalatial, Palatial and Postpalatial period echoes the typical division of the Minoan period, but should not be construed as a generally accepted way of carving up the Mycenaean era. There are problems here with the relative lack of information about the Late Bronze Age. We know quite a lot from some places during certain periods, but are almost wholly ignorant of other regions and other times. A good example is the so-called Shaft Grave period, which is almost entirely based on finds from the shaft graves at Mycenae, and it is undoubtedly not representative of mainland Greece as a whole.

Furthermore, the study of Mycenaean culture in general is often made more difficult by the inappropriate use of the Homeric epics as a source of information on the Late Bronze Age. As stated in this book's prologue, the political framework and the basic plots of Homer's poems probably date back to Mycenaean times, but most of the details – architecture, war-gear, characteristics of society – are almost certainly derived entirely from Homer's own time. One key exception is the so-called boar's tusk helmet that is described in *Il.* 10.261–265 and which is almost certainly a relic of the Mycenaean Bronze Age. Homer may have known of a specimen that had been passed from one generation to another as an heirloom; see, for example, Jan Paul Crielaard's 'Homeric and Mycenaean long-distance contacts: discrepancies in the evidence', *Bulletin Antieke Beschaving* 75 (2000), pp. 51–63.

General references for the Mycenaean period are easy to come by. Despite its age, John Chadwick's *The Mycenaean World* (1976) remains a very readable introduction to the Mycenaean Bronze Age. Publisher Thames & Hudson has, throughout many years now, published affordable books with loads of pictures, and William Taylour's *The Mycenaeans* (revised edition, 1983) is a useful handbook. Similarly useful because of its vast number of pictures and references is Hans-Günter Buchholz and Vassos Karageorghis's *Prehistoric Greece and Cyprus: An Archaeological Handbook* (1973). For more in-depth, scholarly accounts of the Mycenaean period, refer, for example, to Michael L. Galaty and William A. Parkinson's edited volume, *Rethinking Mycenaean Palaces II* (revised edition, 2007), or *Aegean Prehistory: A Review* (2001), edited by Tracy Cullen. The various volumes that make up the series *Archaeologica Homerica* are also useful reference works.

The overviews of the Mycenaean period in the books on arms and armour by Anthony Snodgrass and Tim Everson, cited among the general reference works, are useful as jumping-off points for anyone interested in warfare in the Aegean during the Late Bronze Age. However, the most detailed treatment of Mycenaean warfare can be found in C. Diane Fortenberry's unpublished PhD dissertation *Elements of Mycenaean Warfare* (1990).

For an interesting overview of the Mycenaean armour based on the Dendra panoply, refer to Piotr Taracha's paper, 'Warriors of the Mycenaean "Age of Plate"', in Barry Molloy's *The Cutting Edge: Studies in Ancient and Medieval Combat* (2007), pp. 144–152. Mycenaean swords have been the subject of a select few studies. Refer to N.K. Sandars's 'Later Aegean bronze swords', *American Journal of Archaeology* 67 (1963), pp. 117–153, and I. Killian-Dirlmeier's *Die Schwerter von Griechenland (aussenhalb der Peloponnesos), Bulgarien und Albanien* (1993). Chariots were used extensively by the Mycenaeans; the standard work is Joost Crouwel's *Chariots and Other Means of Land Transport in Bronze Age Greece* (1981).

Modern reconstructions of Mycenaean warriors generally owe a great debt to Peter Connolly's *The Ancient Greece of Odysseus* (1998; first published as *The Legend of Odysseus*, 1986). Unfortunately, Connolly's illustrations are sometimes a little too fanciful. Many of his later emulators continue to suggest that Mycenaeans wore metal armour with embossed decorations – inspired by the very late finds from Kallithea – all through the Late Bronze Age and even into the twelfth century BC. Nicolas Grguric's *The Mycenaeans, c. 1650–1100 BC* (2005) – offers a largely accurate and balanced overview based on the empirical evidence.

Mycenaean fortifications have always attracted a lot of attention. Spyros Iakovides's *Late Helladic Citadels on Mainland Greece* (1983) remains a useful guide; N.C. Scoufopoulos's *Mycenaean Citadels* (1971) is older, but might also be worth a look for interested readers. For a concise and more up-to-date account of Mycenaean fortifications, refer to Nic Field's *Mycenaean Citadels, c. 1350–1200 BC* (2004). An overview of fortifications and other large Mycenaean structures and infrastructure can be found in R. Hope-Simpson and D.K. Hagel's *Mycenaean Fortifications, Highways, Dams and Canals* (2006). With regards to Cyclopean masonry, the most in-depth treatment is N.C. Loader's *Building in Cyclopean Masonry, with Special Reference to the Mycenaean Fortifications on Mainland Greece* (1998). For a relatively recent overview of research at the palace of Pylos, see J.L. Davis and S. Alcock's *Sandy Pylos: An Archaeological History from Nestor to Navarino* (1998). A detailed description of the late fortifications on the island of Salamis can be found in Yannis Lolos's article, 'Salamis', *Archaeological Reports* 47 (2001), pp. 14–15. When I mention the continued use of Helladic fortifications in the Protogeometric and Geometric periods, I cite Jan Paul Crielaard's paper, 'Basileis at sea: elites and external contacts in the Euboean Gulf region from the end of the Bronze Age to the beginning of the Iron Age', in Sigrid Deger-Jalkotzy and Irene S. Lemos's *Ancient Greece: From the Mycenaean Palaces to the Age of Homer* (2006), pp. 271–197.

In discussing the Siege Fresco from Mycenae, I make reference to a remark made by Joost Crouwel in the discussion of a paper by N.R. Thomas, 'The war animal: three days in the life of the Mycenaean lion', in Robert Laffineur's edited volume *Polemos: le context guerrier en Égée à l'âge du Bronze. Actes de la 7e Recontre égéenne international, Université de Liège, 14–17 Avril 1998* (1999), pp. 297–312; the reference is to p. 311.

With regards to Mycenaean burials with arms, the most convenient overview is provided by Sigrid Deger-Jalkotzy's paper, 'Late Mycenaean warrior tombs', in the volume she edited with Irene S. Lemos (cited above), pp. 151–179. For information on the Mycenaean beehive tombs, refer to Oliver Dickinson's *The Aegean Bronze Age* (1994), pp. 222–227, or Donald Preziosi and Louise A. Hitchcock's *Aegean Art and Architecture* (1999), pp. 175–177.

A useful reference work for Mycenaean iconography is Paola Cassola Guida's *Le armi defensive dei Micenei nelle Figurazione* (1973). More general are the various papers collected in E. Rystedt and B. Wells's edited volume, *Pictorial Pursuits: Figurative Painting on Mycenaean and Geometric Pottery: Papers from Two Seminars at the Swedish Institute at Athens in 1999 and 2001* (2006). Diane Fortenberry also discusses the iconographic evidence in her PhD dissertation. Also useful is E. Vermeule and V. Karageorghis's *Mycenaean Pictorial Vase-Painting* (1982).

For relatively recent discussions of the Mycenaean Linear B tablets, refer to Cynthia Shelmerdine's paper, 'Mycenaean palatial administration' in the volume edited by Deger-Jalkotzy and Lemos (2006), pp. 73–86. See also T.F. Tartaron's article, 'Aegean prehistory as world archaeology: recent trends in the archaeology of Bronze Age Greece', *Journal of Archaeological Research* 16 (2008), pp. 83–161, esp. pp. 93–95 and 100–110. Deger Jalkotzy also contributed a useful paper on the subject in Laffineur's edited volume (1999), entitled 'Military prowess and social status in Mycenaean Greece', pp. 121–132. The *o-ka* tablets have naturally been subject to much discussion. A. Uchitel rejects the idea that the tablets have a military purpose, in his article, 'On the "military" character of the *o-ka* tablets', *Kadmos* 23, pp. 136–163. An accessible introduction to the Linear B tablets is John Chadwick's *The Decipherment of Linear B* (second edition, 1967).

The typology of galleys proposed by Michael Wedde can be found in his paper, 'War at sea: the Mycenaean and Early Iron Age oared galley', published in Robert Laffineur's edited volume (cited above), pp. 465–474. Wedde states that the straight keel of the Mycenaean oared galley allowed the ship 'to beach at speed [which] would have offered a tactical advantage, in that the warriors could spring directly on dry land, and not wade ashore, a moment when the defenders would have had a critical advantage' (p. 469). Another very thorough treatment of ships of the Bronze Age – Egyptian, Levantine, as well as Minoan and Mycenaean – can be found in Shelley Wachsmann's *Seagoing Ships and Seamanship in the Bronze Age Levant* (1998). For a more general treatment, refer to Lionel Casson's *Ships and Seamanship in the Ancient World* (1971).

• Chapter 2: Raiders of women and cattle

The focus in this chapter is on the Early Iron Age. Some of the more important works of reference are cited in the text, but an overview here can nevertheless still be useful. The ground work was laid by Anthony Snodgrass in his *The Dark Age of Greece* (1971). Other recommended books on the subject include Nicholas Coldstream's *Geometric Greece* (1977; revised edition, 2003), and *From Citadel to City-State: The Transformation of Greece, 1200–700 BCE* (1999) by Carol G. Thomas and Craig Conant. A more recent monograph that covers the same period is Oliver Dickinson's *The Aegean from Bronze Age to Iron Age: Continuity and Change Between the Twelfth and Eighth Centuries BC* (2006). Ian Morris's *Archaeology as Cultural History: Words and Things in Iron-Age Greece* (2000) is intended to be a readable cultural history of the period and is clear and concise. Of note also are the collected essays in *Ancient Greece: From the Mycenaean Palaces to the Age of Homer* (2006), edited by Sigrid Deger-Jalkotzy and Irene S. Lemos.

This period is generally considered rather inward-looking, but the evidence from Lefkandi shows that the Aegean was not wholly cut off from the outside world. Overseas activities became the purview, initially, of the aristocracy, a subject that my supervisor Jan Paul Crielaard wrote about in his unpublished doctoral dissertation, *The Euboeans Overseas: Long-Distance Contacts and Colonization as Status Activities in Early Iron Age Greece* (1996). Similar ground is covered from a different perspective by David W. Tandy in his *Warriors into Traders: The Power of the Market in Early Greece* (1997). For Greek colonization, the standard reference remains John Boardman's *The Greeks Overseas: Their Early Colonies and Trade* (fourth edition, 1999). More limited in scope, but no less noteworthy, is Irad Malkin's *The Returns of Odysseus: Colonization and Ethnicity* (1998).

There is – as far as I am aware – only one synthesis that deals specifically with ancient Greek burials with arms; namely, Andrea Bräuning's *Untersuchungen zur Darstellung und Ausstattung des Kriegers im Grabbrauch Griechenlands zwischen dem 10. und 8. Jahrhundert v. Chr.* (1995). For further details, the student has to consult the relevant excavation reports. A number of volumes have already appeared on Lefkandi, including two volumes on *The Protogeometric Building at Toumba* (1990). Much has been written on this building; of particular note is 'The hero's home: some relfections on the building at Toumba, Lefkandi', written by Jan Paul Crielaard and Jan Driessen and published in *Topoi* 4 (1994), pp. 251–270. As regards the cemetery at the West Gate of Eretria, the excavation report is C. Bérard's *L'hérôon à la porte de l'oueste* (1970), published as the third volume in the series of reports simply titled *Eretria*. For the Athenian Kerameikos, consult W. Kraiker and K. Kübler's *Kerameikos 1: Die Nekropolen des 12. bis 10. Jahrhunderts* (1939) and K. Kübler's *Kerameikos 5: Die Nektropole des 10. bis 8. Jahrhunderts* (1954). The reports for the Athenian agora are spread across periodicals – mostly

Hesperia – and publications in the series of volumes entitled *The Athenian Agora*. A good introduction to the fieldwork is provided by J.McK. Camp's *The Athenian Agora: Excavations in the Heart of Classical Athens* (1986; revised edition, 1992). For Argos, see Pierre Courbin's *Tombes géométriques d' Argos* (1974) and Robin Hägg's *Die Gräber der Argolis in submykenischer, protogeometrischer und geometrischer Zeit* (1974). For the tomb with the bell-shaped cuirass, consult Courbin's article, 'Une tombe géométrique d'Argos', *Bulletin de correspondence hellénique* 81 (1957), pp. 322–386. For additional burials with arms, consult I. Georganas' 'Weapons and warfare in Early Iron Age Thessaly', published in *Mediterranean Archaeology and Archaeometry* 5 (2005), pp. 63–74. For more background information regarding burials and funerary rites, see Carlo Antonaccio's *An Archaeology of Ancestors: Tomb Cult and Hero Cult in Early Greece* (1995).

With regards to the fortifications, the standard works can be briefly cited here. The starting point is R.L. Scranton's *Greek Walls* (1941), which laid the groundwork for later studies in ancient Greek fortifications. Frederick Winter's *Greek Fortifications* (1971) offers a survey of Greek fortifications, mostly later Archaic and beyond. A.W. Lawrence's *Greek Aims in Fortification* (1979) strives to understand the reasons behind the Greek construction of walls, and bases itself mostly on Classical and later evidence. Specifically as regards Old Smyrna, the standard references are R.V. Nicholls's 'Old Smyrna: the Iron Age fortifications and associated remains on the city perimeter', *Annual of the British School in Athens* 53/54 (1958/1959), pp. 35–137, and Ekrem Akurgal's *Alt-Smyrna I: Wohnschichten und Athenatempel* (1983). For Emporio, see John Boardman's *Greek Emporio: Excavations in Chios, 1952–1955* (1967). More recent work has already been listed in the chapter itself, of which Rune Frederiksen's *Greek City Walls of the Archaic Period* (2010) should really be considered the standard reference for the foreseeable future. Naturally, new walls continued to be discovered. I was fortunate enough to visit the excavations of Prof. Alexander Mazarakis Ainian at Palaioskiathos on the island of Skiathos in 2011, where walls have been unearthed that appear, on the basis of Protogeometric pottery fragments, to be as early as the tenth century BC.

The key publication with regards to the iconographic evidence for this period is Gudrun Ahlberg's *Fighting on Land and Sea in Greek Geometric Art* (1971). The edited volume by Rystedt and Wells has already been mentioned in the section on the Mycenaean period. For more technical details, one may also wish to consult J.M. Davison's *Attic Geometric Workshops* (1961). Another useful source for pictures and accompanying discussion is John Boardman's *Early Greek Vase Painting* (1998). More general is *Tausend Jahre frühgriechische Kunst* (1980) by R. Hampe and E. Simon. For the Argive motif of the horse-leader, see Susan Langdon's 'The return of the horse-leader', in *American Journal of Archaeology* 93 (1989), pp. 185–201. As regards warrior figurines, see Michael Byrne's *The Greek Geometric Warrior Figurine: Interpretation and Origin* (1991), even if I do not believe that most of the figurines necessarily represent deities. For the Parian vases and the *polyandreion* at Paroika, see especially Ph.N. Zaphiropoulou's 'Recent finds from Paros', in *Excavating Classical Cultue: Recent Archaeological Discoveries in Greece* (2002), edited by M. Stamatopoulou and M. Yeroulanou, as well as Zaphiropoulou's contribution to Rystedt and Wells's *Pictorial Pursuits* (2006), pp. 271–277. Also important is Anthony Snodgrass's *Homer and the Artists* (1994); the reference to Snodgrass, with respect to the martial feat of making a 360 degree turn while standing in a chariot, comes from this book, p. 64.

The remark that there is nothing implausible about the Homeric use of the chariot owes a lot to J.K. Anderson's 'Homeric, British and Cyrenaic chariots', published in *American Journal of Archaeology* 69 (1965), pp. 349–352, as well as his 'Greek chariot-borne and mounted infantry', in *American Journal of Archaeology* 79 (1975), pp. 175–187. The standard work for chariots of this period is Joost Crouwel's *Chariots and Other Wheeled Vehicles in Iron Age Greece* (1992). For more details on helmets of this period, see J. Borchardt's *Homerische Helme: Helmformen der Ägäis in ihren Beziehungen zu orientalischen und europäischen Helmen in der Bronze- und frühen Eisenzeit* (1972). Similarly useful are the many volumes in the series *Archaeologica Homerica*, published in the 1970s and 1980s.

• Chapter 3: Men of bronze

The story of Psamtik and the bronze men is found in Herodotus (Hdt. 2.152). Scholarly interest in Egypt's Late Period is not as great as for earlier periods. A good introduction to the Late Period is Alan B. Lloyd's 'The Late Period (664–332 BC)', a chapter in *The Oxford History of Ancient Egypt* (2000), pp. 364–387, edited by Ian Shaw. Lloyd also briefly discusses changes in Egypt's military during this period. As regards the Greek activities in Egypt, Naucratis naturally looms large. A useful publication is A. Möller's *Naukratis: Trade in Archaic Greece* (Oxford). See also G. Vittmann's *Ägypten und die Fremden im ersten vorchristlichen Jahrtausand* (2003). For an English overview of Greeks in Egypt (and elsewhere), consult John Boardman's *The Greeks Overseas*, pp. 111–159.

For the proper interpretation of the Greek inscription at Abu Simbel, see Matthew Dillon's 'A Homeric pun from Abu-Simbel, Egypt (Meiggs & Lewis 7a)', *Zeitschrift für Papyrologie und Epigraphik* 118 (1997), pp. 128–130. The pun refers to the use of the word *oudamos* ('nobody') as a personal name in Odysseus' encounter with the Cyclops Polyphemus (Hom. *Od.* 9.408). The discussion on this inscription mentions *xenoi* and guest-friendship; the most useful book on this subject is Gabriel Herman's *Ritualised Friendship and the Greek City* (1987). I suggest that *epikouroi* should probably be interpreted not just as mercenaries, but – sometimes at least – also as some kind of guest-friends who provide support in exchange for some kind of repayment, be it favours or gifts. For a brief rundown of the evidence, see B.M. Lavelle's 'Epikouroi in Thucydides', American Journal of Philology 110 (1989), pp. 36–39, and especially p. 36 n. 1.

Greek mercenaries are often treated as a phenomenon of the Classical period and the fourth century BC in particular, but Greek warriors were already a familiar sight in many armies of the Near Eastern empires from at least the first half of the seventh century BC onwards. Discussion of these early mercenaries is often limited in general books on the subject, such as Matthew Trundle's Greek Mercenaries from the Late Archaic Period to Alexander (2004) or Stephen English's more recent Mercenaries in the Classical World to the Death of Alexander (2012). A useful study of early Greek mercenaries is N. Luraghi's 'Traders, pirates, warriors: the proto-history of Greek mercenary soldiers in the eastern Mediterranean', Phoenix 60 (2006), pp. 21–47. The reference to Greek encounters with Assyrians and the presence of Greek slaves in Nineveh comes from Amélie Kuhrt's lecture 'Greeks' and 'Greece' in Mesopotamian and Persian Perspectives (2002).

As regards possible Carian contributions to Greek arms and armour, doubts were expressed by Anthony Snodgrass in his article, 'Carian armourers: the growth of a tradition', Journal of Hellenic Studies 84 (1964), pp. 107–118. I do not share these doubts; I think there is ample evidence in the sources – mentioned in the chapter – to suggest that the Greeks did indeed adopt many elements from Anatolian civilizations in particular, just as their stone architecture was indebted to Egypt and their writing system to Phoenicia, while influences from Assyria can be noted in Greek sculptures and figurines of the seventh century BC. Indeed, the difficulty in distinguishing 'Greek' from 'Western Anatolian' argues strongly in favour of an ethnogenesis that encompassed the Aegean basin and its immediate hinterland. Carians and Lydians may have been as different from – or as similar to – Rhodians as Thessalians and Macedonians were compared with Argives.

Much of this chapter is based not only on the written sources, but also considerable amounts of iconographic evidence, especially vase-paintings. My doctoral dissertation included more than 500 items in total, ranging from the Mycenaean period down to the Persian Wars. The Corpus Vasorum Antiquorum is an invaluable resource, but a few other books were incredibly useful in the course of my research. For Corinth, the standard reference is D.A. Amyx's Corinthian Vase-Painting (1988), published in three volumes. Corinthian vases were originally thought to be Sicyonian, hence K.F. Johansen's Les vases sicyoniens: études archéologique (1923). For an interesting approach to Archaic Corinth, in which the pottery plays a significant part, see Michael Shanks's Art and the Greek City-State: An Interpretive Archaeology (1999). For Laconian pottery, refer to Conrad Stibbe's Lakonische Vasenmalerei des sechsten Jahrhunderts v. Chr. (1972). Large quantities of lead figurines of warriors, archers, and horsemen have been unearthed at Sparta; see The Sanctuary of Artemis Orthia at Sparta (1929), edited by R.M. Dawkins. For

Boeotia, see R. Hampe's *Frühe Griechische Sagenbilder in Boötien* (1936), even if the dates are generally a little too early for objects such as engraved fibulae. As regards the islands, useful is A.A. Lemos's two-volume *Archaic Pottery of Chios: The Decorative Styles* (1991). More general is John Boardman's *Early Greek Vase Painting* (1998).

The *hippobatas* and *hippostrophos* phenomenon was first brought to light, I believe, by A. Alföldi in his 'Die Herrschaft der Reiterei in Griechenland und Rom nach dem Sturz der Könige', a paper in *Gestalt und Geschichte: Festschrift K. Schefold* (1967), pp. 13–45. Peter Greenhalgh discusses it further in his *Early Greek Warfare: Horsemen and Chariots in the Homeric and Archaic Ages* (1973). Strangely enough, most modern authors seem not to attach any great significance to the motif of the 'knight and squire', preferring to see early hoplites as regular infantry rather than mounted infantry. But the motif is so common in the Archaic period that it does warrant further consideration and I have tried to do so in this book. The suggestion that the Argive shield was specifically invented to be easily carried by men who spent considerable time on horseback is my own. Anthony Snodgrass's 'The first European body-armour', published in *Studies in Honour of C.F.C. Hawkes* (1971), pp. 33–50, served as an inspiration, as did M. Detienne's 'La phalange: problèmes et controverses', in *Problèmes de la guerre en Grèce ancienne* (1968), edited by Jean-Pierre Vernant, pp. 119–142 (especially pp. 134–138). For more details, see my article, 'From horsemen to hoplites: some notes on Archaic Greek warfare', *Bulletin Antieke Beschaving* 82 (2007), pp. 305–319.

There are quite a few books that deal more generally with cavalry in ancient Greece, most of which focus – rather understandably – on the Classical period, such as G.R. Bugh's *The Horsemen of Athens* (1988), I.G. Spence's *The Cavalry of Classical Greece* (1993), and L.J. Worley's *Hippeis: The Cavalry of Ancient Greece* (1994). R.E. Gaebel's *Cavalry Operations in the Ancient Greek World* (2002) has a very broad scope, but includes a useful amount of introductory material on pp. 17–60 that covers horses, chariots, and horse riding in Greece and the Near East down to 500 BC. A general treatment on horsemanship, with an emphasis on Xenophon, can be found in J.K. Anderson's *Ancient Greek Horsemanship* (1963).

On lyric poetry, refer to D. Mulroy's *Early Greek Lyric Poetry* (1992). A concise history, some of it a little speculative, can be found in M.L. West's 'Greek poetry, 2000–700 BC', *Classical Quarterly* 23 (1973), pp. 179–192. For an interesting slant on exhortation poetry, consult E. Irwin's *Solon and Early Greek Poetry: The Politics of Exhortation* (2005), especially pp. 15–62. Of interest also is P. Murray's 'Poetic inspiration in Early Greece', *Journal of Hellenic Studies* 101 (1981), pp. 87–100.

Archilochus has been dated based on his reference to Gyges of Lydia and a solar eclipse; see M. Cogan and H. Tadmore's 'Gyges and Ashurbanipal: a study in literary transmission', *Orientalia* 46 (1977), pp. 65–85. Regarding Archilochus and the discarding of his shield, see T. Schwertfeger's 'Der Schild des Archilochos', *Chiron*

12 (1982), pp. 253–280. The Parians were interested in Thasos because of the gold mines on the island and the nearby Thracian coast; J.F. Healey, *Mining and Metallurgy in the Greek and Roman world* (1978), pp. 45–47, summarizes the evidence. Of interest also is A.J. Podlecki's 'Three Greek soldier-poets: Archilochus, Alcaeus, Solon', *Classical World* 63 (1969), pp. 73–81.

The poet Tyrtaeus is usually dated to the second half of the seventh century BC, but this has not been uncontested. A.W. Verrall – in his 'Tyrtaeus: a Graeco-Roman tradition', *Classical Review* 10 (1896), pp. 269–277 – argued that Tyrtaeus was active around the time of the Messenian Revolt of 464 BC. There was a little back-and-forth between Verrall and R.W. Macan in *Classical Review* 11 (1897), but on the whole most people simply assumed the original date was correct. Chris Faraone more recently suggested that the poetry attributed to Tyrtaeus includes Classical interpolations; refer to his 'Stanzaic structure and responsion in the elegiac poetry of Tyrtaeus', *Mnemosyne* 59 (2006), pp. 19–52, and especially pp. 43–46 (comparisons with Pindar and epitaphs of the late fifth century BC). The notion that Tyrtaeus was originally an Athenian schoolteacher – as mentioned, for example, by Plato (*Leges* 1.629a–b) – certainly seems to fit more with the fifth century BC than anything earlier; additional care must therefore be taken when using Tyrtaeus as a source for the seventh century BC. On Alcaeus and the connection with Babylon, see J.D. Quinn's 'Alcaeus 48 (B16) and the fall of Ascalon (604 BC)', *American School of Oriental Research* 164 (1961), pp. 19–20.

With regards to ancient Lydia, our knowledge is hampered by a lack of in-depth research into areas outside of the capital city of Sardis, where excavations are still ongoing. Much relevant literature on the subject is also published in Turkish, and is therefore not widely accessible. A recent and comprehensive book on the subject, with an extensive bibliography, is Christopher Roosevelt's *The Archaeology of Lydia, from Gyges to Alexander* (2009). Concerning the date of the Lydian conquest of Old Smyrna (ca. 600 BC), see J.M. Cook's 'On the date of Alyattes' sack of Smyrna', in *Annual of the British School in Athens* 80 (1985), pp. 25–28.

The Lelantine War is the subject of P. Parker's *Untersuchungen zum Lelantischen Krieg und verwandten Problemen der frühgriechischen Geschichte* (1997). The main difficulties with regards to this early war are also treated concisely by Jonathan Hall in his *A History of the Archaic Greek World, ca. 1200–479 BCE* (2007), pp. 1–8; these opening pages to his book should be required reading for anyone interested in ancient history, especially for periods where we have only scraps of information. The other wars and battles discussed in this chapter are likewise often sketchy; Herodotus' 'Battle of the Fetters', like the 'Battle of the Champions', seems strictly anecdotal. (This has not, however, precluded modern scholars from treating these battles as evidence for the existence of ritualistic warfare in the Archaic period.) As regards the expansion of Argos, for which we have sound archaeological evidence in addition to written testimony, see Jonathan Hall's 'How Argive was the

"Argive" Heraion? The political and cultic geography of the Argive plain, 900–400 BC', *American Journal of Archaeology* 99 (1995), pp. 577–613.

A great deal of time and energy has been wasted on scholarly discussions of the hoplite phalanx. The hoplite – characterized as a heavily-armed spearman equipped with Argive shield – appeared a little before 700 BC. Questions then concerned the date and nature of the phalanx (the supposed formation that the hoplite fought in) and whether or not the hoplite was a member of an emerging middle class and an early sign of what would eventually lead to democracy in Athens, in other places in Greece. Tempers flared and eventually two camps emerged. The first was the 'orthodox' camp, which supposed that the phalanx was introduced at the same time or shortly after the hoplite and was indeed a sign of an emerging middle class. The rapidity of this development led some to talk of a 'hoplite reform' around or shortly after 700 BC. Its proponents include A.J. Holladay – who wrote an article entitled 'Hoplites and heresies', *Journal of Hellenic Studies* 102 (1982), pp. 94–103 – and, most famously, Victor Davis Hanson, author of the influential book *The Western Way of War: Infantry Battle in Classical Greece* (second edition, 2000). The 'heretic' camp includes G.L. Cawkwell – author of 'Orthodoxy and hoplites', *Classical Quarterly* 39 (1989), pp. 375–389 – and Peter Krentz, Hans van Wees, and others. The text undoubtedly makes it clear that I belong to the latter camp as well.

One of the characteristics of the orthodox view is that hoplite fighting is typically regarded as ritualized and bound by various rules of honour. These notions generally do not bear close scrutiny; see, especially, Peter Krentz's 'Fighting by the rules: the invention of the hoplite *agon*', *Hesperia* 71 (2002), pp. 23–39, as well as his somewhat broader paper, 'Deception in Archaic and Classical Greek warfare', published in *War and Violence in Ancient Greece* (2000), edited by Hans van Wees, pp. 167–200. With regards to the idea of the hoplites representing some sort of Archaic Greek 'middle class', see now Hans van Wees's 'The myth of the middle-class army: military and social status in ancient Athens', in *War as a Cultural and Social Force: Essays on Warfare in Antiquity* (2001), edited by Tønnes Bekker-Nielsen and Lise Hannestad, pp. 45–71. There are often ideological factors in play when it comes to equating the ancient world with modern notions and wishful thinking; see P.J. Rhodes's *Ancient Democracy and Modern Ideology* (2003).

Terminology tends to be confused when it comes to hoplites and the hoplite phalanx. The word *phalanx*, as a technical term, was "first generally applied to the Macedonian phalanx", that is, only from the fourth century BC onwards, according to F.E. Adcock, *The Greek and Macedonian Art of War* (1957), p. 3 n. 5. The term should therefore really be avoided when talking about Archaic warfare. A second problem concerns the word 'hoplite' itself. It is cognate with the Greek word *hoplon*, but this was not the Greek word for the Argive shield, but rather a general word that could mean any kind of equipment, and even tools; see discussion and examples in J.F. Lazenby and David Whitehead's 'The myth of the hoplite's *hoplon*',

Classical Quarterly 46, pp. 27–33.

The emphasis on the phalanx in modern scholarly literature suggests that the Greeks were the first to field armed men in tight formations. This is difficult to maintain in the light of clear artistic evidence from the Near East and Egypt. One scene on the Sumerian 'Stela of the Vultures' – which dates back to the third millennium BC – depicts warriors with spears and axes in a tight formation; another scene depicts multiple ranks of warriors with spears and shields forming what can only be described as a phalanx. A wooden model from a tomb of the Eleventh Dynasty in Egypt, ca. 2000 BC, depicts spearmen with shields marching in a rectangular formation, four men wide and ten men deep. It seems clear that the use of formations is connected to command structures and state-organized forms of violence. For some much-needed context, consult secondary literature on warfare in other regions of the world, such as Anthony J. Spalinger's *War in Ancient Egypt* (2005) or William J. Hamblin's *Warfare in the Ancient Near East to 1600 BC: Holy Warriors at the Dawn of History* (2006).

On the Chigi Vase, see Jeffrey Hurwit's article 'Reading the Chigi Vase', *Hesperia* 71 (2002), pp. 1–22. Hurwit suggests that the Chigi Vase is actually a kind of manual for the young aristocrat, in that it shows different (violent) stages in a high-ranking young man's life: from hunting hare to hunting lion, and possibly accompanying his father to the battlefield as a mounted squire, to finally fighting other men himself. Others have argued before that the battle scene on the Chigi Vase represents the hoplite phalanx in action, but Christopher Matthew assembles the evidence and deals with it decisively in his *A Storm of Spears: Understanding the Greek Hoplite at War* (2012), pp. 26–28.

One of the characteristics of warfare in this period – as well as the Dark Age – is that it seems to have been the virtually exclusive domain of the aristocracy. Commoners may not have taken part in most battles, except when pressured or as victims of raids or sieges. Henk Singor has emphasized the aristocratic aspect of Archaic Greek warfare in his unpublished Dutch doctoral dissertation, *Oorsprong en betekenis van de hoplietenfalanx in het Archaïsche Griekenland* (Leiden University, 1988). J.B Salmon had earlier remarked that the Greek armies of the Archaic period probably numbered in the hundreds, rather than thousands; see his article, 'Political hoplites?', *Journal of Hellenic Studies* 97 (1977), pp. 87–122. Only from the Persian Wars onward do we begin to see larger Greek armies, precursors of the more socially diverse armies of Classical Greece that numbered in the thousands, and this point is worth keeping in mind when dealing with Greek warfare of the Dark Age and Archaic period.

With respect to Archaic Greek armour, I should again mention Eero Jarva's *Archaiologia on Archaic Greek Body-Armour* (1995), since it offers a very comprehensive catalogue, including references to a large number of vase-paintings and other iconographic material. The linen corslet has recently been the subject of very detailed study by Gregory S. Aldrete, Scott Bartell, and Alicia Aldrete, in their *Reconstructing Ancient Linen Body Armor: Unraveling the Linothorax Mystery* (2013). Of course, the books on Greek arms and armour cited earlier, such as those by Snodgrass and Everson, contain information that is of interest here.

The emergence of tyrants in Archaic Greece is a remarkable phenomenon that still does not seem perfectly understood. A. Andrewes's *The Greek Tyrants* (1956) has cast a long shadow, but his emphasis on the military aspect of tyranny is not supported by the extant evidence. In order to get an idea of the context in which tyranny appeared, and for a stimulating look at how Greek aristocrats interacted with each other, refer instead to Hans van Wees's paper, 'Megara's mafiosi: timocracy and violence in Theognis', in *Alternative to Athens: Varieties of Political Organization and Community in Ancient Greece* (2002), edited by Roger Brock and Stephen Hodkinson, pp. 52–67. Herodotus' story of Pisistratus' rise to power contains much that is almost certainly a fabrication, such as his two earlier attempts to seize control that ended in failure; 'third time lucky' was already a familiar concept in antiquity. A good discussion of the subject can be found in Gregory Cane's 'The prosperity of tyrants: Bacchylides, Herodotus, and the contest for legitimacy', *Arethusa* 29 (1996), pp. 57–85.

It is important to note that tyranny does not seem to have been as common as the historical sources make it seem. Jonathan Hall, in his history of Archaic Greece (cited earlier), points out that "it is important to recognize that it was not a universal phenomenon: according to one estimate, only twenty-seven out of hundreds of states are known to have been subject to a tyranny over a period of 150 years" (p. 142). See also the list of cities affected by *stasis*, in *An Inventory of Archaic and Classical Poleis* (2004), edited by M. Hansen and T.H. Nielsen, pp. 1361–1362.

For further details on Olympia and Delphi, refer to Catherine Morgan's *Athletes and Oracles: The Transformation of Olympia and Delphi in the Eighth Century BC* (1990). On Kalapodi and its finds, see Rainer Felsch's *Kalapodi: Ergebnisse der Ausgrabungen im Heiligtum der Artemis und des Apollon von Hyampolis in der antiken Phocis* (1996). The shift from burials with arms to dedications of metal objects at sanctuaries was already noted by Anthony Snodgrass in his *Archaic Greece: The Age of Experiment* (1980). The numerous finds of weapons and armour from Olympia have been the subject of a number of volumes in the series *Olympische Forschungen*. Among them, E. Kunze's *Archaische Schildbänder* (1950) and *Beinschienen* (1991), A. Furtwängler's *Die Bronzen* (1967), P.C. Bol's *Argivische Schilde* (1989), as well as H. Baitinger's *Die Angriffswaffen aus Olympia* (2001), are useful. Note that, as dedications quickly filled up the temples, priests periodically cleaned them out and deposited the gifts in trenches (hence, some communities in the sixth century started building *thesauroi* or treasuries to keep their votive offerings safe). As a result, most of the weapons and armour found at Greek sanctuaries is hard to date exactly, making the creation of an accurate typology difficult.

In the final section of this chapter, I argue that it is difficult to distinguish Greek material culture from that of western Anatolia. In addition to the earlier cited works by Kuhrt and Luraghi, see also P.W. Haider's 'Griechen in Vorderen Orient und in Ägypten bis ca. 590 v. Chr.', in *Wege zur Genese griechischer identität: die Bedeutung der früharchaischen Zeit* (1996), edited by C. Ulf, pp. 59–115. On the difficulty of identifying Greeks and Greek activities in the East, see J.C. Waldbaum's 'Greeks in the East or Greeks and the East? Problems in the definition and recognition of presence', *Bulletin of the American Schools of Oriental Research* 305 (1997), pp. 1–17. The Lydian objects mentioned in the text can be found in *The Lydian Treasure: Heritage Recovered* (1996) by I. Özgen and J. Öztürk, although the book itself may be difficult to track down. For riders on Lydian pottery, see George Hanfmann's 'Horsemen from Sardis', *American Journal of Archaeology* 49 (1945), pp. 570–581. For more on the Phrygians, see *The Archaeology of Midas and the Phrygians: Recent Work at Gordion* (2005), edited by Lisa Kealhofer. Also of interest is Latife Summerer's 'Indigenous responses to encounters with the Greeks in northern Anatolia: the reception of architectural terracottas in the Iron Age settlements of the Halys basin', in *Meetings of Cultures in the Black Sea Region: Between Conflict and Coexistence* (2008), edited by P. Guldager Bilde and J. Hjarl Petersen, pp. 263–286.

• Chapter 4: Rebels and empire

Much has been written on the Greco-Persian Wars, with a great deal of the available publications based, usually quite directly, on the account by Herodotus, with few additional details gleaned from such sources as Aeschylus' play *The Persians*. Peter Green's *The Greco-Persian Wars* (1996), an updated version of his original *The Year of Salamis* (1970), remains a very readable introduction to the conflicts between the Greeks and the Persians, even if it almost never strays from Herodotus. There are fewer treatments of the Persian Wars or the Persian army from an Achaemenid perspective. Nicholas Sekunda's *The Persian Army, 560–330 BC* (1992) provides a brief, illustrated overview. Persian siege warfare is discussed in detail by Duncan B. Campbell in his *Besieged: Siege Warfare in the Ancient World* (2006), pp. 14–29.

Herodotus has been much maligned, with the epithet 'father of lies' – a play on his original reputation as the 'father of history' – often repeated. In ancient times, there were many who doubted his accounts and some modern scholars have followed suit. While there is some fabrication in Herodotus (his account of the city of Babylon, for example, is largely fictitious), there is also a lot that seems accurate, and some details have been verified archaeologically, such as Thracian burial customs. The Greek historian is probably most reliable when it comes to the period that was still within living memory in his own day: the first quarter of the fifth century. However, his account is far from complete, let alone objective; this subjectivity was no doubt exacerbated by the fact that he relied mostly on oral traditions for his information. Furthermore, his stories often have a moral, in which the stereotypical rise and (hubristic) fall of various historical figures take centre stage. He was also selective in what he included in his writings. A good point would be the role of slaves in the Persian Wars; see Peter Hunt's *Slaves, Warfare, and Ideology in the Greek Historians* (1998).

A compounding problem is that Herodotus is often considered by Classical scholars to be the only source available for the period in question, barring rare instances such as Aeschylus' play *The Persians*, written in 476 BC. However, there are Persian sources available. These reveal, for example, that, to the Persians, the Greeks were a people who lived on the periphery. For a proper evaluation of Greece within the Persian concept of the world, refer to Amélie Kuhrt's important *Greeks' and 'Greece' in Mesopotamian and Persian Perspectives* (2002), cited earlier. More generally on Herodotus, *Brill's Companion to Herodotus* (2002), edited by E.J. Bakker, I.J.F. de Jong, and Hans van Wees, is uneven in quality, but the papers by Boedeker, Forsdyke, and Harrison are recommended.

The iconographic evidence for this period consists largely of Attic vase-painting. The majority of known black-figure vases date from the same period in which Attic workshops also started making red-figure vases. The standard references for Attic wares are John Beazley's *Attic Black-Figure Vase Painters* (1956) and *Attic Red-Figure Vase-Painters* (1963). To these we may add the books written by John Boardman and published by Thames & Hudson, which feature copious amounts of generally small, but still useful illustrations: *Athenian Black Figure Vases* (corrected edition, 1991), *Athenian Red Figure Vases: the Archaic Period* (1975), and *Athenian Red Figure Vases: the Classical Period* (1989).

With regards to specific battles of the Persian Wars, Marathon and Thermopylae loom large. As regards the former, the *Ancient Warfare* magazine special of 2011 provides a good starting point for further reading. As far as Thermopylae is concerned, *Beyond the Gates of Fire: New Perspectives on the Battle of Thermopylae* (2013), edited by Christopher Matthew and Matthew Trundle, offers an accessible and up-to-date examination of the battle and how it was remembered in antiquity. Anyone attempting to reconstruct an ancient battle would do well to read N. Whatley's 'On the possibility of reconstructing Marathon and other ancient battles', *Journal of Hellenic Studies* 84 (1964), pp. 119–139.

The textbox on Sparta was included for one reason: to acknowledge the reputation of Sparta as a military powerhouse, even if it seems to have been largely a fiction. There are very few indicators that Sparta was in any way extraordinary in the Archaic period; even their acquisition of Messenia was not unique, although the scale may have been unusual. Many of the characteristic features of ancient Sparta, which were supposedly ancient, may actually have been fairly recent introductions.

A good example is the dual kingship of Sparta, which was probably created in the sixth century BC; see D.A. Miller's 'The Spartan kingship: some extended notes on complex duality', *Arethusa* 31 (1998), pp. 1–17. There are many good contributions on Sparta to be found in *Sparta: Beyond the Mirage* (2002), edited by Anton Powell and Stephen Hodkinson; Michael Flower's contribution – 'The invention of tradition in Classical and Hellenistic Sparta' (pp. 191-217) – is especially noteworthy.

In this chapter, I argue that the introduction of what we refer to as the 'phalanx' can be dated to the later sixth century BC, based on a number of new developments. The idea that the ropes on the inside of the Argive shield could be used to strengthen the shield wall in the phalanx was first proposed, to my knowledge, by Allen Pittman in his paper, '"With your shield or on it": combat applications of the Greek hoplite spear and shield', in *The Cutting Edge: Studies in Ancient and Medieval Combat* (2007), edited by Barry Molloy, pp. 64–76. Regarding the earliest mention of Athenian *klerouchoi*, see J.A.S. Evans's 'Note on Miltiades' capture of Lemnos', *Classical Philology* 58 (1963), pp. 168–170. In Athens, at least, a centralized mechanism for mobilizing the army may not have been available under the reforms of Cleisthenes at the end of the sixth century, as emphasized by Henk Singor in his paper, 'The military side of the Peisitratean tyranny', in *Peisistratos and the Tyranny: A Reappraisal of the Evidence* (2002), edited by H. Sancisi-Weerdenburg, pp. 107–129; see also H. van Effenterre, 'Clisthène et les mesures de mobilisation', *Revue des études grecques* 89 (1976), pp. 1–17; F.J. Frost, 'The Athenian military before Cleisthenes', *Historia* 33 (1984), pp. 283–294.

• Epilogue: Henchmen of Ares

A key influence for this concluding part of the book is Paul Treherne's article, 'The warrior's beauty: the masculine body and self-identity in Bronze-Age Europe', published in *Journal of European Archaeology* 3 (1995), pp.105–144. A similarly interesting treatment of an ostensibly martial subject can be found in Hans van Wees's paper, 'Greeks bearing arms: the state, the leisure class, and the display of weapons in Archaic Greece', in *Archaic Greece: New Approaches and New Evidence* (1998), edited by Nick Fisher and Hans van Wees, pp. 333–378. In this paper, Van Wees argues that men stopped carrying weapons in everyday life and switched to wearing more elaborate clothes, identifying themselves more and more as men of leisure rather than warriors, a development he associates with the emergence of a stronger central authority.

At one point, I emphasize that high-ranking men claimed power and that this, in turn, obliged them to defend their communities. The same point is argued in a very interesting way by Susanne Ebbinghaus in her article, 'Protector of the city, or the art of storage in Early Greece', *Journal of Hellenic Studies* 125 (2005), pp. 51–72.

In this article, she takes a large, fragmentary *pithos* or storage vessel from Mykonos as her starting point. This vase depicts scenes of the fall of Troy. She writes that the pot should be interpreted as a statement regarding the military obligations of the rich. Important within the context of the vase's scenes is a fallen warrior, whom she plausibly regards as the Trojan hero Hector. She concludes: "The interconnection of a man's prowess in battle, his standing in the community and his wealth, which we find expressed in early Greek poetry, explains why a pithos was felt to be the appropriate place to advertise the importance of leadership by illustrating the suffering of a city that had lost its protector" (p. 68–69).

The text box on the 'The best of the Greeks' is inspired by Gregory Nagy's *The Best of the Achaeans: Concepts of the Hero in Archaic Greek Poetry* (revised edition, 1999). Note that Homer used a variety of names to denote the Greeks and their country, with Achaeans (Achaea) being the most common variant. Hesiod and later Greek poets and writers referred to themselves as Hellenes and their country as Hellas, just as modern Greeks still do. In this book, I simply refer to 'Greeks' and 'Greece'. Aside from Nagy's book, you may also be interested in reading Richard Holway's *Becoming Achilles: Child-Sacrifice, War, and Misrule in the Iliad and Beyond* (2012). It offers a stimulating interpretation of the heroic ideal as encouraging self-destruction to achieve greatness. Delving even deeper into the psychological effects of war in particular is Jonathan Shay's *Achilles in Vietnam: Combat Trauma and the Undoing of Character* (1994).

The translation of the epitaph from the tomb of Arniadas is taken from M.L. Lang's 'The alphabetic impact on Archaic Greece', in *New Perspectives in Early Greek Art* (1991), edited by D. Buitron-Oliver, pp. 65–79. This epitaph is compared with one for an Athenian called Croesus by Katharine Derderian in her *Leaving Words to Remember: Greek Mourning and the Advent of Literacy* (2001). She suggests that the "warrior's epigram transforms the crisis of death into a transition from heroic action and death to a future of memory; it depicts the warrior's past action in death in heroic diction and emphasizes the agency of the reader, who reacts to the epigram's message with recognition, mourning, and aspiration to follow its ethical paradigm" (p. 101).

Sources

What follows is a subject index for the relevant ancient Greek sources in order not to overburden the text with too many references in parentheses. It includes the Homeric epics, the poems of Hesiod, fragments of lyric poets like Archilochus and Tyrtaeus, and Herodotus. Note that while this overview aims to be comprehensive, it is not necessarily exhaustive.

ambush: Hom. *Od.* 4.271–289, 8.492–520 (Troy captured via the ruse of the Wooden Horse); *Il.* 18.520–529, *Od.* 4.842–847 (ambuscades are common in the epic world); Hdt. 6.77–78 and 8.27 (importance of ruses).

ankle-clasps: Hom. *Il.* 11.18 (Agamemnon wears silver ankle-clasps, *argureoisin episphuriois*, with which he fastens his greaves to his legs); *Il.* 18.612 (Achilles also uses silver ankle-clasps).

archers: Hom. *Il.* 2.716–725 (Philoctetes, a great archer among the Greeks, abandoned on Lemnos; his people also said to be skilled archers); *Il.* 4.92–103 (Pandarus shoots Menelaus and thereby violates the truce); *Il.* 5.50–53 (Scamander – a hero killed by Menelaus – said to have been a great huntsman and – therefore? – a skilled archer); *Il.* 5.192–205 (Pandarus greatest of the Trojan archers); *Il.* 5.294–296 (Diomedes kills Pandarus, who falls to the ground, with his armour rattling); *Il.* 8.266–272 (Teucer shoots from behind Ajax's shield); *Il.* 8.277–291 (Agamemnon praises the archer Teucer); *Il.* 8.300–313 (Teucer attempts to shoot Hector, but hits another man instead; when he tries again, he hits Hector's squire); *Il.* 11.385 (Diomedes insults Paris by calling him *toxotes*, "archer"); *Il.* 13.313–314 (Idomeneus praises Teucer as the greatest of the Greek archers, but is careful to also stress his skill at hand-to-hand combat); *Il.* 13.581–600 (Helenus attempts to shoot Menelaus, but his arrows are deflected by the Spartan king's shield and armour); *Il.* 13.712–722 (the Locrian contingent consists entirely of archers who fire in large volleys that confuse the Trojans; they are also equipped with slings, and are specifically said not to wear either helmets or shields and are therefore useless at close-range fighting); *Il.* 15.458–483 (Teucer's bow string snaps and he goes to his tent to fetch shield, helmet and spear in order to fight at close range; the fact that the poet does not mention him putting on his armour suggests that he was already wearing it); *Il.* 14.479 (the Trojan hero Achamas insults the Greeks by calling them *iopmoroi*, "arrow-fighters"); *Od.* 11.601–608 (the ghost of Heracles stalks the underworld with his bow and arrow at the ready); *Od.* 21.403–430 (Odysseus' skill as an archer); Arch. fr. 3 West (reference to lack of archers in a battle, often claimed to refer to the Lelantine War); Tyrt. fr. 19.1 West (mentions archers); Alc. fr. 388 West (Carian helmet-plumes); Hdt. 9.60 (Pausanias hopes that the Athenians will at least send him some archers).

arming scenes: Hom. *Il.* 3.326–339 (Paris dons his armour); *Il.* 11.15–43 (typical arming scene).

army, *stratos*: *Il.* 1.172 (Agamemnon as *anax andron*, the "lord of men", commander-in-chief of the Greek army); *Il.* 2.50–53 (the *plethys* is present at assemblies called by Agamemnon); *Il.* 2.474–483 (*promachoi* or *protoi*, fighters in the front rank, distinct from the *plethys* or *laos*, the bulk of the army); *Il.* 4.422–432 (the Greek army advancing in waves); *Il.* 13.247–248, 13.254–265 (warbands able to resupply in camp while the battle rages on); *Il.* 16.259–261 (the Myrmidons under the command of Patroclus come streaming out of the Greek camp like wasps from a roadside nest); *Il.* 17.354–355 (shield wall formed to defend a fallen comrade); Tyrt. fr. 11.11–14 (*promachoi*); Mimn. fr. 13a West (a group of men made "a fence with their hollow shields"); Hdt. 5.66 (Athenian army mobilized centrally after reforms of Cleisthenes).

banishment: Hom. *Od.* 1.402–404 (threat of being driven from Ithaca).

beautiful death: Hom. *Il.* 6.145–149 (natural death compared to the shedding of leaves in autumn); *Il.* 7.89–90, *Od.* 8.72–82 (excelling in life would grant one an immortal reputation upon a glorious death); *Il.* 22.71–76 (Priam idolizing the death of a young man in battle, while deploring the demise of an older man); Arch. fr. 133 West (everlasting glory mocked); Tyrt. fr. 12.21–34 West (the young warrior that dies in battle will enjoy everlasting glory); Mimn. fr. 1 West (old men are "loathsome and vile"); Hdt. 6.120 (Spartans commend the Athenians on a job well done when they arrive at Marathon and see the Persian corpses); Hdt. 9.78–79 (mutilation of Leonidas' body).

body-armour, see: corslet, cuirass.

booty: Hom. *Il.* 1.225–244 (Achilles bitterly points out that Agamemnon receives far more of the spoils than men who are arguably better fighters); *Il.* 5.165 (chariots and horses captured); *Il.* 7.467–475 (excess booty is traded away for needed supplies, such as wine); *Il.* 11.684–688 (after a successful Pylian raid against the Epeans, the booty is handed over to Neleus, who takes his share and redistributes the remainder among his people); *Il.* 17.760–761 ("many fine pieces of armour littered the ground on both sides of the ditch, as the Greeks fled"); Hdt. 9.85 (distribution of booty takes place shortly after victory, or after the burial of the dead).

bow and arrows: Hom. *Il.* 3.18, 6.322, 8.266 (emphasis on the curved appearance of bows); *Il.* 4.105–126 (detailed description of a composite bow); *Il.* 4.124–140 (Menelaus wounded by an arrow); *Il.* 5.95–100 (Diomedes wounded by Pandarus); *Il.* 8.80–86 (one of Nestor's horses shot by Paris); *Il.* 11.373–383 (Diomedes shot by Paris); *Il.* 11.504–507 (Machaon wounded by Paris); *Il.*11.579–584 (Eurypylus shot by Paris); *Il.* 16.25–27 (Patroclus lists the wounded); *Il.* 16.510–512 (Glaucus hit in the arm by Teucer); *Il.* 19.59–60 (Achilles wishes Briseis had been killed by an arrow); *Il.* 21.110–113 (Achilles tells Hector how he might one day be killed by either spear or arrow); *Il.* 23.850 (archery contest); *Od.* 1.260–263 (Odysseus once travelled to Ephyre in Thesprotia in search of poison to dip his arrows into).

burial: Hom. *Il.* 6.416–420 (Eëtion is not stripped off his armour after death, but instead cremated in his war-gear out of respect); *Il.* 7.326–335 (Nestor recommends building a pyre close to the ships and have the bones collected to bring back to Greece upon the conclusion of the Trojan War); *Il.* 7.421–432 (at the end of a day's fighting, each side collects their dead, try to identify the remains, and then cremate the bodies); *Od.* 11.66–78 (Elpenor's ghost asks Odysseus to cremate him in full armour, even though he was not remarkable for his battlefield prowess, as per *Od.* 10.552–553).

chariots: Hom. *Il.* 3.29, 4.231, 5.13 (heroes dismount to fight); *Il.* 7.13–16 (rare instance of fighting from a chariot); *Il.* 8.184–185, 16.466–476 (teams of either two or four horses); *Il.* 9.123–124, 9.265–266, 11.697, 23.262–538 (chariot races); Hdt. 1.179, 4.170, 4.183, 4.193, 5.9, 7.86–87, 7.184 (chariots still used in war by Libyans and other foreign peoples); Hdt. 7.40–41, 8.115 (Persians still use a chariot to transport their king, even if the chariot was no longer used by the Greeks).

community: Hom. *Od.* 3.81–82 (Telemachus explains to Nestor that he is from Ithaca and that he has come on private business, not on public business); Hdt. 6.92 (the Argive *demos* refuses to send military aid to the island of Aegina, but a thousand volunteers under Eurybates nevertheless join the battle).

companions, *hetairoi*: Hom. *Il.* 1.179, 1.349, 3.259, 5.514, 5.334, 7.115 (followers of a leader); *Il.* 11.585, 13.566, 13.596 (retreating from battle within the throng of one's companions); *Il.* 4.113 (companions shielding a comrade); *Il.* 4.266 (Idomeneus tells Agamemnon that he will be a staunch companion); *Il.* 4.373 (fighting ahead of one's companions); *Il.* 9.205 (Achilles as Patroclus' companion); *Il.* 16.170 (fifty men at oars also companions in battle); *Il.* 1.6, 2.174, 9.177 (Odysseus' companions). Compare: 'henchmen', *therapontes*.

corslet (non-metallic): Hom. *Il.* 2.529 (the lesser Ajax is said to wear a linen corslet); *Il.* 2.830 (two Trojans wear linen corslets).

cuirass (metal): Hom. *Il.* 1.371, 2.163, 10.287 (Greeks referred to as *chalkochitonas*, "bronze-shirted", which suggests that bronze body-armour is a common characteristic of Greek warriors fighting at Troy); Hom. *Il.* 5.180 ("bronze-shirted Trojans"); Hom. *Il.* 22.321–325 (cuirass consists of two halves or "hollows", *gualoi*: undoubtedly a front and back plate); Hdt. 8.27 (hoplites equipped with body-armour).

destruction: Hom. *Il.* 2.226–227, 4.338–339, 8.165, 9.270, 16.830–832 (description of what would happen if Troy were captured: it would be razed to the ground and its population either enslaved or slaughtered); *Il.* 21.522–523 (most towns apparently destroyed through burning).

epikouroi, people who come to the aid of allies or friends, especially in exchange for rich gifts, and especially in order to defend said friend: *Il.* 1.428–431 (Aphrodite comes to aid Ares as an *epikouros*); *Il.* 2.130, 2.803–815, 3.451–456, 5.473, 6.111, 6.227, 7.348, 7.368, 7.477, 8.497, 9.233, 10.420, 11.220, 11.563, 12.61, 12.108, 13.755, 17.14, 17.212, 17.220, 17.335, 17.362, 18.229 (the Trojan contingents, unlike the Greek, are frequently referred to as *epikouroi*, perhaps partly because the Trojans and their allies are not as culturally homogeneous as the Greeks, speaking many different languages, and can thus not be collectively referred to by one name); *Il.* 3.185–189 (Priam says that as a young man he once came to the aid of Otreus and Mygdon to fight against the Amazons); *Il.* 4.376–379 (Agamemnon reminds Diomedes of his father, Tydeus, who once came to Mycenae with Polynices to ask for *epikouroi* to aid in the war against Boeotian Thebes); *Il.* 5.477–478 and 491, 12.101 (Sarpedon tells Hector that he came to Troy as an *epikouros*, making a point that he himself was never threatened by the Greeks at *Il.* 5.482–484); *Il.* 6.234–236 (Glaucus and Diomedes exchange armour on the battlefield when they find that their ancestors were guest-friends of each other); *Il.* 7.244–312 (battle between Hector and Ajax ends inconclusively, with them exchanging gifts at the end); *Il.* 16.538–540 (Polydamas rebukes Hector, telling him that he has forgotten about the *epikouroi* who came to aid Troy in their war against the Greeks); *Il.* 17.220–226 (*epikouroi* fight in exchange for rich gifts); Arch. fr. 15 West ("an *epikouros* is a buddy for just so long as he's prepared to fight"); Arch. fr. 216 (the poet says he will "be called an *epikouros*, like a Carian"); Hdt. 2.152–154 (Ionian and Carian raiders serve as *epikouroi* to Psamtik I); Hdt. 3.4–11 (Greek troops in foreign service).

feast: Hom. *Od.* 3.4–11 (Nestor and the Pylians sacrifice to Poseidon).

fortifications: Hom. *Il.* 2.646, 2.691 (some Greek towns are described as strongholds); *Il.* 6.242–250 (stone was extensively used in Troy's construction); *Il.* 4.239, 7.164, 13.81–87, 16.698–709 (walls in the epic world are taken by storm); *Il.* 6.433–434 (one part of the Trojan walls singled out as being easier to climb); *Il.* 7.327–343 (Nestor advises the Greeks to fortify their camp); *Il.* 7.454–463 (the Greek walls rival those of Troy itself, which were made by Poseidon and Apollo); *Il.* 12/154–155 (part of the Greek camp's walls are made of stone); *Il.* 7.433–441, 8.343–344, 9.348–350, 15.1–2 (the Greeks fix sharp stakes within the ditch outside of the wall, as well as in front of both ditch and wall); *Il.* 12.50–79 (stakes in ditches and walls fixed with the express purpose of keeping out chariots and horses); *Od.* 11.264–265 (Thebes was immediately walled after its foundation, "since without bulwarks they could not have lived, for all their strength, in Thebes of the wide spaces"); Hdt. 3.156, 9.118 (most sizeable towns in Herodotus' *Histories* appear to have been walled); Hdt. 7.139, 6.36 (temporary wooden palisades constructed).

games: Hom. *Il.* 11.698–701 (Nestor's father, Neleus, once sent a chariot to compete in races organized in Elis); *Il.* 2.773–775 (Achilles' Myrmidons amuse themselves on the beach by throwing the discus or spear, or practising with the bow); *Il.* 23.621–623 (various contests at Patroclus' funeral games, including boxing, wrestling, spear-throwing, and running); *Il.* 23.798–825 (friendly duel as part of the funeral games for Patroclus); *Od.* 11.543–555 (the armour of Achilles was the prize in a competition between Odysseus and the greater Ajax).

general, in the sense of army commander or other high-ranking military leader: Arch. fr. 113.1 (use of *archos* to denote a leader); Arch. fr. 114.1 West (earliest attested use of the more familiar term *strategos* for a military commander, cognate with the older word *stratos* – "army" – that was already used by Homer); Hdt. 6.109 (use of *polemarchos* – polemarch – to denote the commander-in-chief of the army at Athens, which was also an archon position); Hdt. 7.83 (one or more *strategoi* as commanders of the army as a whole, often magistrates by the time of the Persian Wars); Hdt. 7.173 (polemarch as the title of a high-ranking military commander at Sparta).

gifts and gift-exchange: *Il.* 9.149–156 (Agamemnon wishes to make peace with Achilles and offers him treasure and slaves, the hand of one of his daughters, and ownership of no fewer than seven towns); *Il.* 11.19–23 (Cinyras, the king of Cyprus, sent Agamemnon a beautiful cuirass as a token of his friendship and support when he learnt that the latter was preparing for war); *Od.* 4.174–179 (Menelaus tells Telemachus that he wanted to "empty" one of his own cities close to Sparta for Odysseus and his people to dwell in); *Od.* 21.33 (Odysseus gave Iphitus a spear and sword in exchange for a bow); *Od.* 16.78–81 and 19.241–243 (Telemachus promises gifts); *Od.* 21.339–342 (Penelope promises Odysseus – disguised as a beggar – a mantle, tunic, spear, sandals and sword if he were to succeed in stringing the bow).

glory: Hom. *Od.* 24.80–84 (a grave mound will keep the memory of a man alive).

greaves: Hom. *Il.* 4.80, 6.529 (the Greeks are called *euknemides*, "strong-greaved"); *Il.* 7.41 (the Greeks are called *chalkoknemides*, "bronze-greaved"); *Il.* 18.612 (Achilles' greaves, fashioned by Hephaestus, are either decorated with or made of tin and fastened using silver ankle clasps).

greed: Hom. *Il.*1.231 (Achilles accuses Agamemnon of eating his own people).

guest-friendship, *xenia*: Hom. *Il.* 7.362–364 (Menelaus insulted when his guest Paris abducts Helen and also steals valuables from the Spartan king's home).

harangues: Hom. *Il.* 7.94–102 (Menelaus complains to the Greeks about their cowardice and prepares to face Hector himself).

healers, *iatroi*: *Il.* 11.506–507 (the best healer of the Greek army, the warrior Machaon, is wounded by Paris); *Il.* 11.514–515 (a healer is said to be knowledgeable when it comes to cutting out arrows and treating wounds with medicines: in other words, battlefield triage); *Il.* 827–831 (Achilles said to be skilled at healing wounds, since he was trained by the centaur Chiron).

heirlooms: Hom. *Il.* 16.143–144 (Achilles uses his father's spear in battle); *Il.* 17.194–197 (father gives to son); *Od.* 21.128–130 (Telemachus comes close to stringing his father's bow).

helmet: *Il.* 3.8, 5.680 ("shining" helmets, implied to be metal); *Il.* 3.371–372 (horsehair crests); Hom. *Il.* 4.495, 7.12 (metal helmets); *Il.* 5.182, 13.529–530 (helmet with "hollow eyes"); *Il.* 10.259 (Diomedes receives a *kataitux*, leather skull cap, lacking "horn and crest"); *Il.* 10.261–265 (boar's-tusk helmet worn by Odysseus); *Il.*12.384 (helmet said to be *tetraphalon*, "four-sheeted"; presumably hammered out of four sheets of bronze); *Il.* 16.106 (Ajax' helmet has cheek pieces); Tyrt. fr. 11.32 West (helmets with crests or plumes); Hdt. 1.171 (use of the familiar word *kranos*); Hdt. 4.180 (one helmet type referred to as Corinthian).

henchmen, *therapontes* (sometimes translated as 'servants'): Hom. *Il.* 2.110, 6.67, 7.382, 15.733, 19.78 (the Greeks referred to as "henchmen of Ares"); *Il.* 5.48 (the henchmen of Idomeneus); *Il.* 6.18 (Axylus and his henchman); *Il.* 8.79, 10.228 (the two Aiantes referred to as "henchmen of Ares"); *Il* 8.119 (charioteer as henchman);

16.464 (henchman of Sarpedon); *Il.* 16.653, 18.152 (Patroclus referred to as the henchman of Achilles); *Il.* 19.47 (Odysseus and Diomedes referred to as "henchmen of Ares"); *Od.* 16.253 (henchmen as helpers in carving meat); Arch. fr. 1 West (Archilochus refers to himself as a "henchman of the lord god of war"). Compare: 'companions', *hetairoi*.

heralds, *kerukes*: *Il.* 7.273–282 (heralds can apparently determine when men ought to stop fighting); *Il.* 9.9–12 (heralds call men to assembly following an order of the *basileis*); *Il.* 12.342–363 (heralds carry messages, even in the thick of battle); *Il.* 11.684–685 (heralds serve as town-criers); *Il.* 24.148–151 (heralds serving as attendants); Hdt. 9.12 (heralds).

horses: Hom. *Il.* 2.230 (Trojans as "breakers of horses"); *Il.* 2.237 (Castor as "breaker of horses"); *Il.* 3.75 (Argos said to provide good pasture for horses); *Il.* 3.185–186 (horses very common in Phrygia); *Il.* 4.202 (Trikka also good horse country); *Il.* 8.194 (Diomedes a "breaker of horses"); *Il.* 10.431 (reference to Phrygian "riders", *hippodamoi*); *Il.* 11.150–152, 15.269–270 (horses ridden instead of yoked to a chariot); *Il.* 15.262–270 (Hector compared to a horse breaking from its stable); *Il.* 16.584 (Patroclus referred to as a "lord of horses"); Mimn. fr. 14 West (bravery of a Greek warrior in the face of Lydian cavalry); Hdt. 1.67, 8.124 (Spartan *Hippeis*; perhaps they once rode to battle?); Hdt. 1.79–80 (Lydians famed as horsemen and used lances in combat); Hdt. 4.87, 5.98, 6.29, 7.21, 7.40–41, 7.55, 7.84 and 87–88, 7.177, 8.113, 9.14, 9.20–25, 9.39–40, 9.49, 9.50–52 and 56–57, 9.60, 9.71, 9.85 (Persians use greater numbers of horse troops, often to the detriment of Greek armies); Hdt. 4.121, 7.208 (mounted scouts); Hdt. 5.14 (Persians use mounted messengers); Hdt. 5.63 (ground near Phaleron levelled to make it better suited for horses); Hdt. 6.112 (the Athenians at Marathon had neither archers nor horsemen); Hdt. 6.58, 9.54, 9.60 (horsemen used by Greeks as dispatch riders); Hdt. 7.173, 7.196, 8.28 (Thessalians renowned as horsemen); Hdt. 7.154, 7.158 (Syracusans used horsemen); Hdt. 8.138 (cavalry used to hit specific targets); Hdt. 9.13 (Attica said not to be suited for horses, apart from the area around Marathon at 6.102); Hdt. 9.17 (Persian horsemen used javelins); Hdt. 9.68–69 (Boeotians have a *hipparchos*, a cavalry commander); Hdt. 9.32 (horse troops operate separately from warriors on foot).

hospitality, *xenia*, see: guest-friendship.

missiles, *bele*: *Il.* 3.79–80 (the Greeks fire arrows and hurl stones in an attempt to hit Hector); *Il.* 11.540 (Hector wades through the *stiches* - lines – and fights not just with spear and sword, but throws large rocks as well); *Il.* 13.323 (the greater Ajax described by Idomeneus as a man who could not be broken by bronze or great stones).

mitre, probably a bronze belly-guard, used to protect the abdomen: Hom. *Il.* 4.134–140 (Menelaus is shot by Pandarus, with the arrow first piercing his *zoster*, then his cuirass, and then his *mitre*, "which he wore to protect his skin and keep the spears off"); *Il.* 4.185–187 (Menelaus' *mitre* is fixed in front of or beneath the *zoster* and *zoma*, "flap"); *Il.* 4.215–16 (Menelaus removes the *zoster*, then the *zoma* and finally the *mitre*); *Il.* 5.855–857 (with the help of Athena, Diomedes drives a spear through Ares' *mitre* and into his belly); *Il.* 16.419 (the Lycians specifically said not to use the *mitre*).

mercenaries, see: *epikouroi*.

oaths: Hom. *Il.*10.329–330 (Zeus is the protector of oaths).

patriotism: Hom. *Il.* 15.496–498 (honourable to die in the defence of one's country); Tyrt. fr. 10.15–16, 10.23–24, 12.15 West (fighting for the whole community, one's *patridos* or 'fatherland'); Cal. fr. 1.6–11 West (fighting in defence of one's country and family).

physical appearance: Hom. *Il.* 3.166–170 (Agamemnon said not to be very tall); *Il.* 3.191–198 (Odysseus said to be short); *Il.* 5.801 (Tydeus said to have been fairly short).

prisoners: Hom. *Il.* 2.237 (prisoners considered "prizes of honour"); *Il.* 6.46–47 (the Trojan Adrestus tells Menelaus not to kill him, but to take him prisoner, as his father is rich and will pay a fine ransom); *Il.*10.378–457 (Dolon hopes to be taken prisoner, but Diomedes ruthlessly beheads him); *Il.* 11.104–106 (prisoners are sold off or kept for ransom); *Il.* 23.20–23 (Achilles sacrifices Trojan prisoners at Patroclus' pyre); Hdt. 1.151, 6.45, 6.106 (prisoners of war are enslaved); Hdt. 1.167, 4.202, 8.127, 9.120 (prisoners of war executed); Hdt. 5.77, 6.79, 9.99 (prisoners of war held for ransom); Hdt. 7.180 (prisoners of war sacrificed).

public assembly: Hom. *Od.* 2.6–259.

raiding: Hom. *Il.* 9.328–329 (Achilles recounts having destroyed no fewer than 23 towns in the vicinity of Troy); *Il.* 11.669–704 (Nestor leads a party of young men on a raid and steals a considerable amount of livestock; they also take a number of prisoners); *Od.* 3.71–74, 9.252–255 (visitor asked by his host whether he is on some specific business or "roving as pirates do"); *Od.* 3.103–108 (Achilles led the Greeks on raids for plunder while they were at Troy); *Od.* 14.234–291, 17.419–444 (Odysseus lies about being a Cretan who tried to raid Egypt); *Od.* 16.425–427 (Eupeithes, father of Antinous, once raided the Thesprotians, angering the Ithacans because they feared the victims might retaliate); *Od.* 21.15–21 (Odysseus sent to Messene by Laërtes and the other elders of Ithaca to ask for compensation after they had been the victim of a Messenian raid).

recruitment: Hom. *Il.* 1.152–600 (Achilles explains that he and his fellow leaders came to Troy as a favour, *charis*, to Agamemnon); *Il.* 23.295–296 (Echepolus sent Agamemnon a beautiful mare to avoid having to go to Troy); *Il.* 24.399–400 (a Myrmidon, Argeïphontes, tells Priam that he and his six brothers cast lots, and he was chosen to accompany Achilles on the expedition to Troy); *Od* 4.642–644 (Telemachus takes "chosen men" with him on his expedition).

reprimands: Hom. *Il.* 2.188–206 (Odysseus scolds the Greeks who want to sail home).

rewards: Hom. *Il.* 12.310–314 (*temenos*, "public land", for services rendered); *Il.* 6.194–195 (Bellerophon receives *temenos* from the Lycians); *Il.* 9.573–580 (awarded by the elders on behalf of the entire community).

scouts, *episkopoi*, *kataskopoi* or simply *skopoi*: Hom. *Il.* 2.791–794 (Polites takes up position on the burial mound of Aesyetes to keep an eye on the Greeks); *Il.* 8.553–865, 9.1 (the Trojans keep lookouts on the plain); *Il.* 10.204–205 (Nestor asks if there are any Greeks brave enough to go and spy on the Trojans); *Il.* 10.206–210 (the objective of the spying mission of Odysseus and Diomedes is to capture a lone enemy warrior or to overhear the plans that the Trojans are forging); Hdt. 1.152 (small, fast ships like fifty-oared galleys used as naval spies); Hdt. 6.101, 6.21, 7.219 (Persians rely on traitors and deserters for intelligence); Hdt. 7.192 (lookouts posted; runners report back with news).

seers, *manteis*: *Il.* 1.106–108 (Calchas is the chief seer in the Greek army); Hdt. 7.113 (few commanders undertake anything without consulting a seer); Hdt. 8.27 (a seer gives direct tactical advice).

servants: Hom. *Il.* 3.268–270 (heralds lead lambs to the slaughter in a sacrifice to mark an oath; they also wash the hands of their superiors and mix wine, like young men); *Il.* 9.173 (young men, *kouroi*, fill a mixing-bowl with wine that they pass from one man to the next); *Il.* 9.658–659 (Patroclus orders his *hetairoi* and slave-girls to make a bed ready for Phoenix); *Il.* 24.572–586 (Achilles tells his henchmen to take care of Priam's mules, horses, and herald, while female slaves wash Hector's body); Hdt. 5.111, 9.82 (commanders, at least, had servants and shield-bearers); Hdt. 7.229, 9.50 (servants and attendants in the army).

shield: Hom. *Il.* 7.250, 11.434 and 13.405 (*aspis* described as *omphaloessa*, "bossed", and round); *Il.* 3.135 (leaning on an *aspis*); *Il.* 3.335 (Paris' *mega sakos*); *Il.* 4.201–202 (shields are common); *Il.* 5.126 (*sakos* of Tydeus); *Il.* 5.452 and 12.105 (*sakos* said to be made of ox-hides and resembling a *purgos*, "tower"); *Il.* 6.117–118 (Hector's bossed *aspis* reaches from the neck to the ankles; compare *Il.* 15.645–646); *Il.* 11.32–40 (Agamemnon's round *aspis* is covered with bronze, features ten concentric circles, twenty tin bosses and a central boss made of cobalt, with the face of a Gorgon inscribed at the centre, flanked by Fear and Terror; the strap is decorated with silver); *Il.* 7.219–220 (Ajax' shield is made of bronze and seven layers of ox-hide); *Il.* 8.193 (Nestor's *aspis* features *kanones* or "cross-rods"); *Il.* 15.474, 22.4 (shield held aslant against one's shoulder); 18.478–607 (the new *sakos* of Achilles made by Hephaestus); Arch. fr. 5 West (Archilochus had to abandon his shield in a battle against a Thracian tribe); Tyrt. fr. 11.24 West (broad shield that reaches to the shins); Tyrt. fr. 11.31–34 (shield pressed against shield); Tyrt. 12.24 West (shield that is "bossed"); Solon fr. 5.5–6 West (metaphorical use of shield); Hdt. 8.27, 9.74 (Greeks equipped with large, blazoned shields).

shield strap, *telamon*: Hom. *Il.* 2.388–389, 5.798, 14.404–405 (described); *Il.* 4.478 (presence of strap implied); *Il.* 12.400–402 (Sarpedon's strap is used to keep the shield in front of his chest; compare also *Il.* 12.425–426).

ships: Hom. *Il.* 2.509–510 (the Boeotians said to have ships that carry 120 men rather than the normal 50); *Il.* 16.168–170 (ship with fifty oarsmen as normal); *Od.* 2.209–217 (Telemachus asks the men at assembly to give him a ship and a crew); *Od.* 2.285–295 (Athena, disguised as Mentor, tells Telemachus that she will find both ship and crew for him); *Od.* 9.322–323 (ship with twenty oars referred to as an *eikosoros*); Arch. fr. 116 West (reference to "life on the sea"); Arch. fr. 192 (refers to a man who survived a shipwreck); Hdt. 5.71 (Athenian naucraries); Hdt. 6.137 (ship with fifty oars referred to as a *pentekontoros*); Hdt. 7.100, 7.180–181, 8.83, 9.32 (reference to marines, *epibatai*, used in boarding actions); Hdt. 8.9 (use of the *diekplous*); Hdt. 8.85 (captain of a trireme referred to as a *trierarchos*).

sieges: Hom. *Il.* 6.447–465 (siege ends when town is sacked and razed to the ground, with the men and some children killed, and the women and remaining children enslaved); *Il.* 12.160–161 (the Greeks defend the walls of their camp against the Trojans by tearing stones out of the towers and throwing these at the besiegers); *Il.* 12.257–261 (stakes used to topple enemy walls); *Il.* 12.287–289 (both the Greeks and the Trojans throw large numbers of stones at each other around the walls of the camp); *Il.* 12.445–446 (some heroes use boulders to smash gates and walls); *Il.* 18.207–213 (inhabitants of a besieged island-town light signal-fires during the night in the hope that men from neighbouring islands would come to their aid;

during the day, smoke billows up as the town itself is ablaze); *Il.* 18.509–512 (war is represented on the new shield of Achilles by a city under siege); *Il.* 21.514–517 (the gods prevent the Greeks from capturing Troy by scaling their walls); *Il.* 22.111–122 (Hector suggests they end the siege by giving back to the Greeks everything that Paris took, including Helen, and giving them further compensation); Hdt. 3.54 (siege of Samos).

single combat: Hom. *Il.* 3.15–75 (single combat between Paris and Menelaus to decide the outcome of the Trojan War); Hdt. 6.92 (Eurybates killed by the fourth man he challenged to single combat); Hdt. 9.27 (the Battle of Marathon referred to as *monomachia*, in this case a test of strength between two specific groups, the Athenians and the Persians).

slaves: Hom. *Od.* 14.276–297 (in a false story, Odysseus claims that he travelled with a Phoenician to Libya, who was intent on selling the Greek there as a slave); *Od.* 21.370–371 (a slave can be chased off after offending his master).

spear: Hom. *Il.* 3.179 (use of *aichmetes* – "spearfighter", "spearmen" – as a common word to denote a Greek or Trojan warrior who is not an archer); *Il.* 6.319 (Hector's massive thrusting spear measuring eleven cubits or nearly five metres in length); *Il.* 10.24, 10.31, 10.135, 10.178, *Od.* 2.10 (men in the epic world apparently never go anywhere without a spear); *Il.* 10.76, 11.212, 12.464–465, 13.241 (heroes equipped with two spears); *Il.* 10.153 (spears apparently equipped with a butt-spike to drive them into the ground when not in use, as seen by Nestor and the other leaders when they visit the shelter of Diomedes at night); *Il.* 11.357 (attempt to retrieve a thrown spear); *Il.* 15.674–678, 15.472–476 (use of *naumacha xusta* or "ship-spears", said to be a whopping twenty-two cubits or ten metres in length, and used by Ajax to defend the ships from the Trojans when the latter wish to set fire to them); *Il.* 16.142–144, 19.387–391 (Achilles' spear – inherited from his father – is so heavy only he can wield it); *Il.* 21.144–163 (the ambidextrous hero Asteropaeus throws two spears at once and does not use a shield); *Od.* 1.120–129 (when a guest visits a house, his spear is put in a spear-rack upon arrival); Arch. fr. 2 West (Archilochus said to eat and drink with, as well as recline on, his spear); Arch. fr. 24.13 (typical warrior is the spearman); Tyrt. fr. 11.25–30 West (spear and sword as common weapons); Tyrt. fr. 11.35–38 (*gymnetes* with spears, and *panoploi*); Tyrt. fr. 19.12 (reference to "spearmen"); Solon fr. 37 West (reference to the *metaichmios*, the 'land between the spears', quite literally the no-man's land between two opposing armies).

stripping of the dead: Il. 4.466, 4.506, 4.532, 5.164, 5.435, 6.28, 6.71, 7.77–80, 11.110, 13 and 15 *passim*, 16.246–247, 22.258–259 (battle over the bodies of fallen comrades to prevent them from falling into the hands of the enemy); *Il.* 13.260–265 (Idomeneus strips an enemy corpse and keeps the booty); *Il.* 17.122 (Hector strips Achilles' armour from Patroclus' corpse, with the spirit of the war god entering him when he dons the armour at *Il.* 17.210–212).

sword: Hom. *Il.* 1.190–191 (Achilles contemplates striking Agamemnon down with his sword); *Il.* 1.219 (Achilles' sword has a silver hilt);*Il.* 2.45, 3.334 (sword studded with silver nails); *Il.* 3.355–369 (a sword is used on the battlefield when a spear is no longer available); *Il.* 10.254–261 (on the night expedition, Odysseus and Diomedes leave their spears behind, but take their swords); *Od.* 2.3 (when Telemachus leaves home, he takes both his spear and sword); *Od.* 20.125, 21.119 (Telemachus carries his sword while at home: if this had been an abnormal show of strength, the suitors would certainly have commented on this); *Od.* 22.74–75 and 79–80 (the suitors wish to rush upon Odysseus with swords, apparently the only weapons that high-ranking men are never parted from); Hdt. 7.224 (sword used as a backup weapon after the spear had snapped).

taxation: Hom. *Il.* 4.257–263 (*gerousios oinos*, "wine of the elders").

thetes, landless labourers: Hom. *Od.* 11.489–491 (life as a *thes* considered dreadful by the shade of Achilles).

treasures, *keimelia*: Hom. *Il.* 2.373–374 (the Greeks ponder the great wealth that is in store for them once Troy is finally captured); *Od.* 2.337–347 (Odysseus' palace features a store-room filled with all sorts of treasure and weapons); *Od.* 9.263–265 (when a man dies, his treasure – and thereby his honour or *time* – passes to his heirs); *Od.* 19.1–34, 22.23–25 (the weapons are removed from the hall where the suitors spend most of their time); *Od.* 22.101–115 (Telemachus runs off to fetch equipment from an inner room); Alc. fr. 140.3–15 Voigt (description of the *megas domos* of Alcaeus).

units, subdivisions of the army: Hom. *Il.* 4.221–231, 16.173 (*stiches* used to denote ranks and files of men, as well as simply large bodies of men); *Il.* 4.334, 4.347 (*pyrgos*, 'tower', used to denote a dense group of fighters); *Il.* 6.187–190 (use of *lochos* to denote a small group of men hiding in ambush); *Il.* 11.90, 19.158 (*phalanges* as throngs of men); *Il.* 16.168–199 (Achilles divides the Myrmidons into five different sections, each with its own leader); *Il.* 20.236 (*stiches* of horses); *Od.* 4.277 (the Trojan Horse is referred to as a "hollow *lochos*", a "hollow ambush"); *Od.* 10.203–205 (Odysseus divides his crew in half and appoints Eurylochus as commander of one half); *Od.* 20.49 (use of the term *lochos* to denote a smallish body of men, a military unit); Hdt. 6.37 (use of *lochos* to denote men hiding in ambush); Hdt. 8.6 (use of *lochos* to refer to ships stationed somewhere); Hdt. 6.37, 8.86 (fighting *kata taxein*, "in good order", also applied to ships); Hdt. 9.21 (the Athenian commander Olympiodorus leads a *lochos* of three hundred picked men); Hdt. 9.53 (*lochos* used to refer to a body of men, commanded by a *lochagos*).

votives: Hom. *Il.* 7.705 (the Pylians sacrifice to the gods after a successful raid); *Il.* 7.726–728 (the Pylians sacrifice to the gods to ask for help); *Il.* 7.81–86 (Hector vows to hang the armour of his victim in Apollo's temple if he is kept safe); Alc. fr. 401B Voigt (Alcaeus had to abandon or even surrender his shield, which the enemy then hung up in the temple of their principal goddess, Athena); Hdt. 9.81 (part of the spoils, usually a tithe, was dedicated to the gods).

words and deeds: Hom. *Il.* 1.490–492 (leading men engage in both politics and war); *Od.* 2.273 (Odysseus a man of words and deeds).

zoster, probably a belt made of fabric: Hom. *Il.* 4.134–140 (Menelaus hit by an arrow through his *zoster*); *Il.* 10.77–78 (Nestor's *zoster*); *Il.* 7.305 (Ajax gives Hector a purple *zoster*); *Il.* 11.234–237 (Agamemnon wears a silver-plated *zoster* beneath his cuirass).

Acknowledgements

This book is largely a reworked and revised version of my doctoral dissertation, which I defended at the VU University in Amsterdam on 16 March 2010. The dissertation featured separate chapters on each category of evidence (burials with arms, dedications from sanctuaries, fortifications, iconographic evidence, the Homeric epics, Archaic poets and inscriptions, and finally Herodotus). One of the aims of the dissertation was to establish regional differences and to trace developments across time. In the end, it was clear that, while there was certainly diversity in material culture from one region to the next, this may have been – to a large extent – a function of the uneven distribution of the evidence throughout the Aegean. The changes through time were more significant. The results of my PhD research therefore suggested a subdivision into the four periods that are each treated in the separate chapters of this book.

The dissertation – and therefore this book – would not have been possible without the encouragement and helpful advice of my supervisor at the VU University, Dr Jan Paul Crielaard. His enthusiasm and knowledge of the subject matter were a constant source of inspiration. I thank him for his support, which dates back to when the PhD dissertation was still only a smaller master's thesis. All in all, he has guided me through a period of nearly ten years, which I still believe is extraordinary. Naturally, I alone am responsible for any errors that remain in the text.

I would also like to thank my promotor at the VU University, Prof. Douwe Yntema. In addition, I extend my gratitude to the members of the committee for taking the time to read my PhD dissertation and for providing me with stimulating questions that have helped in fine-tuning some of my ideas for the present book. The members included Prof. Nico Roymans and Dr Mieke Prent (VU University Amsterdam), Dr Henk Singor (Leiden University), Prof. Josine Blok (University of Utrecht), and Prof. Hans van Wees (University College London). Prof. Van Wees has supplied ample criticism regarding some of my interpretations, as well as further comments and corrections, for which I am grateful. Again, any errors that remain and the viewpoints expressed in the text are, of course, mine alone.

A substantial part of my work on the dissertation was made possible thanks to a PhD grant awarded by the Faculty of Arts at the VU University in Amsterdam. This grant allowed me to work at the university for a little over two years, gaining valuable experience as both a researcher and a teacher. Furthermore, I was subsequently awarded a Rubicon grant by the Netherlands Organisation for Scientific Research (NWO) to conduct two years' worth of further study into Greek fortifications at the University of Thessaly in Volos. Some of the results of this research have been incorporated into this book. My time in Greece was very pleasant and I would like to thank Prof. Alexander Mazarakis Ainian of the Department of History, Archaeology and Social Anthropology for his hospitality and help in getting me settled there. My thanks are also due to Dr Christina Mitsopoulou, Themis Dallas, and other colleagues at the University of Thessaly for their warmth and hospitality.

My thanks also, of course, to Karwansaray Publishers for publishing this book and therefore making the results of my research available to a large audience. In particular, I thank the editor-in-chief, Jasper Oorthuys, and the publisher, Rolof van Hövell tot Westerflier, for supporting this project. I extend particular gratitude to Jona Lendering, who was an excellent editor of the book. He has weeded out some silly mistakes and hopefully managed to steer it towards a cohesive and comprehensible whole. Gratitude also to Dr Duncan Campbell, who served as copy editor and has helped improve the overall quality and flow of the text.

The visual appeal of the book has been aided greatly by the beautiful work done by the illustrators of *Ancient Warfare* magazine. In alphabetical order, I warmly thank Rocío Espín, Angel García Pinto, Milek Jakubiec, Sebastian Schulz, Johnny Shumate, and Graham Sumner, for their efforts and their patience. Andrew Brozyna designed the book's wonderful cover and created two pictures for the chapter on the Mycenaeans. Sandra Elzinga and Merel Teunissen of MeSa Design have done a great job regarding the internal layout of the book. My thanks also to Christianne Beall in making all of the illustrations ready for print.

Finally, words cannot express the gratitude that I owe to my partner, Arianna Sacco, for supporting me in all my endeavours over the course of the last few years. I therefore dedicate this book to her, with love.

Index

References to the List of Dates, Bibliographic Notes, Sources, or Acknowledgements are not included in this index. Page numbers in *italic* refer to illustrations and/or captions.

A

M

T